# PUBS
## for Families

ADRIAN TIERNEY-JONES

**BOOKS**

Published by CAMRA, The Campaign for Real Ale
230 Hatfield Road, St Albans, Hertfordshire AL1 4LW
T 01727 867201
F 01727 867670
E camra@camra.org.uk
www.camra.org.uk
*Managing Editor*: Mark Webb

First published 1998
Fourth edition 2003

Printed in the United Kingdom at
the University Press, Cambridge

*Design/typography*: Dale Tomlinson
*Fonts*: The Antiqua &Taz (lucasfonts.com)
*Maps*: John Macklin
*Illustrations*: Christine Jopling
*Cover design*: Rob Howells

ISBN 1 85249 183 3

*Every effort has gone into researching the contents of
this book, but no responsibility can be taken for errors.*

# Contents

5 Introduction

9 First XIII

13 **East Anglia**
Cambridgeshire, Essex, Norfolk, Suffolk

31 **London**
Greater London

38 *Warning! Bouncy Castles and Bottle-warming Ban-alert!*

39 **Midlands**
Bedfordshire, Derbyshire, Herefordshire, Leicestershire, Lincolnshire, Northamptonshire, Nottinghamshire, Oxfordshire, Shropshire, Staffordshire, Warwickshire, West Midlands, Worcestershire

76 *What makes a Child-friendly Pub?*

77 **North East**
Tyne & Wear, Durham and Northumbria

85 **North West**
Cheshire, Lancashire & Cumbria, Merseyside, Greater Manchester

101 **The South**
Berkshire, Buckinghamshire, Hampshire, Hertfordshire, Isle of Wight, Jersey *(Channel Isles)*, Kent, Surrey, Sussex

123 **The South West and West Country**
Cornwall, Devon, Dorset, Gloucestershire & Bristol, Somerset & Wiltshire

157 **Yorkshire**

169 *Is Pub Food making our children sick?*

171 **Scotland**

197 *How the Children's Certificate failed to make Pubs more Family-friendly*

199 **Wales**

219 Index of pub amenities and nearby attractions

# Acknowledgements

To JAMES – who has always behaved impeccably in pubs since the age of three weeks. May he long continue to do so!

Thanks to all the CAMRA members who sent in pub recommendations, also to friends who sent in suggestions; thanks are also due to Charlie who helped me out when things were looking a bit hairy. Finally, thanks as ever to Jane.

# Introduction

Do pubs and kids go together like a pint of ale and a decent pie? Or are they a marriage made in hell? While researching this book I had some interesting answers to this question. When I asked one pub in the north if they were family-friendly I received the priceless reply that 'children and cask beer don't mix'. Er, hello? Does he mean that youngsters give off death rays which effect the quality of real ale? In the last year or so I have also noticed a lively exchange in the letters pages of CAMRA's *What's Brewing*. Some members were bemoaning the unfriendliness of some pubs to children, while others wrote in congratulating the vehemently anti-child licensee.

This, hopefully, is where this book should help. With the help of CAMRA members (with families) across the UK we've pinpointed the pubs which actively welcome children – so you know you can enter their thresholds without walking into a Cold War situation. Equally we can steer you away from the kind of boozers which are ankle-deep in lager and dedicated to drunken brawls. The good news is that, in general, pubs are becoming much more family friendly.

It wasn't always thus. When I was growing up children and pubs certainly didn't mix. A pub was a place of grown-up illicit mystery – its arcane goings-on well hidden behind smoked-glass windows. When the door opened, out would come the pungent perfume of beer and tobacco. Sounds pretty disgusting nowadays but, as a youngster, it symbolised all that was secretly adult and I thought it the most alluring scent around.

The fascination was such that I couldn't wait to get to the bar and I finally made it inside the mystic portals when I was a distinctly underage 15. Four of us sneaked into a hotel bar in Llandudno and ordered halves of Greenall Whitley's bitter. I can't remember what it tasted like but it was undoubtedly an unimpressive introduction to the world of beer.

Not long afterwards I became a schoolboy regular at a remarkably tolerant hotel bar where we tried Manns Brown (like drinking brown paper I remember), Stone's keg bitter, Strongbow and Wrexham Lager. Fortunately I discovered real ale at college and have been a devoted real beer and pub man ever since. This has meant that our four-year-old son James has been going to pubs (and beer festivals) since the tender age of three weeks.

Pubs hold no mystery for James – and hopefully he won't grow up feeling the need to break in and overdo the ale (though, ten to one he'll be a teetotaller just to spite me – or, even worse, become a fan of nitrokeg). Because we take him to a wide variety of pubs, including some very traditional ones, he doesn't see them as playgrounds and doesn't expect to be entertained by clowns or given plastic toys alongside a pappy hamburger. However that's not to say we've come through unscathed. I still wince at the memory of the time at the King & Castle station bar at Kidderminster when James (then two) pinched the bottom of a big looking bloke standing next to me at the bar. Said bloke turned round, totally overlooking James, and nearly decked me.

All of us, parents or not, have suffered from children misbehaving in the pub. A full-on toddler tantrum is not a pretty sight or sound (and certainly not what you need as a background to a quiet lunch). We are all entitled to a decent standard of behaviour in a place where we are spending our hard-earned cash. We're not talking 'sit and be silent', but equally not condoning using a bar as a venue for games of tag or unbridled screaming fits (see the feature What makes a Child-friendly Pub?). My own view is that by taking children into pubs from an early age, they soon learn what's acceptable behaviour – it happens on the continent, why not here?

Mind you, it's not always the children who misbehave. In the course of researching this book, I was told a tale by one landlord about a fight which broke out between two fathers on a bouncy castle in the back garden of a pub!

This book is pretty picky. We could have made it twice or even treble the size but we were looking for a very special kind of pub. There are plenty of themed pubs which cater for children but try getting a decent pint of real ale in them.

All the pubs here serve at least one real ale, with some of them offering up to eight handpumps. Equally we're not suggesting landlords should dress up as clowns and put a bouncy castle up in the snug. We're celebrating good pubs, good beer and a friendly atmosphere.

Each one is different. Some pubs suit all ages while some are ideal for older children and some have the needs of toddlers and young kids at heart. Where this is obvious we've pointed it out – and also taken care to indicate any potential dangers – such as nearby canals, ponds or gardens which open onto the carpark. Obviously, it goes without saying, that you should keep your children firmly within your sights and under your control at all times – but hopefully this information will help you in picking the best pub for you.

Some pubs go to town and have hosts of seasonal special events for children while others are plain, simple village boozers used by local families. Food is served in most of them, but out of the small number which do not have food some allow families to bring in picnics. Unlike the last edition of *The Best Pubs For Families*, we have included pubs which only serve children if you are eating – going on the principle that most people out with their children are looking for food. There are pubs on the beach, pubs overlooking the sea, pubs in the shadow of great mountains and pubs right in the middle of towns and cities. Some have traditional games such as chess, draughts and dominoes behind the bar, while others provide colouring books and crayons. Some even give away small toys with the meal (useful if your child is addicted to McDonald's). One pub has a miniature railway doing a circuit of the pub garden on which children can take a ride; another has a train set circling the length of the bar. Many pubs organise special events: one in Hertfordshire has a living history exhibit with native American Indians in a tepee village over a weekend, while one in Norfolk is home to a Guy Fawkes bonfire. All in all, this book offers you a really wonderful selection of the most brilliant pubs – I'm already planning our next five years of holidays around some of them!

The pubs in this book have been hand-picked and vetted by CAMRA members and myself. All the information was checked by telephone prior to inclusion. However changes do occur to pubs and it's inevitable that, over the course of the life of this book, some will change hands and the policy towards children (as well as the real ales, food etc.) may be different. If you're travelling a distance, it's always worth a quick phone-call to check nothing has changed. Also, we would really welcome feedback about the pubs in this book, good or bad. There is a form at the back of this book where you can recommend a pub to be included in the next edition – or suggest we boot it out unceremoniously. If a pub really impresses please let us know: there are plans to institute a CAMRA family-friendly pub of the year and we'd love your input.

A few final points. Where we have said that kids are allowed everywhere this does not include the bar area, which is a big no-no whether the pub has a Children's Certificate or not. Don't forget that a lot of garden toys and entertainments are seasonal and slides and swings are usually packed away during the winter. Otherwise, my advice is to get out there and enjoy the pubs listed here – as well as the real ales. You won't find any Greenall Whitley anymore – praise be.

*Cheers*

ADRIAN TIERNEY-JONES

# First XIII

*Choosing one 'gold star' pub from each region is a hard job.
All the pubs in this book are present because they offer a
warm welcome to families as well as good real ales.
However, some pubs go that little bit further to entertain
children without losing their essential character, so here is the
best family-friendly pub for each region. Please contact us if
you have any thoughts on the selection or want to put your
own favourite forward for an accolade in the next edition.*

## The South West

**The Old Station House Inn** at
Blackmoor Gate on the fringes
of Exmoor where the staff are
especially trained to recognise
the needs of families and their
parents, without turning this
large roomy establishment
into a Butlins lookalike.

## The South

**The Chequers Inn** at Rookley on the Isle of Wight, an 18th-
century pub which was closed by Whitbread in 1988 because
they deemed it to be unprofitable. The current owners
bought it and have made a real success of it, complete with
lots of play facilities in the garden, colouring books handed
out inside and even a Braille menu.

## London

The editor's choice for London is not a pub. There are many family-friendly pubs in the city, but few have that extra something which makes them stand out. However, Wetherspoons gets an honourable mention because all their London establishments offer dedicated family and no-smoking areas, as well as a good selection of real ales.

## East Anglia

**Five Miles From Anywhere No Hurry Inn** at Upware in Cambridgeshire, which sits by the River Cam in four acres of landscaped gardens, has a large secure play area from which it will be difficult to prise away your hard-playing children.

## Midlands

Outside Scotland, the Midlands region covers the largest amount of pubs in this book and for that reason I have gone for a couple of pubs which I really think are outstanding.

**The Royal Oak Inn** at Old Tupton in Derbyshire, where there's an adventure playground and the presence of a magician on special occasions; there are also eight real ales usually on tap.

**The Fancott Arms** in Fancott, Bedfordshire, is home to a small light railway on which children can ride as it tours the garden. If that's not enough, there's a big climbing frame and a football pitch. When you're inside waiting to eat you get 'Freddy' bags which contain colouring pads and crayons.

## North West

**The Royal Oak** at Rode Heath in Cheshire where the play area includes swings, a slide and even go-karts. A bouncy castle and magician turn up during the pub's two beer festivals and during the rest of the time there are colouring books kept inside and a free ice cream with the kids' menu.

## Yorkshire

For rugby league-mad kids, the **Boat Inn** at Allerton Bywater is a must as it is full of sporting mementoes of the career of former Great Britain captain Brian Lockwood, whose son is landlord. There's also a newly built play area which shows that the pub is taking children very seriously. The Boat Brewery can also be found behind the back of the pub.

## North East

**The Travellers Rest** at Slaley because of its adventure playground and the chance for kids to try such delights as tortilla wraps and stir fries. Nice surrounding countryside as well.

## Wales

**The Barn** at Mwyndy, who book a clown for their summer beer festival and a magician for the winter one.

 **The Snowdonia Parc Hotel** at Waunfawr has a big playground outside, while inside there's a large family room with a fantastic selection of large toys such as pedal cars. There's also a brewpub attached. What more can you want?

## Scotland

**The Bridge Inn** in Ratho to the west of Edinburgh. Landlord Ronnie Rusack got the MBE for his work on getting the neighbouring Union Canal open to traffic and he also pioneered the use of Children's Licences. The Bridge is a very family-friendly place with an excellent kids' menu, a well-stocked play area, which includes a carousel, and children's parties on canal boats.

**The Sligachan Hotel** on the Isle of Skye which has won an award for being the most child-friendly pub on the island. If it's raining there's an indoor ball pool while outdoors there's an assault course play area.

# East Anglia

Cambridgeshire
Essex
Norfolk
Suffolk

*Fox & Hounds*
RAMSDEN HEATH, ESSEX

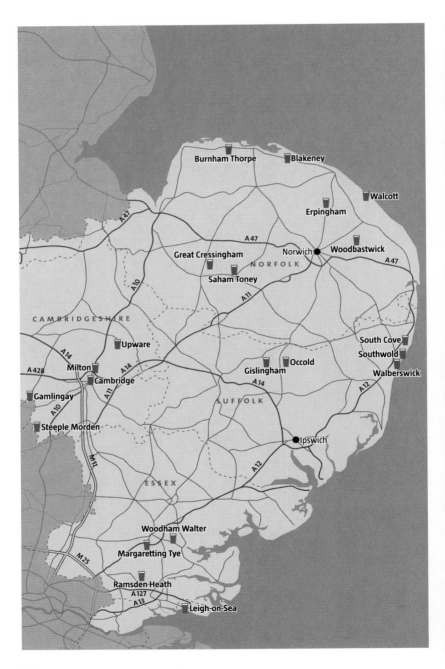

Noel Coward was never that complimentary about EAST ANGLIA. 'Norfolk, very flat,' was his sole comment. While the region is certainly vertically challenged, it is in many other ways blessed with some of the most beautiful countryside in England as the likes of Constable and Gainsborough realised when they set up their easels.

This is the home of the wide open skies of the Fens, the gentle greenness and picturesque villages of Suffolk, the popular beaches of north Norfolk, the sandy, tree-spotted expanses of the Brecklands, the Norfolk Broads where life passes at the pace of a narrow-boat. Not forgetting, of course, the cheerful, kiss-me-quick brashness of Southend.

It's an area with something for families with children of all ages, whether you want to walk the many nature trails and observe the wildlife, take a ride on a steam train, go boating on the Broads, build a sandcastle outside a brightly coloured beach hut, investigate the history of flying or go wild among the rides of a theme park.

As for the pubs, this is olde worlde territory with plenty of wooden beams, rustic furniture and even a collection of hats in one establishment. Most have outside playing areas, while several provide bouncy castles in the summer. One pub even organises an annual fireworks display.

Essex is the nearest county to London and even though it's the most built-up, especially in the south, it has its fair share of rural pubs. Seaside pleasures feature large among its attractions and Southend offers an aquarium and an indoor play area for days when beach play is rained off. Elsewhere, on brighter days, how about a splash on the beach or a spot of bird-spotting?

Suffolk is a county of unspoilt beaches and charming coastal villages, including the historic site of Dunwich which used to be a major city in the Middle Ages but has since fallen prey to the sea's progress. Its inspirational countryside means that Suffolk is also an ideal place for a walking or cycling holiday. Further inland, there is a wealth of small towns and villages, mainly unchanged for centuries, while more up-to-date pleasures are provided by leisure parks and an aircraft museum.

Despite Noel Coward's slight, Norfolk remains a favourite holiday destination, with the beaches at Cromer, Sheringham, Wells-next-the-Sea and Hunstanton particularly popular, while a holiday spent boating on the Norfolk Broads will be a favourite for most children. Other places to visit include a zoo, steam railway line and a reconstructed Celtic village.

At the heart of Cambridgeshire lies Cambridge with its museums, colleges and walks along the Cam. Or you might want to take out a punt. Away from the city, there are aircraft museums, plenty of countryside walks and a zoo. Check out the Five Miles From Anywhere Inn, a place where I guarantee you'll have a job getting the kids to leave. With attractions like these who needs Noel Coward?

## CAMBRIDGESHIRE

### CAMBRIDGE

## Cambridge Blue

85–87 Gwydir Street, Cambridge CB1 2LG
**T** 01223 361382
**E** cambridgeblue@fabdial.co.uk
*Licensees*: Chris and Debbie Lloyd
*Opening times*: 12–2.30 (3 Sat), 6–11; 12–3, 6–10.30 Sun
*Real ales*: Beer range varies

I remember this friendly back street pub back in the late 1970s when it was called the Dewdrop and owned by Tolly Cobbold. Now it's an enterprising freehouse run by the same couple who made such a success of the Free Press, which can be found nearer to the city centre. Gratifyingly, this is a completely non-smoking pub (no mobile phones allowed either). There's a lounge and main bar, conservatory and large secure rear garden which backs onto a cemetery; the internal decor is livened up by the presence of rowing memorabilia. The Anglia Polytechnic University is close and students are still known to nip over the back wall to get to the pub.

Children are allowed in the light and airy conservatory, where colouring books and games are provided, and also enjoy the garden populated by a Wendy House and a couple of rabbits. This is a wonderful place to sit in the summer.

Even though the pub majors on a good choice of real ales, including selections from Nethergate, Woodforde's, City of Cambridge and Milton, the food is equally tempting with some inspired vegetarian choices. The **kids' menu** thankfully avoids the chicken nugget syndrome, instead going for beans on toast, sausage and mash and jacket potatoes; be warned no chips or anything fried. Child-sized portions off the main menu can also be served where possible, including soup, paté, veggie chillis, burritos and nut roasts. Roast lunches (small portions available) are served on Sundays alongside the main menu. Food is available lunchtimes and evenings all week.

As for family attractions, Gwydir Street is about a mile from the city centre and the beautiful River Cam with its chance for punting, the Fitzwilliam Museum which has a massive collection of coins, paintings, antiquities and arms and armour (great for the bloodthirsty child!) and the Cambridge University Botanic Gardens. Much nearer there is Parkside swimming baths opposite Parkers Piece.

✓ children restricted to certain areas
✓ family room
✓ garden
✓ garden toys
✓ lunchtime meals
✓ evening meals
✓ food lunchtime and evening
✓ children's menu
✓ bottle warming
✓ no smoking area
✗ accommodation
✗ nearby camping and caravan sites

✘ nappy changing
✘ entertainment
✘ children's certificate
✘ high chairs
✓ time limit – 9pm

## GAMLINGAY

# Cock

25 Church Street, Gamlingay SG8 0NJ
**T** 01767 650255
*Licensee*: Roger Collins
*Opening times*: 11.30–3, 5.30–11; 11–30-11 Sat;
12–4, 7–10.30 Sun
*Real ales*: **Greene King Abbot, IPA**; guest beers

Back in the early 1600s this small village was almost totally destroyed by fire, with the Cock the sole survivor. Not surprisingly the inside of this Greene King-owned pub is multi-beamed with a rustic feel, including pew-style seating and an inglenook fireplace, while lots of pictures of cockerels and decorative brasses line the walls.

Children are allowed in the lounge bar which is designated as the family room. Here there are cards and dominoes. Families are also welcome in the no-smoking dining room. Out in the gated garden there is a play area with Wendy House and climbing frame, as well as a small menagerie consisting of goats, a Vietnamese pot-bellied pig, rabbits, guinea pigs and a couple of hens.

Food is served lunchtimes and evenings throughout the week apart from Sunday and Monday evenings. The **kids' menu** has the usual culprits with chips, but half-sized portions off the main menu can also be ordered where possible. Selections include tandoori chicken, fish dishes, small steaks, sandwiches, baguettes and jacket potatoes. Grandparents might like to note the special senior citizen lunches from Wednesday to Sunday.

After lunch take a walk around the village which has a nature conservation area; also nearby are Waresley and Grandsden woods. Over the border into Bedfordshire the Shuttleworth Collection of aircraft near Biggleswade is a short drive away.

✓ children restricted to certain areas
✓ family room
✓ garden
✓ garden toys
✓ lunchtime meals
✓ evening meals
✓ food lunchtime and evening
✓ children's menu
✓ bottle warming
✓ no smoking area
✘ accommodation
✘ nearby camping and caravan sites
✘ nappy changing
✘ entertainment
✘ children's certificate
✓ high chairs
✓ time limit – 9.30pm Fri, Sat

## MILTON

# Waggon & Horses

39 High Street, Milton CB4 6DF
**T** 01223 860313
*Licensee*: Nick Winnington
*Opening times*: 12–2.30 (3 Sat), 5 (6 Sat)–11;
12–3, 7–10.30
*Real ales*: **Elgood's Black Dog Mild, Cambridge Bitter, Pageant Ale**, seasonal beers, guest beers

Purpose-built 'Tudorbethan' 1930s pub which was once thought to be owned by Lacon's of Great Yarmouth; it's now an Elgood's house. The current landlord used to run the Cambridge Blue (see entry) and has amassed a large collection of hats which are on show in the pub. 'I always wore a bowler hat,' he tells me enigmatically when I ask about the display. Most of the hats are given to him by customers who get a pint in exchange. 'A decent hat, mind you.'

Children are allowed in the no-smoking part of the bar and the secure garden at the back of the pub, where swings and slides can be found. There used to be chickens but Reynard the Fox got to them.

Traditional bar food is served lunchtimes and evenings all week, with small portions off the main menu available for children. These include chips with ham, sausage, scampi or the ubiquitous chicken nugget, but there are also chillis and curries for adventurous older palates. Sundays sees a roast lunch alongside the main menu, with children being provided for with small portions.

Real cider is supplied by local producers Cassels.

Milton is a small village just north of Cambridge over the A14 so it's handy for visiting the city while nearer to the pub there's the Milton Country Park with plenty of walks.

✓ children restricted to certain areas
✗ family room
✓ garden
✓ garden toys
✓ lunchtime meals
✓ evening meals
✓ food lunchtime and evening
✗ children's menu
✓ bottle warming
✓ no smoking area
✗ accommodation
✗ nearby camping and caravan sites
✗ nappy changing
✗ entertainment
✗ children's certificate
✗ high chairs
✓ time limit – 9pm

## STEEPLE MORDEN

# Waggon & Horses

19 Church Street, Steeple Morden SG8 ONJ
**T** 01763 852829
*Licensee*: David Mumford
*Opening times*: 12–3, 7–11; 12–11 Sat; 12–10.30 Sun
*Real ales*: **Greene King XX Mild**; **IPA**; guest beers (summer)
*Directions*: off the A505 between Baldock and Royston

There was once a gallows and pillory in this rural south Cambridgeshire village, but nowadays life is much more sedate, especially in the traditional 300-year-old village pub. Inside, the main bar area leads to a cosy wood-beamed lounge where there's a large inglenook fireplace. Photos of the village at the turn of the last century can be found on the walls and in the words of the landlord there is also 'lots of bric-a-brac'. It's a friendly place catering to the community, but strangers are soon made to feel welcome.

Children are allowed in the lounge/family room and the very secure garden has swings and slides; there is plenty of room for children to let off steam.

No food is served apart from sandwiches at lunchtime (not on Sundays) so maybe this would be more suitable for a quick visit on the way to Linton Zoo or Duxford Air Museum, both of which are within easy driving distance. There is a Caravan Club registered site at the rear of the pub which must be booked.

✓ children restricted to certain areas
✓ family room
✓ garden
✓ garden toys
✗ lunchtime meals
✗ evening meals
✗ food lunchtime and evening
✗ children's menu
✗ bottle warming
✗ no smoking area
✗ accommodation
✓ nearby camping and caravan sites
✗ nappy changing
✗ entertainment
✗ children's certificate
✗ high chairs
✓ time limit – 9pm

## UPWARE

# Five Miles From Anywhere No Hurry Inn

Old School Lane, Upware CB7 5ZR
**T** 01353 721654    **F** 01353 722425
**E** office@fivemilesinn.co.uk
www.fivemiles.co.uk
*Licensees*: Mark and Christine Lewis
*Opening times*: 11–3, 7–11 (12.30am Wed, 2am Fri, Sat); closed Mon; 11–2am summer Sat; 12–10.30 Sun
*Real ales*: **City of Cambridge Hobson's Choice**; guest beers
*Directions*: two miles off A1123, between Wicken and Stretham

Unique modern pub which sits beside the River Cam and attracts a varied clientele, from boating types (there is a slipway and moorings) to walkers and families. There are also regular music nights. Set in over four acres of landscaped grounds, there are two airy and bright bars – a lounge bar and games bar with large-screen TV, video game machines and pool tables. There is also a restaurant which overlooks the gardens and river.

Children are allowed everywhere, though during the summer it would be hard to keep them away from the large secure play area with a tree house, slide, swing and other play activities, as well as a large bouncy castle.

Food is served every day, 11am–2.30pm Monday to Saturday and 12.30pm–3.30pm on Sundays when there is a carvery with child-sized portions (under-fives eat free, main course only); evening serving starts at 7pm all week, going through to 9.30pm (later on Wednesday, Friday and Saturday). The **kids' menu** has familiar choices with chips or new potatoes; sandwiches are also available.

As the name of the pub suggests this is a very rural location and is excellent for walks, especially at Wicken Fen National Nature Reserve, which has nature trails, children's activities and a visitor centre. Other attractions in the area which might interest historically-minded children include Oliver Cromwell's house in Ely, as well as the magnificent cathedral.

✗ children restricted to certain areas
✗ family room
✓ garden
✓ garden toys
✓ lunchtime meals
✓ evening meals
✓ food lunchtime and evening
✓ children's menu
✓ bottle warming
✗ no smoking area
✗ accommodation
✗ nearby camping and caravan sites
✓ nappy changing – women's toilet
✓ entertainment
✓ children's certificate
✓ high chairs
✓ time limit – 9pm

## ESSEX

### LEIGH-ON-SEA

# Broker

213–217 Leigh Road, Leigh-on-Sea SS9 1JA
T 01702 471932
www.brokerfreehouse.co.uk
*Licensee*: Alan Gloyne
*Opening times*: 11–3, 6–11; 11–11 Thu–Sat; 12–10.30 Sun
*Real ales*: **Ridleys IPA, Shepherd Neame Spitfire,** guest beers
*Directions*: 500 yards from A13

Leigh-on-Sea may be eclipsed by its brasher and bolder neighbour Southend, but it's still worth seeking out the Broker which can be found near a shopping centre. A family-run establishment, it's a large open-planned pub with a separate dining area and a small beer garden patio outside; in the summer there may be several outdoor toys for kids to play with. Inside there is also a Pacman machine.

Children are allowed in a designated no-smoking area in the main bar and the dining area. Food is served lunchtimes-only Monday–Wednesday, all day until 8.30pm on Thursday, Friday and Saturday and lunchtimes-only again on Sunday. There's no kids' menu as such but smaller portions are widely available off the extensive menu, many accompanied with chips. These might include omelettes, pasta dishes, bangers and mash and sandwiches, while Sunday lunch sees a roast in a baguette (child-sized portions available) or roast meat in a Yorkshire Pudding. There are also vegetarian options.

There is plenty to do in the area, including a local bowling alley and park with swings etc, while Southend with all its seaside glory is only 10 minutes away. Highlights for the kids include the Kids Kingdom indoor adventure play area at Garon Park in Southend and the Sealife Aquarium on the Esplanade.

✓ children restricted to certain areas
✗ family room
✓ garden
✓ garden toys
✓ lunchtime meals
✓ evening meals
✓ food lunchtime and evening
✗ children's menu
✓ bottle warming
✓ no smoking area
✗ accommodation
✗ nearby camping and caravan sites
✓ nappy changing – women's toilets
✗ entertainment
✓ children's certificate
✓ high chairs
✓ time limit – 7.30pm

## MARGARETTING TYE

## White Hart

Swan Lane, Margaretting Tye CM4 9JX
**T** 01277 840478    **F** 01277 841178
www.thewhitehart.uk.com
*Licensee*: Liz Haines
*Opening times*: 11.30–3, 6–11; 12–10.30 Sun
*Real ales*: **Adnams Bitter**, **Broadside**, **Mighty Oak IPA**, guest beers
*Directions*: between Stock, Galleywood and Margaretting

Even though Chelmsford is but a few miles to the south, the White Hart is in the middle of a rural area which is sometimes called Tigers Island. This apparently refers to the chaps working on the railway in the 19th century who liked to spend their time engaged in bareknuckle fighting. Nowadays, things are more peaceful in this very traditional, multi-roomed, single-bar hostelry which was built in the 16th century but enlarged in the 1960s. Inside, a profusion of old beams crisscross the ceiling, while there are exposed brick walls and a large no-smoking conservatory at the back where children are allowed. In here the decor is slate flooring, cane furniture and a light, airy, spacious feel.

Outside there is a large, fenced-in garden which I'm told should be gated by the summer of 2003; here there is a play area with swings, a slide and climbing frame.

There is also a pets corner with goats, birds and guinea pigs, while ducks use the fenced-off pond. Food is served lunchtimes and evenings all week, and from midday–8.30pm on Sundays. The **kids' menu** offers up familiar choices and during the school holidays it is joined by specials such as pizzas, pies and bangers and mash. On Sundays, small roasts are served alongside the children's menu.

Between 7–9 real ales are available, while two beer festivals are held throughout the year, in June and November. The summer festival has a sweet stall, ice cream stand and is very child-friendly. The pub used to have a bouncy castle during the summer, but sadly due to reckless, potentially dangerous behaviour by a minority of unsupervised children it was stopped. This is something, sadly, I have heard quite often during my research for this book.

This is an area popular with walkers, who make the pub their base.

✓ children restricted to certain areas
✓ family room
✓ garden
✓ garden toys
✓ lunchtime meals
✓ evening meals
✓ food lunchtime and evening
✓ children's menu
✓ bottle warming
✓ no smoking area
✗ accommodation
✓ nearby camping and caravan sites
✓ nappy changing – disabled toilets
✗ entertainment
✗ children's certificate
✓ high chairs
✗ time limit

## RAMSDEN HEATH

## Fox & Hounds

Church Road, Ramsden Heath CM11 1PW
**T** 01268 710286    **F** 01268 711988
www.pickapub.co.uk
*Licensee*: Jill Young
*Opening times*: 11–11; 12–10.30 Sun
*Real ales*: **Greene King IPA**, **Old Speckled Hen**, guest beers

Purpose-built pub dating from the 1920s which can be found just outside the village. Inside there's a bar and a spacious lounge area with oak barrels converted into tables and sepia pictures of the area on the wall. There's also a no-smoking restaurant.

Children are allowed anywhere and can be entertained with small games and colouring books; there's also a monthly karaoke in which the young ones take part. Outside at the back there's a large secure beer garden with a swing, slides and climbing frame as well as a pets' corner.

In July there's a family-friendly beer festival with a bouncy castle, entertainers, music and a barbecue. Beers come from local small breweries and Weston cider is also sold.

Food is served lunchtimes and evenings Monday-Saturday, while on Sundays it is available 12.30pm–6pm. The **kids' menu** has familiar choices with chips, while smaller portions off the main menu can be served if possible. These include traditional bar food standbys such as lasagne, cod and chips and scampi, as well as sandwiches and baguettes. On Sundays there is a carvery (small portions available) as well as the main menu.

Hanningfield Reservoir and its nature reserve is close, while Southend and its seaside pleasures are a short drive away.

- ✘ children restricted to certain areas
- ✘ family room
- ✔ garden
- ✔ garden toys
- ✔ lunchtime meals
- ✔ evening meals
- ✔ food lunchtime and evening
- ✔ children's menu
- ✔ bottle warming
- ✔ no smoking area
- ✘ accommodation
- ✘ nearby camping and caravan sites
- ✘ nappy changing
- ✔ entertainment
- ✘ children's certificate
- ✔ high chairs
- ✔ time limit – 9pm

## WOODHAM WALTER

# Bell

The Street, Woodham Walter CM9 6RF
T 01245 223437
*Licensee*: Alan Oldfield
*Opening times*: 12–3, 7–11; 12–3 Sun
*Real ales*: **Adnams Broadside**; **Greene King IPA**; guest beer
*Directions*: off A414, near Danbury

Black-and-white timber and plaster-faced hostelry from the 16th century in a village off the old Colchester-London road. Nowadays, it's popular with walkers and visitors to the nearby town of Maldon where a famous pre-Norman Conquest battle between Vikings and the locals is commemorated. Inside the Bell, it's very comfortable and traditional with plenty of wooden beams, log fires in the winter and old photos of the pub on the wall.

There's a bar area, a no-smoking family room and restaurant, with children allowed in the latter two spaces. There's a secure garden to the rear but care must be taken with toddlers as it runs down to a small stream. Food is served lunchtimes and evenings throughout the week, though not Sunday evenings when the pub closes. No kids' menu as such, but small portions off the main menu are usually served. These include sausage and chips, chicken dishes, sandwiches, salads, pies and on Sunday lunchtimes small roasts; the main menu is also available then.

As for things for the family to do, there's a nature trail around the village and plenty of walks in the surrounding countryside with opportunities to see the local birdlife. Further afield Colchester Zoo and the town's Castle Museum are easily reached by car.

- ✔ children restricted to certain areas
- ✔ family room
- ✔ garden
- ✘ garden toys
- ✔ lunchtime meals
- ✔ evening meals
- ✔ food lunchtime and evening
- ✘ children's menu
- ✔ bottle warming
- ✔ no smoking area

✘ accommodation
✘ nearby camping and caravan sites
✘ nappy changing
✘ entertainment
✘ children's certificate
✓ high chairs
✘ time limit

# NORFOLK

## BLAKENEY

### Kings Arms

Westgate Street, Blakeney NR25 7NQ
**T** 01263 740341
www.blakeneykingsarms.co.uk
*Licensees*: Howard and Marjorie Davies
*Opening times*: 11–11; 12–10.30 Sun
*Real ales*: **Adnams Bitter; Marston's Pedigree; Woodforde's Wherry**
*Directions*: just west of Blakeney Quay

Blakeney is a quaint old town on the north Norfolk coast which is popular with the yachting fraternity as well as birdwatchers and walkers. Regular ferry trips leave the quay to take visitors to see the unique seal colony at Blakeney Point, a three-mile long sand and shingle spit, which is also one of Britain's foremost bird sanctuaries. The 18th-century Kings Arms (look out for the distinct lettering 'FH 1760' on the roof) has been run by the same licensees for nearly 30 years and there are photographic mementos of their previous career in the London theatre dotted about on the walls; a must-see is a red telephone kiosk which acts as a compact cartoon gallery.

There are six rooms (three are non-smoking) in all, with children allowed everywhere apart from at the bar; a garden room has been recently added which can seat up to 40 people. Traditional pub games available include darts, table skittles and dominoes. Outside in the safe beer garden there are swings.

During the week food is served at lunchtimes and evenings until 9.30pm; it is available all day during the weekend; there are roast lunches on Sunday, adult portions only, but the kids' and main menus are available. The **kids' menu** includes familiar choices with chips, but also has homemade fish fingers, while smaller portions off the main menu are available including salads, pasta, sandwiches and jacket potatoes. The Kings Arms is specifically noted for fresh fish and shellfish which come from local suppliers.

This is a beautiful part of Norfolk with plenty of opportunities for exploring the coastline and seeing the wildlife, while the North Norfolk Railway runs nearby and there is also Holt Country Park with plenty of picnic areas, walks and organised seasonal events.

✘ children restricted to certain areas
✘ family room
✓ garden
✓ garden toys
✓ lunchtime meals
✓ evening meals
✓ food lunchtime and evening
✓ children's menu
✓ bottle warming
✓ no smoking area
✓ accommodation
✘ nearby camping and caravan sites
✓ nappy changing – disabled toilet
✘ entertainment
✘ children's certificate
✓ high chairs
✘ time limit

## BURNHAM THORPE

### Lord Nelson

Walsingham Road, Burnham Thorpe PE31 8HN
**T** 01328 738241
**E** enquiries@nelsonslocal.co.uk
www.nelsonslocal.co.uk
*Licensee*: Lucy Tagg
*Opening times*: 11–2.30, 6–11; 12–3.30, 7–10.30 Sun
*Real ales*: **Greene King Abbot, IPA; Woodforde's Nelson's Revenge, Wherry**

As the name of the pub suggests, Burnham Thorpe was the birthplace of Horatio Nelson. In his adult years, he lived in the village for several years before leaving for sea and fame in 1793, but not before he gave a farewell party for the villagers. At the time it was called the Plough, but the old sea dog's national fame eventually encouraged the renaming of the pub. Nowadays, Nelson is also commemorated with paintings, books and memorabilia on display and for sale. A rum-sounding rum concoction called Nelson's Blood is also served!

Time hasn't changed it that much since Nelson's days. For a start don't look for a serving bar – there isn't one. Staff serve drinks directly to your table and the real ale is tapped straight from the cask. Inside the pub, the decor is also traditional with high-backed settles in the Nelson Bar, while an open fireplace warms the Ward Room, which also doubles up as a family room and dining area; it is non-smoking. Children are allowed anywhere throughout the pub while outside there is a large beer garden with a play area.

The previous licensee's idea of food was apparently a bag of crisps, but that has all changed now with food being served at lunchtimes and in the evening until 9pm. The **kids' menu** has the usual favourites, while smaller portions off the excellent main menu are served where possible – these include filled baguettes, soups and vegetarian options. There are roast lunches on Sundays in the winter; small portions are served. Food is available 12pm–2.30pm and 6pm–9pm throughout the week. There are plenty of places to visit in this corner of Norfolk, including Royal Sandringham, Holkham Hall, the beaches of north Norfolk and the Sea Life Centre at Hunstanton. Please note: the pub is usually shut in January.

✗ children restricted to certain areas
✓ family room
✓ garden
✓ garden toys
✓ lunchtime meals
✓ evening meals
✓ food lunchtime and evening
✓ children's menu
✓ bottle warming
✓ no smoking area
✗ accommodation
✓ nearby camping and caravan sites
✓ nappy changing – disabled toilet
✗ entertainment
✗ children's certificate
✓ high chairs – booster seats
✗ time limit

## ERPINGHAM

# Spread Eagle

Eagle Road, Erpingham, NR11 7QA
T 01263 761591    F 01263 768609
*Licensee*: Billie Carder
*Opening times*: 11–3, 6.30–11; 12–3, 7–10.30 Sun
*Real ales*: **Adnams Bitter, Broadside; Greene King's Old Speckled Hen; Woodforde's Nelson's Revenge, Norfolk Nog, Wherry**
*Directions*: north of Aylsham, off the A140

Flint is used a lot for building in this part of the world and the 17th century Spread Eagle is no exception with its brick and flint frontage. Inside it's large and open-planned with a long comfortable bar, a games room, a non-smoking dining room and, during the summer, an outside garden bar. A wood-burning stove adds to the cosy atmosphere – but supervise toddlers!

There's a relaxed atmosphere as children are allowed everywhere apart from sitting at bar stools, though under-16s have to be out by 9.30pm. The games room is the designated family room and has a pool table plus books and board games. Outside the large garden is secure and popular with families during the summer when children can work off their energies on the climbing frame.

There's a **kids' menu** offering familiar choices such as sausages or fish fingers with chips, but smaller portions off the main menu can also be had. These include bar food staples such as scampi and sausages, plus choices off the specials board which may include spaghetti bolognese and chicken madras ('you'd be amazed how many kids like curries,' I'm told by the landlady). Roasts and the main menu are available on Sundays, which again feature small portions. Food is served all week, midday–2pm, 7pm–9pm.

Real ale scholars interested in the history of Woodforde's are directed to the barn in the car park which was the second home of the brewery, before they moved to Woodbastwick. An ideal stopping place on the way to the coastal resort of Cromer (the Norfolk Shire Horse Centre is nearby), where the carnival takes place in August, while the Norfolk Broads are very close. At Aylsham, just down the road there's Norfolk's longest narrow gauge steam railway, the Bure Valley Railway.

- ✗ children restricted to certain areas
- ✓ family room
- ✓ garden
- ✓ garden toys
- ✓ lunchtime meals
- ✓ evening meals
- ✓ food lunchtime and evening
- ✓ children's menu
- ✓ bottle warming
- ✓ no smoking area
- ✗ accommodation
- ✓ nearby camping and caravan sites
- ✗ nappy changing
- ✗ entertainment
- ✗ children's certificate
- ✓ high chairs
- ✓ time limit – 9.30pm

## GREAT CRESSINGHAM

# Olde Windmill Inn

Water End, Great Cressingham, Watton IP25 6NN
**T** 01760 756232   **F** 01760 756400
**E** halls232@aol.com
*Licensees*: Michael and Caroline Halls
*Opening times*: 11–3, 6–11; 12–3, 6–10.30 Sun
*Real ales*: **Adnams Bitter**, **Broadside**; **Greene King IPA**; guest beers.
*Directions*: Off the A1065 between Watton and Swaffham

The same family has owned this spacious rural inn for nearly half a century. It sits just north of the forested sandy heathland known as the Brecklands. Dating from 1650, the inn has been sympathetically extended over the years and now has ten separate drinking,

eating and socialising areas, including two conservatories and a games room. The decor is rustic throughout with log fires, agricultural bric-a-brac on the wall, such as old traps and brasses, and wooden beams.

Children are allowed in eight of the rooms, four of which are dedicated family rooms possessing the same olde worlde charm as the rest of the inn. There is no time limit and even though country music is played on Tuesday evenings it does not permeate through the rest of the inn. Use of the pool room has to be supervised by adults. There is access to the large secure beer garden from the family rooms, where a sand pit and play area can be found.

Food is served from 12pm–2pm every day throughout the week, while in the evenings it is available from 6.30pm–10.30pm (6pm on Sat, 6.30pm–10pm sun). The Tasty Toddlers menu includes familiar choices such as fish-shaped pieces of cod, burger or sausage with chips and beans. Smaller portions off the main menu are available where possible, such as scampi, coriander mushrooms and beef bourguignon. There are also specials. On Sundays there are two roasts (small portions available) plus the normal extensive menu. The licensees say that bottle and food warming can be done by special arrangement, so phone ahead.

No accommodation but there are two adjacent Caravan Club sites plus camping by arrangement. Nearby attractions include Thetford Forest Visitor Centre at Santon Downham, the Iceni Village at Cockley Cley and the Ecotech Centre at Swaffham. The Peddlars Way also passes close by.

- ✓ children restricted to certain areas
- ✓ family room
- ✓ garden
- ✓ garden toys
- ✓ lunchtime meals
- ✓ evening meals
- ✓ food lunchtime and evening
- ✓ children's menu
- ✓ bottle warming – by special arrangement
- ✗ no smoking area
- ✗ accommodation
- ✓ nearby camping and caravan sites

✓ nappy changing ladies – women's toilets
✗ entertainment
✗ children's certificate
✓ high chairs
✗ time limit

## SAHAM TONEY

# Old Bell

Saham Toney, Watton IP25 7HD
T 01953 884934
Licensees: Sally-Ann and Binzy Leeder
Opening times: 11–3, 5–11; 11–11 Sat; 12–10.30 Sun
Real ales: **Adnams Bitter**; guest beers
Directions: one mile outside Watton

Baseball caps, including one from the New York Fire Department in the aftermath of September 11, cover the walls and beams of this friendly 17th-century pub. The landlord is a mad keen sports fan so there is lots of other related memorabilia hanging on the wall. It all makes for a warm and cosy atmosphere complemented by the excellent food which includes organic meat from an award-winning butcher.

Children are allowed in the no-smoking dining room and also in the snug to the left of the wooden floored bar. The latter hosts a TV and is classed as the family room. Outside, to the left of the pub, there is a secure garden with a Wendy House. It is reached by going over a small bridge built by the landlord. A bouncy castle may appear on the odd occasion during the summer, and barbecues are held. There is also a patio at the back of the pub.

The **kids' menu** has familiar choices, though smaller portions off the main menu can be served where possible. These include sandwiches, pasta, jacket potatoes and salad as well as the pub's biggest seller, steak and kidney pie. In the summer homemade ice creams are a welcome part of the menu. Roasts and the main menus are served on Sunday with small roasts for children. Food is served at lunchtimes and evenings every day.

Even though it's a small village, Saham Toney has one of the oldest meres (Old English for an artificial pool) in the country and it is also close to Wayland Wood, where the Babes in the Woods tale is supposed to have originated back in the 16th century. There are plenty of walks in the area, with the Peddars Way and Thetford Forest close by. Other attractions include Banham Zoo and an Iceni Village and Museum at Cockley Cley.

✓ children restricted to certain areas
✓ family room
✓ garden
✓ garden toys
✓ lunchtime meals
✓ evening meals
✓ food lunchtime and evening
✓ children's menu
✓ bottle warming
✓ no smoking area
✗ accommodation
✓ nearby camping and caravan sites
✗ nappy changing
✗ entertainment
✗ children's certificate
✓ high chairs
✓ time limit – 9.30pm

## WALCOTT

# Lighthouse Inn

Coast Road, Walcott NR12 0PE
T 01692 650371
E info@lighthouseinn.co.uk;
www.lighthouseinn.co.uk
Licensee: Steve Bullimore
Opening times: 11–11; 12–10.30 Sun
Real ales: **Adnams Bitter; Tetley Bitter**; guest beers

This warm and friendly pub, situated on the coast, halfway between Great Yarmouth and Cromer, is very popular with locals and organises many events such as one of the largest fireworks displays in the area.

However it is also a magnet for visiting families, especially on those August evenings when discos, barbecues and children's entertainments (including a clown) are organised, weather permitting. Children are allowed in a spacious family room (where there is plenty to amuse them), the no-smoking dining room and the enclosed and spacious beer garden (with rides and games).

When hunger strikes, the **kids' menu** has familiar choices served with chips while smaller portions of the good value main menu, which uses locally grown vegetables, quality meat and homemade pastry, are also available. These include a variety of salads, homemade pies, homemade lasagne, bar standards with chips, fish dishes and sandwiches. On Sundays both a roast and the main menus are available; with child-sized portions of the roast served. Food is available all day until late in the evening throughout the whole week.

No accommodation, but there is a camping and caravan site at the back of the pub. Walcott is in an ideal position for visiting the many attractions in the area, including the Woodland Leisure Park at Trimingham, the shopping village Roys of Wroxham and a beautiful picnic spot at Bacton Wood.

✓ children restricted to certain areas
✓ family room
✓ garden
✓ garden toys
✓ lunchtime meals
✓ evening meals
✓ food lunchtime and evening
✓ children's menu
✓ bottle warming
✓ no smoking area
✗ accommodation
✓ nearby camping and caravan sites
✗ nappy changing
✓ entertainment
✗ children's certificate
✓ high chairs
✗ time limit

## WOODBASTWICK

### Fur & Feather Inn

Slad Lane, Woodbastwick NR13 6HQ
T 01603 720003
www.furandfeatherinn.co.uk
*Licensee*: Tim Ridley
*Opening times*: 11.30–3, 6–11 (11.30–11 summer); 12–10.30 Sun
*Real ales*: **Woodforde's Mardler's Mild, Fur and Feather, Wherry, Great Eastern, Nelson's Revenge, Norfolk Nog, Admiral's Reserve, Headcracker**
*Directions*: off B1140 east of Norwich, follow brown signs for Woodforde's Brewery

Welcoming pub and restaurant in an idyllic spot which was converted from three thatched cottages. It's also the 'tap' for next door's Woodforde's brewery, so you are always guaranteed an excellent pint. There is also a visitor centre for the brewery so you can buy their beers and other souvenirs to take home. Inside the big open bar, it's traditional rustic decor with exposed brick and beams, quarry stone tiled floor and heavy oak furniture.

Children are allowed in the no-smoking area of the bar and the restaurant, which is also no smoking. There are tables outside in the front garden which has a pond; there is a two-foot fence around it but do keep an eye on toddlers and young children. During the summer, barbecues are occasionally held outside.

Food is served both lunchtimes and evenings all year round and the **kids' menu** features standards such as beans on toast, cheesy pasta bites, lasagne and ham & chips. Other selections off the main menu can also be served where possible; these include bangers and mash, scampi, sandwiches and salads. On Sunday lunchtimes, child-sized roasts are served alongside the main menu. As well as the full range of Woodforde's beer, the brewery's bottle-conditioned barley wine Norfolk Nips can also be supped.

Norwich and Great Yarmouth are within easy driving distance, while Woodbastwick is on the edge of that unique combination of lakes and rivers the Norfolk Broads; here there are plenty of opportunities for exploring, boating and general outdoor fun.

✓ children restricted to certain areas
✗ family room
✓ garden
✗ garden toys
✓ lunchtime meals
✓ evening meals
✓ food lunchtime and evening
✓ children's menu
✗ bottle warming
✓ no smoking area
✗ accommodation
✗ nearby camping and caravan sites
✓ nappy changing – disabled toilet

✗ entertainment
✗ children's certificate
✓ high chairs
✗ time limit

## SUFFOLK

### GISLINGHAM

## Six Bells

High Street, Gislingham IP23 8JD
T 01379 783349
*Licensees*: Roy and Margaret Buttle
*Opening times*: 12–3, 7 (6 Fri)–11 (closed Mon);
12–3, 7–10.30 Sun
*Real ales*: **Adnams Bitter**; guest beer
*Directions*: between Eye and Stowmarket

Friendly Victorian village local named after the six ancient bells hanging in Gislingham's church tower. It's a roomy pub consisting of a bar with a large collection of brewery pump clips on the walls (the landlord is a CAMRA member and a strong supporter of micro-breweries), a comfortable lounge area within the bar and a no-smoking dining room called the Columbine Room. This was opened in 1991 and a well was uncovered in the course of building; it has been covered with glass and illuminated providing a feature in the tastefully decorated room.

Children are allowed everywhere, while outside there is a safe garden adjoining the pub with swings and a climbing frame; there's also a village playground close to the pub.

Food is served lunchtimes and evenings throughout the week. The **kids' menu** has familiar choices while smaller portions off the menu can be ordered where possible; this includes traditional bar food choices such as scampi and ham, egg and chips, home-cooked casseroles, curries and sandwiches. Sunday lunches see a roast as well as the main menu; small roasts are available.

A very welcoming pub, run by the same licensees for 13 years. It's close to Thornham Walks where there are 12 miles of footpaths through the Thornham estate. These includes ones through ancient parkland, woodland, farmland and water meadows; there is also an extensive programme of activities throughout the year. Also close by is Thornham Parva whose ancient thatched church traces its history back to the Norman times.

✗ children restricted to certain areas
✗ family room
✓ garden
✓ garden toys
✓ lunchtime meals
✓ evening meals
✓ food lunchtime and evening
✓ children's menu
✓ bottle warming
✓ no smoking area
✗ accommodation
✓ nearby camping and caravan sites
✗ nappy changing
✗ entertainment
✓ children's certificate
✓ high chairs
✗ time limit

### OCCOLD

## Beaconsfield Arms

Mill Road, Occold IP23 7PN
T 01379 678033
*Licensees*: Wendy and Gerald Turner
*Opening times*: 12–3, 6–11; 12–3, 6.30–10.30 Sun
*Real ales*: **Adnams Bitter**; **Greene King Abbot**, **IPA**; occasional guest beer

Time stands still in this friendly village pub. Landlady Wendy Turner remembers the time when this very old pub was full of Sealed Knot members after an engagement at a county show in nearby Eye. Not only did these enthusiastic recreators drink the pub dry, but dressed in their Civil War uniforms and carrying their own pewter mugs they did not look out of place among the low ceilings, wooden beams, church pews, inglenook fireplace and rustic furniture. The profusion of hanging flower baskets at the front also invites comment. One customer told the Turners that he knew they were running the place as soon as he passed, as their previous pub in the district had been similarly floral. Inside there's a main bar area, a games room and a non-smoking dining room.

Children are allowed in the dining room only – but it's fine to sit there with a drink and a bag of crisps – you don't have to eat a full meal. At the back of the pub, there's a secluded, hedged garden with slide, tree house and swings. Food is served lunchtimes and evenings all week, with the **kids' menu** featuring familiar choices, while smaller portions off the main menu are also available where possible. These include freshly prepared, value-for-money choices such as pies, beef in red wine, chicken tikka and lamb in mint.

A very friendly and traditional pub close to the beautiful old town of Eye, while further afield it's a short drive to the Norfolk and Suffolk Aviation Museum at Flixton and to Banham Zoo over the border in Norfolk.

✓ children restricted to certain areas
✗ family room
✓ garden
✓ garden toys
✓ lunchtime meals
✓ evening meals
✓ food lunchtime and evening
✓ children's menu
✓ bottle warming
✓ no smoking area
✗ accommodation
✗ nearby camping and caravan sites
✗ nappy changing
✗ entertainment
✓ children's certificate
✓ high chairs
✓ time limit – 8.30pm

## SOUTH COVE

# Five Bells

Southwold Road, South Cove NR34 7JF
**T** 01502 675249
*Licensee*: Colin Harbour
*Opening times*: 11.30–3, 6.30–11; 12–3, 6.30–10.30 Sun

*Real ales*: **Adnams Bitter, Broadside**; occasional seasonal beer
*Directions*: on the B1127 between Southwold and Wrentham

Traditional community pub to be found in a small village which lies just off the A12 which makes it a handy stop if you're travelling up to Lowestoft or Great Yarmouth. Inside the comfortable interior there's a public bar, no-smoking lounge/family room and small dining area at the back. On the walls there are old pictures of the pub before its refurbishment, as well as various bits of brass, swords and spears.

Children are allowed in the lounge and dining area, while there's also a garden to the side. Food is served lunchtimes and evenings all week. There's a small **kids' menu** with the ubiquitous chicken nuggets or fish fingers served with chips. Smaller portions off the main menu can also be ordered; choices include honest pub food such as sausages, ham, bangers and mash and a pasta bake. Child-sized roasts are available throughout the week, including Sundays when the main menu can also be chosen from.

There's a caravan site at the back of the pub but please call in advance to arrange bookings. Attractions in the immediate area include the Suffolk Wildlife and Country Park at Kessingland, while Lowestoft has New Pleasurewood Hills leisure park with plenty of thrilling rides and lots of other attractions for the family.

✓ children restricted to certain areas
✓ family room
✓ garden
✗ garden toys
✓ lunchtime meals
✓ evening meals
✓ food lunchtime and evening
✓ children's menu
✓ bottle warming
✗ no smoking area
✓ accommodation
✓ nearby camping and caravan sites
✗ nappy changing
✗ entertainment
✗ children's certificate
✓ high chairs
✗ time limit

## SOUTHWOLD

# Lord Nelson

East Street, Southwold IP18 6EH
**T** 01502 722079
*Licensee:* John Illston
*Opening times:* 10.30–11; 12–10.30 Sun
*Real ales:* **Adnams Bitter; Broadside**; seasonal ales

Friendly and bustling 18th-century brick-built Adnams pub yards from the beach; there is a small smuggler's window on the roof from where the revenue-running men of yesteryear signalled their illegal intentions. As the name suggests, Horatio Nelson is celebrated with gusto within, with lots of memorabilia, including old prints and pictures.

Inside there's one large bar with a snug on the left and a family room-cum-dining area on the right; children are allowed in the very compact snug and family room – this is probably best for the over-fives. There is also an enclosed garden at the back of the pub.

Food is served both lunchtimes and evenings all week. The **kids' menu** has the usual favourites with chips, while smaller portions off the bar menu can also be ordered; these include ham, scampi, sandwiches and salads. On Sundays, the general menu is available. Southwold is an idyllic seaside place to visit all round the year, with lots of small shops, Adnams pubs and in the summer a great beach lined with the famous beach huts. Outside the town, sights to visit include Walberswick Nature Reserve just over the Blyth estuary, Henham Park at Wangford, which usually hosts a Grand Steam Rally in September and also has plenty of beautiful walks, and the Suffolk Wildlife and Country park at Kessingland.

✓ children restricted to certain areas
✓ family room
✓ garden
✗ garden toys
✓ lunchtime meals
✓ evening meals
✓ food lunchtime and evening
✓ children's menu
✓ bottle warming
✗ no smoking area
✗ accommodation
✓ nearby camping and caravan sites
✗ nappy changing
✗ entertainment
✗ children's certificate
✗ high chairs
✗ time limit

## WALBERSWICK

# Bell Inn

Ferry Road, Walberswick IP18 6TN
**T** 01502 723109    **F** 01502 722728
**E** bellinn@btinternet.com
www.blythweb.co.uk/bellinn
*Licensee:* Sue Ireland-Cutting
*Opening times:* 11–3, 6–11; 11–11 Sat and summer; 11–10.30 Sat
*Real ales:* **Adnams Bitter, Broadside**; seasonal ales

Wonderful 16th-century inn opposite the village green and a few yards from the beach. Southwold lies to the north over the River Blyth where you can always find a ferry; on some days the aroma of Adnams brewing over in Southwold is in the air. Inside the multi-roomed Bell, there are low beams, well-worn flagstone floors, open fires, an inglenook fireplace and plenty of photos of village folk, many of whom still use the inn. The ghost of an old fisherman reputedly haunts the place, while George Orwell, who was a regular at the pub when he lived in Southwold, saw a spirit in the village churchyard.

Children are allowed in three rooms and the no-smoking dining area, but not around the bar. Steps lead down into the family room to the left of the bar, where there are colouring books and toys to keep the young ones occupied. The garden round the back looks out over the sea, but is open to the car park so do keep an eye on the kids.

The food is good here with plenty of fresh fish, while the **kids' menu** has familiar choices alongside salads, fish, sandwiches and macaroni cheese pasta. Some dishes off the main menu are also available, such as scampi, chilli and pasta. There are Sunday roasts in the winter and child-sized ones can be served if needed. Food is served lunchtimes and evenings all year round, though it starts an hour later in week evenings during the winter.

This is situated right on the beautiful Suffolk coast, and adventurous kids will be intrigued by the sunken village of Dunwich which is not too far away; it used to be a thriving port in the Middle Ages but the sea took it all away and all that remains now are ever-eroding sand dunes. Other nearby attractions include the riverside centre of Snape Maltings, with its unusual shops and galleries, and the major RSPB reserve at Minsmere near Westleton, a village which also has a large, barn-like second-hand bookshop.

✓ children restricted to certain areas
✓ family room
✓ garden
✗ garden toys
✓ lunchtime meals
✓ evening meals
✓ food lunchtime and evening
✓ children's menu
✓ bottle warming
✓ no smoking area
✓ accommodation
✗ nearby camping and caravan sites
✓ nappy changing
✗ entertainment
✗ children's certificate
✓ high chairs
✗ time limit

# London

Greater London

*The White Horse*
PARSONS GREEN, SW6

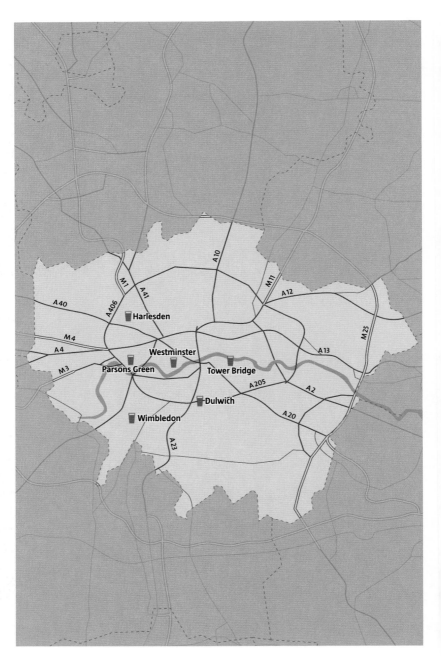

LONDON is one of the great world capitals, packed with history, culture – and shopping! Bloodthirsty kids will revel in the Tower of London – have a total chill-thrill by arriving by boat at Traitors' Gate. Just up the road older children will adore the London Dungeon (a sort of Madame Tussauds of Torture and Horror). The museums are legendary (and full of interaction fun) and the whole family should be awed by the view from the London Eye. Historical sites are beyond count – Buckingham Palace, Westminster Abbey, St Pauls, Houses of Parliament for starters. You can catch a movie or, even better, a live show (check out the half-price ticket booth on Leicester Square which sells cut-price tickets on the day).

All that activity brings on a thirst and the large expanses of Wetherspoon-owned pubs have been a blessing with their no-smoking family areas, but there are also several traditional pubs with excellent food and regular beer festivals that are (perhaps surprisingly for the capital) family-friendly.

## NORTH-WEST LONDON

### NW10: HARLESDEN

## Grand Junction Arms

Canal Bridge, Acton Lane NW10 7AD
T 0208 965 5670
*Opening times*: 11–11; 12–10.30 Sun
*Licensee*: Terry Hills
*Real ales*: **Young's Bitter**, **Special**, seasonal beers

Young's-owned pub situated alongside the Grand Union Canal. If by any lucky chance you're narrow-boating with the family in this area, mooring facilities are available. Children are only allowed in at weekends until 7pm, but this is when the pub has a particularly family-orientated feel. There is no family room, but children are allowed in the large back bar and in fine weather there's a garden and patio which overlooks the canal; keep an eye on wandering toddlers. There's also a playground at the back.

Food is served all day (cold snacks only 3–6pm), with the **kids' menu** offering familiar choices. Sunday lunchtime sees a roast (small portions available) alongside the main menus. The Grand Junction's attitude to children is welcoming and relaxed and if you are in the area this is fine place to visit. As for family attractions, the main one is the canal and you could walk (or narrow-boat) all the way to Manchester if you had the inclination – and the time.

✓ children restricted to certain areas
✗ family room
✓ garden
✓ garden toys
✓ lunchtime meals
✓ evening meals
✓ food lunchtime and evening
✓ children's menu
✓ bottle warming
✗ no smoking area
✗ accommodation

✗ nearby camping and caravan sites
✗ nappy changing
✗ entertainment
✓ children's certificate
✗ high chairs
✓ time limit – 7pm, weekends

## SOUTH-EAST LONDON

### SE1: TOWER BRIDGE

## Pommelers Rest

196–198 Tower Bridge Road SE1 2UN
T 0207 378 1399
*Licensee*: Chris Haigh
*Opening times*: 11–11; 12–10.30 Sun
*Real ales*: **Courage Directors**; **Fuller's London Pride**; **Shepherd Neame Spitfire**; **Theakston Best Bitter**; guest beers

Wetherspoon's pub which is very handy if you're visiting the nearby attractions of the Tower of London, the London Dungeon and Tower Bridge. Like a lot of the pub chain's conversions, the Pommelers had a totally different function before becoming a pub, in this case a hotel. By the way, the name of the pub derives from a tool used by saddlers who were prominent in the area once upon a time.

Children are allowed in the no-smoking area which is designated as a family area but they must be eating with adults and leave by 9pm.

Food is served from 10am (no alcohol until 11am) until 10pm and there's a **kids' menu** which includes familiar choices – crayons and drawings to colour in accompany their food. Some of the main menu can also be served in smaller portions; these include bangers and mash and burgers. Sunday lunchtime sees a choice of roast (small portions available) alongside the main menus.

A big and spacious pub which is ideal for relaxing in after you've exhausted the tourist sights in the area (and are totally exhausted yourselves).

✓ children restricted to certain areas
✓ family room
✗ garden
✗ garden toys
✓ lunchtime meals
✓ evening meals
✓ food lunchtime and evening
✓ children's menu
✓ bottle warming
✓ no smoking area
✗ accommodation
✗ nearby camping and caravan sites
✓ nappy changing – disabled toilets
✗ entertainment
✓ children's certificate
✓ high chairs
✓ time limit – 9pm

## SE21: DULWICH

# Crown & Greyhound

73 Dulwich Village, London SE21 7BJ
**T** 0208 299 4976   **F** 0208 693 8959
*Licensee*: Catherine Boulter
*Opening times*: 11–11; 12–10.30 Sun
*Real ales*: **Adnams Bitter; Fuller's London Pride; Young's Special**

During the latter years of the Victorian age, there were two pubs opposite each other in Dulwich Village. The Crown was on the site of the present-day pub, while the Greyhound (a favourite of Charles Dickens) sat opposite. The landlord of the Crown reckoned two pubs was one too many and so he bought the Greyhound and promptly pulled it down. He also demolished the Crown (no planning in those days) and built a new pub which is why we have this hybrid of a name - to make things even more confusing the pub is also known locally as the Dog! It's a large and imposing building with three bars, a restaurant, conservatory and split-level garden which is secure for small children. Inside, the decor is traditional with wooden floorboards, pictures of the old Greyhound and massive windows to the front which

helps to keep things light and airy.

Children are allowed in a no-smoking area at the front, the restaurant and the conservatory. There is a sandpit in the garden which also has plenty of seating; there are barbecues during the summer.

Food is served all day throughout the week and midday–3pm, 4pm–9pm on Sundays. No kids' menu or chips either, but smaller portions off the main menu are available for most dishes. One favourite is sausage and mash, while there are also pasta dishes and sandwiches. Sunday lunchtime sees a roast and carvery only with small portions available; the second Sunday food session sees the pub revert back to its normal menu. A popular place which is near Dulwich Picture Gallery.

✓ children restricted to certain areas
✗ family room
✓ garden
✓ garden toys
✓ lunchtime meals
✓ evening meals
✓ food lunchtime and evenings
✗ children's menu
✓ bottle warming
✓ no smoking area
✗ accommodation
✗ nearby camping and caravan sites
✓ nappy changing – women's toilets
✗ entertainment
✓ children's certificate
✓ high chairs
✓ time limit – 9pm

# SOUTH-WEST LONDON

## SW1: WESTMINSTER

# Lord Moon of the Mall

16–18 Whitehall SW1A 2DY
**T** 0207 839 7701
*Licensee*: Mary Jane Iverach
*Opening times*: 11–11; 12–10.30 Sun

*Real ales*: **Courage Directors; Fuller's London Pride; Greene King Abbot; Shepherd Neame Spitfire**; guest beers

Former bank which has been imaginatively converted by Wetherspoon's, leaving the high ornate ceilings and other features from the days when clerks rather than drinkers ruled the roost. There's also a cash dispenser, wood panelling, rows of books on shelves and pictures and prints of local sights on the walls. Children are allowed in a designated family area to the back of the pub, where there are also some no-smoking tables.

Food is served all day throughout the week with the **kids' menu** offering pizza, spaghetti bolognese and bangers and mash; there are no chips or fried food. Cottage pie off the main menu can also be served in a small portion. Sunday lunchtime sees a choice of roast (small portions available), alongside the main menus. A free colouring set of crayons and a sheet is handed out with each kids' meal.

An ideal place to get a drink and something to eat if you are sight-seeing in central London as Westminster, Trafalgar Square, Downing Street and Piccadilly Circus are all within easy walking distance.

✓ children restricted to certain areas
✗ family room
✗ garden
✗ garden toys
✓ lunchtime meals
✓ evening meals
✓ food lunchtime and evening
✓ children's menu
✓ bottle warming
✓ no smoking area
✗ accommodation
✗ nearby camping and caravan sites
✓ nappy changing – disabled toilets
✗ entertainment
✓ children's certificate
✓ high chairs
✓ time limit – 5pm

## SW6: PARSONS GREEN

# White Horse

1–3 Parsons Green SW6 4UL
**T** 0207 736 2115
www.whitehorsesw6.com
*Licensee*: Mark Dorber
*Opening times*: 11–11; 12–10.30 Sun
*Real ales*: **Adnams Broadside; Draught Bass; Harveys Sussex Best Bitter; Oakham JHB; Roosters Yankee**; guest beers

Large Victorian building which sits on the corner of the northern edge of Parsons Green. A former coaching inn and Victorian gin palace, it's justifiably popular with anyone who likes excellent beers and wonderful food. Inside, there's a traditional mahogany bar with large wooden tables and benches and comfy sofas. The walls are covered in posters and photos relating to beer and there's a glass display case containing dozens of foreign beers, revealing the landlord's passion for John Barleycorn and all his works.

Children are allowed in all the areas where food is served which amounts to the whole pub; the coach house restaurant is at the back of the pub and is totally no-smoking. Outside the pub there's a large seated area where there are occasional barbecues in the summer. Keep an eye on children as the area is open onto the road. There are no nappy-changing facilities as such, but the pub say that the loos are big enough or if you ask they will direct you to a space upstairs.

Delicious food is served all day throughout the week. No kids' menu but smaller portions of what the landlord calls 'real food' are served. These can include pan-roasted pork chop with caramelised apples and crackling, braised lamb shank with cous cous and sausage and mash. The chips are real as well. There are always two roasts served during Sunday lunch in the winter (small portions available), alongside the main menu and specials. A bustling and busy pub which hosts regular beer festivals and also serves several Belgian, German and even American micro-brewery beers on tap. It's a short walk from Parsons Green tube, and very handy for getting to places like South Kensington with its museums and Kings Road.

x children restricted to certain areas
x family room
✓ garden
x garden toys
✓ lunchtime meals
✓ evening meals
✓ food lunchtime and evening
x children's menu
✓ bottle warming
✓ no smoking area
x accommodation
x nearby camping and caravan sites
x nappy changing
x entertainment
x children's certificate
✓ high chairs
x time limit

## SW19: WIMBLEDON

# Hand In Hand

7 Crooked Billet SW19 4RQ
**T** 0208 946 5720
*Licensee*: Sarah Marley
*Opening times*: 11–11; 12–10.30 Sun
*Real ales*: **Young's Bitter**, **Special**, seasonal beers

Attractive, cosy and friendly old pub off the south-west corner of Wimbledon Common. There's a main bar with local prints on the wall and quarry tiling on the floor and a comfortable no-smoking family room which is where children are allowed. Games such as dominoes, Monopoly and Cluedo are available from the bar to keep them entertained while the older ones might like a go at the bar billiards. Outside at the front there's a small courtyard; parents need to remain vigilant as it opens onto the road, so this is the sort of place which is best for over-sixes. Food is served lunchtimes and evenings throughout the week with a **kids' menu** featuring familiar choices with chips. However, smaller portions are available off the main menu including penne pasta and scampi. Sunday lunchtime sees a choice of roast (small portions available) alongside the main menus. Intriguingly enough, until 1974 the Hand In Hand only had a licence for selling beer which was very rare in those days. Continuing the beer connection it is also allegedly built on the site of a house originally owned by one of the Watney family; no Red Barrel thankfully. An ideal place to relax after a walk on Wimbledon Common where you can regale the children with worthy litter-collecting tales of the Wombles. Also, if you're in the area around November 5, King's College School opposite the pub has one of the best firework displays in London.

✓ children restricted to certain areas
✓ family room
✓ garden
x garden toys
✓ lunchtime meals
✓ evening meals
✓ food lunchtime and evening
✓ children's menu
✓ bottle warming
✓ no smoking area
x accommodation
x nearby camping and caravan sites
x nappy changing
x entertainment
x children's certificate
x high chairs
x time limit

# Warning!
# Bouncy Castles and Bottle-warming Ban-alert!

As pub-going parents, it's the little things that count: friendly staff happily heating up a bottle; a pile of toys under a seat. If we catch sight of swings and slides our spirits soar. If there's a bouncy castle, we think we've died and gone to real pub heaven.

But all these godsends are under threat. And, before you start groaning about nanny states and government red tape, let me say it's the landlords themselves who are considering this grim and grisly step. Yes, bouncy castles could be banned. And, when it comes to bottle warming, landlords could well be losing their bottle.

Even as children's certificates are being replaced by a system which lets the licensee make his own mind up about kids, and pubs are getting family-friendly makeovers, the things that help make a pub family-friendly are looking increasingly precarious. Whilst researching this book, I have come across several landlords who have dispensed with bouncy castles because they have been unable to get insurance for them. In these litigious times, companies are apparently nervous over parents contacting their lawyers at the merest hint of a scratch.

The Wheel & Compass at Market Harborough used to have a bouncy castle but in 2002 their normal insurers turned them down. Landlord David Woolman was totally bemused: 'We never had any accidents but because the bouncy castle didn't have a member of staff supervising all the time the insurers turned me down. The kids were going free on it but the parents didn't give a monkeys about looking after them.'

The issue is making Woolman seriously consider the whole question of outdoor play equipment which the pub also has. 'I am frightened that some kids might hurt themselves and I can't help but think about the claims adverts on the TV. Sometimes I ponder getting rid of that too. The risk falls back on me as the parents don't seem to care. They bring footballs in and kick them about while there are people eating and drinking.'

Jim Slavin, manager at the Bridge Inn at Ratho, near Edinburgh, agrees: 'Litigious parents are becoming a problem. I've noticed at one or two of the larger themed pubs which have indoor play areas that there are signs saying that children have to be supervised by adults. You also have to be very careful with food being served. If a pint of beer went over a child it was an early introduction to alcohol, but hot food and drink are a different matter.'

It's not just bouncy castles either. Family-friendly pubs have always understood that little things like warming up a bottle or a jar of food make all the difference to harried parents. But many landlords told me that now even this innocent attempt to help is backfiring and some of them have gone so far as to refuse to heat bottles or food. Jim Slavin again: 'We tell parents about the strength of our microwaves compared to theirs and that we are being very careful.' The Fancott Arms in Bedfordshire also seems to be eminently sensible in that they hand out bowls of hot water to parents so that they can work out their own temperature.

Yes, catering microwaves can be very powerful and a bottle could come out too hot. But whatever happened to parents testing a bottle on the inside of their wrists? How simple a test is that? What on earth is happening to this country? Without going too much down the 'disgusted of Tunbridge Wells' route, it does seem that our society is following America and suing at the drop of a hat.

Certainly pubs should look after their customers. It's their duty to ensure that play equipment is in good order for instance and that parents should be warned if a plate is exceedingly hot. But, come on, parents also have their role to play. Just because there's a bouncy castle on tap, it's not a case of sit back and let the kids get on with it – they should always be supervised. Many landlords expressed dismay at the way parents allowed their children to rampage around the pub in a totally free-ranging manner. Not good manners for starters but certainly not a great idea when staff are carrying hot food around. It's an accident waiting to happen – and it's the pub which would get the blame.

Come on parents. Give your landlords support on this one. Otherwise you just might find all those extras which make a great family pub just fade away.

# Midlands

Bedfordshire
Derbyshire
Herefordshire
Leicestershire
Lincolnshire
Northamptonshire
Nottinghamshire
Oxfordshire
Shropshire
Staffordshire
Warwickshire
West Midlands
Worcestershire

*The White Hart*
FYFIELD, OXFORDSHIRE

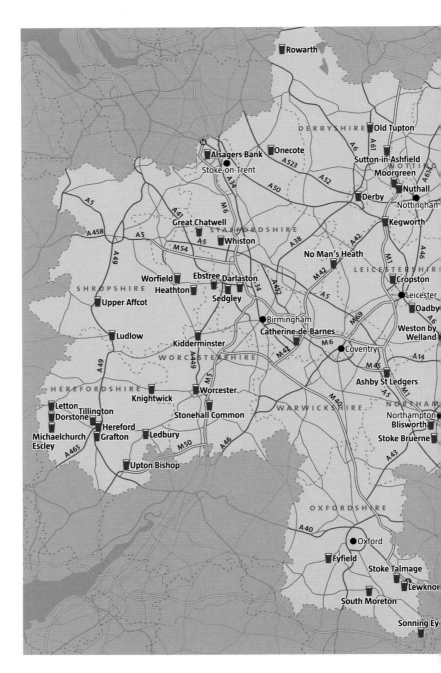

Rowarth

DERBYSHIRE Old Tupton

Onecote

Alsagers Bank

Stoke-on-Trent

Sutton-in-Ashfield

Moorgreen

Nuthall

Derby

Nottingham

Great Chatwell

Kegworth

STAFFORDSHIRE

Whiston

No Man's Heath

LEICESTERSHIRE

Worfield

Ebstree

Darlaston

Cropston

Heathton

Sedgley

Leicester

SHROPSHIRE

Oadby

Upper Affcot

Birmingham

Weston by Welland

Ludlow

Catherine-de-Barnes

Kidderminster

Coventry

WORCESTERSHIRE

Ashby St Ledgers

NORTHAM

Knightwick

Worcester

HEREFORDSHIRE

Letton

Tillington

WARWICKSHIRE

Northampton

Dorstone

Stonehall Common

Blisworth

Michaelchurch

Hereford

Ledbury

Stoke Bruerne

Escley

Grafton

Upton Bishop

OXFORDSHIRE

Oxford

Fyfield

Stoke Talmage

Lewknor

South Moreton

Sonning Ey

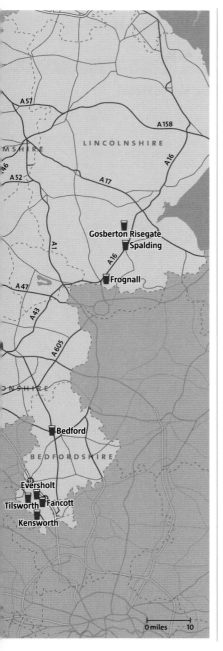

Popularly known as the heart of England, the Midlands stretch from the cider and hop county of Herefordshire to Derbyshire where the Peak District National Park starts its ascent northwards. In the southern region there's magnificent scenery in Worcestershire and Herefordshire, with the Wye Valley and Malvern Hills exquisite places to meander away a summer's afternoon. For more organised entertainment there are plenty of farm parks, falconry centres and the counties' eponymous cities. While you're in this part of the world venture across the border to the Shakespearean country of Warwickshire. All's well that ends well, especially when there's a decent pub in sight.

History is also all around the traveller in Oxfordshire with the university city of Oxford a major draw. For a very regal attraction try Blenheim Palace outside Woodstock which was built for the Duke of Marlborough after he won the battle of Blenheim. A beautiful house and lots of attractive grounds where you can picnic or the kids can run about to their heart's content.

Turn eastwards and you find the counties of Bedfordshire and Northamptonshire. They tend to be overlooked as tourist destinations – rather unjustly. Bedfordshire, for instance, has two top attractions in the shape of Whipsnade Wild Animal Park and Woburn Safari Park, while canalside walks and the historic battlefield of Naseby are two reasons to visit Northamptonshire. For a canalside drink and meal check out the Boat Inn at Stoke Bruerne which has been run by the same family since the 1870s.

The West Midlands offers a mix of urban sprawl and beautiful stirring countryside. Shropshire has the Long Mynd, Wenlock Edge and small villages hidden away in the area which inspired A E Housman's *A Shropshire Lad*. The pubs are pretty good as well. There is also the beautiful foodie town of Ludlow and the Shropshire Hills Discovery Centre at Craven Arms which will elicit cries of "eh oh" with its Teletubby-esque turf roof.

**41**

The West Midlands is the home of mild – drink it at its best at the Beacon Hotel, Sedgley where the Sarah Hughes Brewery produces the award-winning Ruby Mild. Walk off this ale with a stiff stroll up to Sedgley Beacon.

Staffordshire is home to the former brewing capital of Burton-upon-Trent and the Potteries but your family are more likely to want to make their way to Alton Towers, one of the UK's premier theme parks. Other (more sedate) attractions include Shugborough Hall, where the log-fired Victorian micro-brewery is occasionally pressed into service, while the southern edge of the Peak District edges into the county.

Derbyshire, Leicestershire, Nottingham-shire and Lincolnshire are the north-easterly parts of the Midlands where the likes of Batemans, Hardy and Hansons and Everards rule the brewing roost. The city of Derby is noted for its staggering amount of real ale pubs (of course you only go for the fact it's steeped in history), while Sudbury on the A516 between Derby and Uttoxeter has the National Trust Museum of Childhood.

Nottinghamshire is Robin Hood country with Sherwood Forest's visitor centre spinning many a yarn about the man in Lincoln green. At the end of the middle ages, the history of England was changed by the battle of Bosworth Field in Leicestershire. The battlefield is now on the county's heritage trail and if your children are interested in history then this is a must-see. Other attractions in the county include the Great Central Steam Railway at Rothley and the world's largest collection of single-seater racing cars at Donington Grand Prix Collection.

I sometimes think that Lincolnshire is a much-overlooked county. There are few hills, but the fens have their own charm – big skies, church towers spotting the landscape and the incomparable Batemans beers to be found in many pubs. For playtime there's bright and breezy Skegness and Spalding with its monster garden centre where budding young horticulturists should be tempted by the play area onsite.

# BEDFORDSHIRE

## BEDFORD

## De Parys Hotel

45 De Parys Avenue, Bedford MK40 2UA
**T** 01234 352121   **F** 01234 352889
*Licensee*: Jo Worth
*Opening times*: 12–11; 12–10.30 Sun
*Real ales*: **Eagle IPA**; guest beers
*Directions*: off A6, end of High Street

The back garden of this Victorian city hotel literally explodes with laughter on summer bank holidays thanks to fabulous family fundays. There are magicians, a bouncy castle and face-painting (amongst other activities), so if you're going to be in the area around these times, call and find out what's going on. The rest of the time, there's still plenty for the kids to do with a play area in the fully enclosed garden, where you'll also find a fish pond with Koi carp swimming about (don't worry about safety, there's a cover on the top). Inside colouring books and crayons are available. Described as an old-fashioned and cosy hotel, the De Parys has a bar area, no-smoking restaurant and conservatory where you might meet Bruno, an African Grey parrot. Children are allowed everywhere.

Food is served lunchtimes and evenings Monday–Saturday and from midday–10pm on Sunday. If you're eating with your children, their meals (from the **kids' menu** which features familiar choices) come free with an ice cream and glass of coke. Smaller portions off the main menu are available as well; these include scampi and chicken dishes. No roasts on Sunday, but the main menus and specials are served instead.

Things to do in the area include the Bedford Museum with plenty of curiosities, while before having lunch why not make a splash at the Bedford Oasis Beach Pool. Just outside the town there is the Bedford Butterfly Park at Wilden.

✗ children restricted to certain areas
✗ family room
✓ garden
✓ garden toys
✓ lunchtime meals
✓ evening meals
✓ food lunchtime and evening
✓ children's menu
✓ bottle warming
✓ no smoking area
✓ accommodation
✗ nearby camping
✓ nappy changing – women's toilets
✓ entertainment
✓ children's certificate
✓ high chairs
✗ time limit

## EVERSHOLT

# Green Man

Church End, Eversholt MK17 9DU
**T** 01525 280293
*Licensee*: Linda Owen
*Opening times*: 12–11; 12–10.30 Sun
*Real ales*: **Banks's Bitter; Theakston Best Bitter**;
guest beers
*Directions*: Junction 13 from the M1, follow the signs

Two miles from Woburn Abbey and Safari Park you will find the village of Eversholt and the Green Man. As is the case with a lot of villages, the local is opposite the church – an old hangover of the days when the pub vied with the pulpit for the custom of locals. Inside, it's a roomy rustic bar with bay windows at the front giving drinkers a view of the church, while there's a pool table at the other end; children are allowed everywhere apart from at the bar. For parrot fanciers try to catch a glimpse of the African-grey. There's also a no-smoking restaurant which can double up as a family room; it's mainly used on Sundays but can be opened up other times for families who want to use it. In the summer, the garden comes into its own with an aviary, guinea pigs and even a bouncy castle for the kids to work off surplus energy.

There's also an orchard and a covered eating area outdoors. Occasionally there are barbecues accompanied by live music.

There's a well-priced **kids' menu** of familiar choices (a tub of ice cream is thrown in with their meals). Smaller portions off the main menu of bar snacks can also be served, including lasagne, scampi and sandwiches. On Sundays there is a mini-roast available as well as the children's menu. Food is served every day from 12pm–5pm.

As well as Woburn Abbey and Safari Park, there are two excellent walks in the area, and the village itself has a well-maintained open-air swimming pool which is open in the summer.

✗ children restricted to certain areas
✓ family room
✓ garden
✓ garden toys
✓ lunchtime meals
✗ evening meals
✗ food lunchtime and evening
✓ children's menu
✓ bottle warming
✗ no smoking area
✗ accommodation
✓ nearby camping
✗ nappy changing
✓ entertainment
✓ children's certificate
✓ high chairs
✓ time limit – 8pm

## FANCOTT

# Fancott Arms

Fancott near Toddington LU5 6HT
**T** 01525 872366
**E** kevin@thefancott.co.uk
www.thefancott.co.uk
*Licensee*: Kevin Wallman
*Opening times*: 11–11; 12–10.30 Sun
*Real ales*: **Fuller's London Pride; Greene King IPA**;
guest beers
*Directions*: off the M1, Junction 12

During weekends and school holidays in the summer, the garden at the back of the Fancott is a hive of industry as the Fancott Light Railway takes the strain. The enterprising folks who run this friendly 200-year-old pub have a miniature train ('Herbie') and carriage on which children can hitch a ride as it performs a circuit of the garden. As you can imagine, this is wildly popular but, while they're waiting for the next ride, there's a big climbing frame that looks like a castle, complete with wobbly bridge to keep them merrily amused. As if that's not enough, there's even a football pitch at the end of the garden and footballs can be hired for a deposit of £5 – how are you ever going to get them to leave?

Inside the pub, which features a decor of rustic bric-a-brac, children are allowed everywhere apart from the bar area, though most families will probably make for the fairly new restaurant annexe which is partly no-smoking. Children are once again provided for with 'Freddy' bags, which contain colouring pads and crayons.

Food is served 11am–11pm Monday–Saturday and 12pm–10.30pm on Sundays. The **kids' menu** features chicken nuggets, sausage, pizza and fish fingers, all with chips, while older children can choose from a menu which includes scampi, small steaks, cajun chicken; there is also an all-day breakfast. Sunday lunchtimes feature two roasts (small portions available), as well as the main menus. As for bottle warming, the pub hands out hot water so that parents with babies can do it themselves, thus minimising the risk of making the food too hot.

Ideal for stopping off from the M1, while Whipsnade and Woburn are also within easy driving distance.

✗ children restricted to certain areas
✗ family room
✓ garden
✓ garden toys
✓ lunchtime meals
✓ evening meals
✓ food lunchtime and evening
✓ children's menu
✗ bottle warming
✓ no smoking area
✗ accommodation
✗ nearby camping
✓ nappy changing – disabled toilets
✓ entertainment
✗ children's certificate
✓ high chairs
✗ time limit

## Farmer's Boy

216 Common Road, Kensworth LU6 2PJ
**T** 01582 872207
*Licensee*: Pamela Laverty
*Opening times*: 11–11; 12.10.30 Sun
*Real ales*: **Fuller's London Pride, ESB**

Back in the 1970s, comedian Michael Bentine devised a game called Dwyle Flunking which involved two teams of twelve. One side formed a circle while a member of the other team stood in the middle and tried to hit them with a beer-soaked rag on the end of a stick. Everyone had a go and the forfeits usually meant drinking lots of beer. Darts seems a safer bet, but the Farmer's Boy is one of the few pubs where this lunatic activity still takes place during one of their beer festivals.

If you don't fancy that, pop inside this traditional village pub which is very welcoming to families and dogs and is only half a mile away from Whipsnade Zoo. Inside there is a compact public bar and a welcoming lounge area and adjoining no-smoking restaurant; pub historians might be interested to note the original Mann, Crossman and Paulin leaded windows. There are also nooks and crannies to hide away in if you're feeling in need of a little peace.

Children are allowed everywhere apart from the main bar area. On dry days, the garden is where the kids will want to be as there is a safe play area with swings and a climbing frame. The **kids' menu** includes familiar choices, and smaller portions off the main menu can also be served. These include pasta specials, steaks, homemade pies, scampi, sandwiches and jacket potatoes. There's also a Sunday roast with children's portions being available then. Food is available all day in the summer, while in the winter it is served 12pm–3pm and 6pm–9pm. There is no food Tuesday evenings.

✗ children restricted to certain areas
✗ family room
✓ garden
✓ garden toys
✓ lunchtime meals

✓ evening meals
✓ food lunchtime and evening
✓ children's menu
✓ bottle warming
✓ no smoking area
✗ accommodation
✗ nearby camping
✓ nappy changing – large cloakroom
✗ entertainment
✓ children's certificate
✓ high chairs
✗ time limit

## TILSWORTH

### Anchor

1 Dunstable Road, Tilsworth LU7 9PU
T 01525 210289    F 01525 211578
E tonyanchorinn@aol.com
www.nicepub.com
*Licensee*: Tony Williams
*Opening times*: 12–11; 12–10.30 Sun
*Real ales*: **Greene King Abbot**; guest beers
*Directions*: One mile off the A5

'The days of kids in pubs being taboo are long gone,' says landlord Tony Williams and when you see what he's got in the garden you know he means it. As well as an adventure playground with swings etc, he's been busy converting an old coach into something interesting for children. The seats have all been taken out and there will be a ball pond, playhouse and slides all connected up to the vehicle. Small child heaven.

The Anchor was built in the 1870s and has one horseshoe-shaped bar with lots of sections off it. The decor has a piratical theme with loads of little figurines of pirates to which locals add all of the time. They're not all diddy though, one of the pirates is a three-foot tall, particularly bloodthirsty looking chap.

Children are allowed in the partly no-smoking dining area (only with meals), which is designated as the family room, though if you and the family are only popping in for a drink in the summer then there's no problem about being in the garden. Inside, there are colouring books and crayons and Jenga for children to entertain themselves.

Food is served 12pm–2.30pm, 6pm–9.30pm throughout the week with the exceptions of Sunday and Monday evenings. There is a **kids' menu** with familiar stuff such as chicken nuggets, though Tony is keen to promote healthy eating and serves small portions off the main menu. These include chillis, pasta and small steaks. On Sunday lunchtimes there are four roasts with a vegetarian option (small portions available), and no chips are served. A friendly and busy pub which isn't far from the Grand Union Canal with its excellent opportunities for walking.

✓ children restricted to certain areas
✓ family room
✓ garden
✓ garden toys
✓ lunchtime meals
✓ evening meals
✓ food lunchtime and evening
✓ children's menu
✓ bottle warming
✓ no smoking area
✗ accommodation
✗ nearby camping
✗ nappy changing
✗ entertainment
✗ children's certificate
✓ high chairs
✗ time limit

## *DERBYSHIRE*

## DERBY

### Smithfield

Meadow Road, Derby D1 2BH
T 01332 370429
*Licensees*: Roger and Penny Myring
*Opening times*: 11–11; 12–10.30 Sun
*Real ales*: **Draught Bass; Fuller's London Pride; Oakham Bishop's Farewell, JHB; Whim Arbor Light, Hartington IPA**; guest beers
*Directions*: downriver from marketplace

Comfortable riverside pub originally built to provide sustenance for those visiting the cattle market (since moved to another location) and a bit of a Mecca for real ale lovers. Inside, there's a backroom lounge, bar area and games room which doubles up as a family room. Decor throughout includes old photos of Derby, beer memorabilia and old railway clocks, representing the city's industrial heritage. There are usually 7–10 real ales on.

Children are allowed in the family room where there are board games such as snakes and ladders, draughts and chess to entertain them. Outside, the patio and beer garden overlook the River Derwent with sensible railings to prevent kamikaze toddlers from launching themselves into the river.

Food is served lunchtimes Monday to Saturday with no food on Sundays. There is no kids' menu as such, but half portions of the bar snack menu are available for children. These include sandwich platters, salads and burgers with fries and there are often barbecues in the summer.

For some unknown (but highly welcome) reason Derby has lots of pubs and is highly regarded for its choice of real ales; it's also steeped in history with the Derby Heritage Centre and Derby Gaol well worth visiting. Also try the National Trust Museum of Childhood at Sudbury which is on the A516 between Derby and Uttoxeter.

✓ children restricted to certain areas
✓ family room
✓ garden
✗ garden toys
✓ lunchtime meals
✗ evening meals
✗ food lunchtime and evening
✗ children's menu
✓ bottle warming
✗ no smoking area
✗ accommodation
✗ nearby camping and caravan sites
✗ nappy changing
✗ entertainment
✗ children's certificate
✗ high chairs
✓ time limit – 9pm

## OLD TUPTON

# Royal Oak Inn

Derby Road, Old Tupton S42 6LA
**T** 01246 862180
*Licensee*: John Angus
*Opening times*: 12–11; 12–10.30 Sun
*Real ales*: **Daleside Bitter; John Smith Bitter**; guest beers
*Directions*: on the A61, three miles south of Chesterfield

Traditional red-brick inn which was built in 1830 and now offers a selection of up to nine real ales. Even though just outside Chesterfield, it's ideally suited for walking, with the Peak District National Park not too far away. Regular charity walks are also organised by the locals. Inside, following a recent refurbishment, the pub is open-planned with four separate spaces: games room, tap room, best room and snug. Photos of the Peak District line the walls.

Children are allowed everywhere while the garden has a secure play area with tyre swings and an adventure playground. There is a magician on special occasions at Easter, summer and Christmas.

Good value food is served 12pm–8pm Monday–Saturday, except Tuesdays when it's 12pm–2.30pm only. Sundays is 12pm–4pm only. The **kids' menu** has familiar choices with chips, while smaller portions off the main menu are available. These include scampi, omelettes, sausage, egg and chips, sandwiches and chip cobs. On Sundays there are roast lunches only, with small portions available.

Other attractions in the area include the towns of Chesterfield and Mansfield, and the National Trust owned Hardwick Hall.

✗ children restricted to certain areas
✗ family room
✓ garden
✓ garden toys
✓ lunchtime meals
✓ evening meals
✓ food lunchtime and evening
✓ children's menu
✓ bottle warming
✗ no smoking area

**x** accommodation
**x** nearby camping and caravan sites
**x** nappy changing
**x** entertainment
**x** children's certificate
**x** high chairs
**✓** time limit – 9pm

## ROWARTH

# Little Mill Inn

Rowarth SK22 1EB
**T** 01663 743178    **F** 01663 742686
www.littlemillrowarth.co.uk
*Licensee*: Chris Barnes
*Opening times*: 12–11; 12–10.30 Sun
*Real ales*: **Banks's Bitter**; **Cameron's Strongarm**;
**Marston's Pedigree**; guest beers
*Directions*: signed off Siloh Road

Whitewashed waterside inn built in 1781 when its main function was a candlewick mill; there was also a bar and shop which supplied the workers. Back in 1930 flooding swept away part of the mill as well as the landlord who, sadly, was found several miles downstream. There are plenty of before and after photos on the wall in the pub relating to the floods. Inside, the pub is open-planned with the bar at the back, while there is also a separate dining area, pool room and a restaurant upstairs, part of which is no-smoking.

Children are allowed everywhere and there is a smattering of games to amuse them. The garden is at the front and borders a stream, so keep an eye on toddlers (and watch out for older ones getting soggy with a spot of Swallows and Amazons). There is also a climbing frame and swings.

Food is served midday–10pm daily, with familiar choices on the **kids' menu**. Smaller portions off the main menu are also available when possible; these include scampi, pasta, salads and sandwiches, plus specials which make use of local game (don't dismiss the latter as a choice for children – it often goes down very well). Small roasts are available alongside the main menu on Sundays; there is a separate carvery open all day Sunday and weekday evenings. Adventurous older

children might like to try a dish from the Thai menu which is available evenings Monday–Thursday.

The pub owns land on which camping is possible but please give prior notice. Even though the pub is in Derbyshire, it's literally yards away from Cheshire while Manchester's city centre is only eight miles away. Walks in the Peak District are close. Also, from May to September, keep an eye out for the famous Well Dressings (wells are elaborately decorated with pictures made from flowers and petals), a tradition which goes back into the mists of antiquity. Local tourist information centres have lists and dates or check out www.derbyshireuk.net for a programme.

**x** children restricted to certain areas
**x** family room
**✓** garden
**✓** garden toys
**✓** lunchtime meals
**✓** evening meals
**✓** food lunchtime and evening
**✓** children's menu
**✓** bottle warming
**✓** no smoking area
**✓** accommodation
**✓** nearby camping and caravan sites
**x** nappy changing
**x** entertainment
**x** children's certificate
**✓** high chairs
**x** time limit

# *HEREFORDSHIRE*

## DORSTONE

# Pandy Inn

Dorstone HR3 6AN
**T** 01981 550273    **F** 01981 550277
www.pandyinn.co.uk
*Licensees*: Paul and Marja Gardner
*Opening times*: 12–3, 6–11; 12–11 Sat; 12–3, 6–10.30 Sun

*Real ales*: **Wye Valley Butty Bach, Dorothy Goodbody's Bitter** or seasonal beer
*Directions*: signed off B4348

Half-timbered inn which claims to be the county's oldest hostelry. Its history stretches back to 1185 when the original inn was apparently built by one of the killers of Thomas à Beckett as a penance (a curious form of penance but it's a good yarn). Inside it's very traditional and atmospheric with plenty of timber framing, hanging garlands of hops, exposed stone walls and a massive fireplace. There's also a parrot called Oscar who likes nothing better than to have a chat. There are two main drinking areas (with a no-smoking space) plus a restaurant.

Children are allowed everywhere and there are books, toys and games to keep them entertained; there are also bar games such as dominoes, quoits, darts and pool. Outside there's a secure garden and drinking area with climbing frame, seesaw and swings, as well as a set of stocks which the pub jokes is kept for unruly parents (though a veiled threat to children might give you a few minutes peace).

Food is served lunchtimes and evenings all through the week apart from Monday lunchtimes; there is no food on Monday evenings either in January and February. There's a **kids' menu** with familiar choices, while smaller portions are served off the main menu where possible. As the licensees are South African these might include dishes from their home country such as a casserole called tomato bredie, as well as more traditional choices such as pasta and homemade soup and traditional bar snacks. Sunday lunchtimes sees roasts (small portions available) alongside other selections. Bottled local cider is also available.

This is very handy for visiting the nearby Arthur's Stone – reputedly the grave of a king foolish enough to start a fight with King Arthur. Also nearby is the Wye Valley with opportunities for canoeing, while the second-hand book capital of the UK, Hay-on-Wye, is only six miles away on the Welsh border.

- ✗ children restricted to certain areas
- ✗ family room
- ✓ garden
- ✓ garden toys
- ✓ lunchtime meals
- ✓ evening meals
- ✓ food lunchtime and evening
- ✓ children's menu
- ✓ bottle warming
- ✓ no smoking area
- ✗ accommodation
- ✓ nearby camping and caravan sites
- ✓ nappy changing
- ✗ entertainment
- ✗ children's certificate
- ✓ high chairs
- ✗ time limit

## GRAFTON

### Grafton Inn

Ross Road, Grafton HR2 8ED
**T** 01432 355233
*Licensee*: Chris Roberts
*Opening times*: 11–3, 6–11; 12–3, 7–10.30 Sun
*Real ales*: **Spinning Dog Top Dog**; guest beers
*Directions*: on A49 on southern outskirts of Hereford

After being closed for a while this roadside pub reopened in 2002 to show off a smart and tasteful refurbishment. Set in the middle of rolling countryside outside Hereford, it's spacious and fresh-looking inside with lots of old sporting prints on the wall and exposed wooden beams.

Children are allowed throughout the pub. Whilst clearly aimed at the dining market, there are two areas reserved for drinking with a local real ale being served. There is also a no-smoking restaurant and spacious conservatory which looks out onto a large garden with a play area and a duck pond. Parents are advised to keep an eye on their children.

The **kids' menu**, which features all the usual choices, also comes with an ice cream cone and is good value. Smaller portions are available from the lunchtime menu which might include liver and bacon, soups and salads. In the evening there's a varied menu and specials. Roasts are served at Sunday lunchtime; small portions are available as well as selections off the kids' menu with chips. Food is served lunchtimes and evenings throughout the week.

Handy if you're visiting Hereford with all its historic sites including the cathedral and the Cider Museum. The city also has the adventure and activity centre, Jungle Mania.

- ✗ children restricted to certain areas
- ✗ family room
- ✓ garden
- ✓ garden toys
- ✓ lunchtime meals
- ✓ evening meals
- ✓ food lunchtime and evening
- ✓ children's menu
- ✓ bottle warming
- ✓ no smoking area
- ✗ accommodation
- ✗ nearby camping and caravan sites
- ✓ nappy changing – women's toilets
- ✗ entertainment
- ✗ children's certificate
- ✓ high chairs
- ✓ time limit – 9.30pm, younger kids

## HEREFORD

# Grandstand

Grandstand Road, Hereford HR4 9NH
**T** 01432 370867
*Licensee*: Susan Price
*Opening times*: 11–11; 12–10.30 Sun
*Real ales*: **Greene King Abbot, IPA, Ruddles County**

Modern pub overlooking the racecourse which opened in the late 1980s under the name of Canny Brook. Recently it's been refurbished by Greene King as one of their Hungry Horse outlets. The open-plan interior is divided into an over-18s bar, which includes a pool table, lounge and family lounge (part of which is no-smoking) with eating facilities throughout.

Children are allowed everywhere apart from the bar area. There's an extensive **kids' menu** with familiar choices though smaller portions off the extensive, good value menu are also possible. These include 'light bites' such as scampi, fish and chips, steak and chicken. On Sundays there are roasts

alongside the main menu with child-sized portions available. Food is served 11.30am–9.30pm throughout the week; 12pm–9.30pm Sundays. Outside there's a secure garden with play equipment including a fort and slide. The real ales are kept under cask breather. As is common with a large brewery's themed pub, this is very family-friendly with a unisex baby-changing room and a relaxed atmosphere though reasonable control is expected to be maintained with small (and large!) children.

As the pub is just over a mile outside Hereford city centre this an ideal place to recover after visiting some of the historic sites of this beautiful city. For the younger families there is also the adventure and activity centre Jungle Mania.

- ✓ children restricted to certain areas
- ✓ family room
- ✓ garden
- ✓ garden toys
- ✓ lunchtime meals
- ✓ evening meals
- ✓ food lunchtime and evening
- ✓ children's menu
- ✓ bottle warming
- ✓ no smoking area
- ✗ accommodation
- ✗ nearby camping and caravan sites
- ✓ nappy changing – unisex changing room
- ✗ entertainment
- ✗ children's certificate
- ✓ high chairs
- ✓ time limit – 9pm

# Victory

88 St Owen Street, Hereford HR1 2QD
**T** 01432 274998
*Licensees*: James Kenyon and Rebecca Brookes
*Opening times*: 11–11; 12–10.30 Sun
*Real ales*: **Spinning Dog Chase Your Tail, Mutley's Dark Mild, Revenge, Top Dog**, seasonal beers; guest beers

Down-to-earth, CAMRA award-winning town pub which is home to the Spinning Dog brewery. The curious name derives from the dizzying antics of the pub dog Cassie – children will love seeing who can spot the dog first. They'll also fall head over heels for the interior (particularly if they're piratically minded). The bar is in the shape of a galleon, while the back of the pub continues in the same naval theme with lots of rigging and netting. There's even a sort of crow's nest. Children are allowed in the back bar which functions as the family room; here traditional pub games include bar skittles and shove ha'penny as well as pool and darts.

Food is served 11am–5pm throughout the week (12pm–5pm, Sundays), and although there's not a kids' menu as such, children are catered for with an unpretentious bar selection from which small portions are available. These include small steaks, chilli and scampi – all with chips. There are roast lunches on Sundays with small portions available. At the back of the pub there's a small beer garden/patio where picnic tables and seats are available, but it is recommended that children are supervised at all times. Brewery visits are available on request. Traditional cider is served too.

Not far from the city centre and ideal after exploring the ancient city of Hereford.

✓ children restricted to certain areas
✓ family room
✓ garden
✗ garden toys
✓ lunchtime meals
✗ evening meals
✗ food lunchtime and evening
✗ children's menu
✓ bottle warming
✗ no smoking area
✗ accommodation
✗ nearby camping and caravan sites
✗ nappy changing
✗ entertainment
✓ children's certificate
✓ high chairs
✓ time limit – 9pm

## Full Pitcher

The Wharf, New Street, Ledbury HR8 2EN
T 01531 632688
E martinwells@thepitcher.fsbusiness.co.uk
*Licensee*: Linda Simpson
*Opening times*: 12–11; 12–10.30 Sun
*Real ales*: **Greene King Abbot Ale** or **Old Speckled Hen**; guest beer
*Directions*: near A438/A449 junction

Large edge-of-town country pub which was originally called the Biddulph Arms after the family estate to which it belonged. Very family-friendly with children allowed in all areas apart from the bar.

There is also a comfortably furnished separate family room with colouring books and crayons provided (this is also the no-smoking area). Outside in the secure garden, there's a wood-chip surfaced play area with climbing frame, slide, fireman's pole and rope bridge. There are familiar choices on the **kids' menu**, all served with chips or potato letters and peas or beans, while on Sundays smaller portions of the lunchtime roast (as well as the kids' menu) are also available. Food is served lunchtimes and evenings throughout the week and all day at the weekend.

The old market town of Ledbury is very handy for exploring the nearby Malvern Hills, while closer by there is a falconry centre and farm park.

✗ children restricted to certain areas
✓ family room
✓ garden
✓ garden toys
✓ lunchtime meals
✓ evening meals
✓ food lunchtime and evening
✓ children's menu
✓ bottle warming
✓ no smoking area
✗ accommodation
✓ nearby camping and caravan sites
✓ nappy changing – disabled toilets
✗ entertainment
✓ children's certificate
✓ high chairs
✗ time limit

## LETTON

# Swan

Letton HR3 6DH
**T** 01544 327304
*Licensee*: Michael Boardman
*Opening times*: 11–3, 6–11; 11–11 Wed–Sat;
12–10.30 Sun
*Real ales*: Beer range varies
*Directions*: on the A438

Friendly and relaxed roadside inn which started out catering for drovers in the 16th century and was added to during the Victorian era. Children are allowed throughout the premises which includes a small public bar with pool table, a large comfortably furnished lounge split into several areas and a separate dining room. There are board games available. The beer garden is at the back and opens onto the car park so keep an eye on the young ones.

The **kids' menu** includes familiar choices while there are also sandwiches, made with home-baked bread, and soup, plus an extensive menu of home cooked meals, including a blackboard of specials. Small portions are available when possible. On Sundays there are roasts (kids' portions served) as well as vegetarian choices. Food is served during opening hours. The house beer comes from Wye Valley.

Local attractions include a rare breeds farm at Kington, while Hereford, with its superb cathedral and the Cider Museum which traces the history of traditional cider in Herefordshire, is close.

✗ children restricted to certain areas
✗ family room
✓ garden
✗ garden toys
✓ lunchtime meals
✓ evening meals
✓ food lunchtime and evening
✓ children's menu
✓ bottle warming
✗ no smoking area
✓ accommodation
✓ nearby camping and caravan sites
✗ nappy changing
✗ entertainment
✗ children's certificate
✓ high chairs
✗ time limit

## MICHAELCHURCH ESCLEY

# Bridge Inn

Michaelchurch Escley HR2 0JW
**T** 01981 510646
*Licensees*: Emily Robb and Jane Straker
*Opening times*: 11–11; 12–10.30 Sun
*Real ales*: **Wye Valley Butty Bach**, **HPA** or seasonal beer
*Directions*: OS 318341; south of the B4348, just east of its junction with the B4347

Friendly 16th-century pub boasting a rare Welsh stone roof, located in the wild, beautifully wooded country of the Herefordshire side of the Black Mountains. Escley Brook runs through the grounds and enterprising older kids can entertain themselves by using the rope swing over the stream! Not surprisingly, the interior is rustic traditional with a beamed ceiling and an inglenook fireplace separating the public bar, where there's a pool table, from the main bar; there's also a restaurant which is no-smoking.

Children are allowed throughout, though at the time of writing, there were plans to develop a family room. If you can avoid them seeing the rope swing, younger children will be more than happy letting off steam in the secure garden.

Locally sourced, home cooked food is served in the bars and restaurant, with no kids' menu as such but smaller portions off the main menu, including sausage and chips and homemade meatballs with spaghetti always available. In summer 2003, the pub also hopes to be selling its own homemade burgers. Food is served lunchtimes and evenings throughout the week from Easter to September, while during the winter food is definitely served lunchtimes and evenings Thursday–Sunday, but for the rest of the week the pub advises that you call.

This is in the middle of beautiful countryside with plenty of walking, pony trekking and canoeing opportunities, while there's also the outdoor activity centre Mountain Mayhem, offering delights for older kids such as paintballing, rock climbing and go-karting.

x children restricted to certain areas
x family room
✓ garden
✓ garden toys
✓ lunchtime meals
✓ evening meals
✓ food lunchtime and evening
x children's menu
✓ bottle warming
✓ no smoking area
x accommodation
✓ nearby camping and caravan sites
x nappy changing
x entertainment
x children's certificate
✓ high chairs
x time limit

## TILLINGTON

## Bell

Tillington HR4 8LE
**T** 01432 760395
*Licensee*: Jacqueline Williams
*Opening times*: 11–3, 6–11; 11–11 Sat; 12–6, 7–10.30 Sun
*Real ales*: **Draught Bass; Highgate Saddlers; Wye Valley Bitter**; guest beer
*Directions*: on the Hereford–Weobley road, NW of the village

Popular, predominantly food pub which is welcoming to families and has a public bar, large lounge and separate no-smoking restaurant. Children are allowed anywhere except in the bar. Outside there's a large secure garden at the back with a play area including a tree house, tunnel and swing.

Food is home cooked with the **kids' menu** serving all the familiar favourites while smaller portions can be ordered off the main menu. Bar snacks are served at lunchtimes, such as sandwiches and ham, egg and chips, while in the evening there are daily specials alongside the main menu including curry, scampi and Caesar salad. Food is served 12pm–2.20pm and 6.30pm–9.30pm during the week while Sundays is from 12pm–2.30pm; no Sunday evening servings. On Sundays there is a three-course carvery in the dining room,

while in the bar and lounge a roast lunch (small portions served), specials and choices from the main menu are served. The pub and its patrons are very relaxed about youngsters but parents are expected to be in control all the time.

Hereford is only a few miles away, while there are also plenty of walks in the Wye Valley and surrounding countryside. Further afield over the border in Worcestershire you will find the Pig Pen, a working pig farm near Bromyard.

x children restricted to certain areas
x family room
✓ garden
✓ garden toys
✓ lunchtime meals
✓ evening meals
✓ food lunchtime and evening
✓ children's menu
✓ bottle warming
✓ no smoking area
x accommodation
x nearby camping and caravan sites
x nappy changing
x entertainment
x children's certificate
✓ high chairs
✓ time limit – 9.30

## UPTON BISHOP

## Moody Cow

Crow Hill, Upton Bishop, Ross-on-Wye HR9 7TT
**T** 01989 780470
**E** james@moodycow.co.uk
www.themoodycow.co.uk
*Licensee*: James Lloyd
*Opening times*: 12–2.30, 6.30–11; closed Monday lunchtimes in the winter; 12–3 Sun
*Real ales*: **Draught Bass, Hook Norton Best Bitter, Worthington Best Bitter**
*Directions*: At the junction of B4221 and B4224

Friendly attractive-looking stone built pub in a sleepy village a couple of miles north of the M50. Inside there's lots of exposed brickwork with farmhouse furniture, hanging hops and cow-themed objects. Children are not allowed in the main bar, but they can go into the dining room, called the Fresco, and the restaurant (both no-smoking) in an attached barn conversion; colouring books are supplied.

The emphasis is on freshly prepared and home-cooked food, though those popping in for a drink are also welcomed with open arms. There's an interesting **kids' menu** which offers two or three courses, with homemade soup or fishcakes for starters, sausage and mash, battered chicken fillets and chips or spaghetti bolognese for the main choice followed by puddings; small portions can also be served off the main menu including a selection of salads and sandwiches as well as homemade curries, pork and leek sausage and coriander mash, lambs liver and homemade pies – be warned, as the food is freshly prepared, some dishes can take up to 25 minutes to prepare. Food is served midday–2.30pm and 6.30pm–9.30pm; there is no food all day Monday or Sunday evening. No garden but there is a patio between the car park and the entrance to the pub. It is not secure for smaller children.

Nearby attractions include the Queen's Wood Walk, the Forest of Dean Railway at Norchard over the border in Gloucestershire and the National Birds of Prey Centre just of Newent.

✓ children restricted to certain areas
✗ family room
✗ garden
✗ garden toys
✓ lunchtime meals
✓ evening meals
✓ food lunchtime and evening
✓ children's menu
✓ bottle warming
✓ no smoking area
✗ accommodation
✗ nearby camping and caravan sites
✗ nappy changing
✗ entertainment
✓ high chairs
✗ children's certificate
✗ time limit

## LEICESTERSHIRE

### CROPSTON

## Bradgate Arms

15 Station Road, Cropston LE7 7HD
T 0116 234 0336
*Licensee*: David Holden
*Opening times*: 11.30–11; 12–10.30 Sun
*Real ales*: **Banks's Bitter; Marston's Pedigree;** guest beers

Before this welcoming village local was bought by Wolverhampton & Dudley, it had been run by the same landlord since the 1920s. What's more, he's still around and occasionally drops into the pub for a drink. There's been a licensed establishment on this site for 500 years apparently, so it's not surprising that there's a very traditional feel to this multi-roomed establishment. The interior is rustic with wooden beams, old pictures of the area on the wall, mahogany-style furniture and various bric-a-brac on display; a no-smoking restaurant has been added at the back of the pub.

Children are allowed everywhere though an area near the main door is designated as the family room. The garden, which can be found at the rear, is fenced in and although there's no play area, there's plenty of room for young children to run off surplus energy.

Food is served midday–3pm, 5pm–9pm Monday to Friday, and all day Saturday and Sunday. The **kids' menu** has familiar choices, while some dishes on the main menu, such as scampi, sausage and gammon, can be served in smaller portions. A small roast is served on Sunday lunchtimes, when the other menus are also available.

Situated in a rural area, the Bradgate Arms is very close to Bradgate Country Park which has lots of country walks and a visitor centre with information on Lady Jane Grey; she spent a happy time at Bradgate before her brief nine-day reign as Queen and subsequent beheading (a suitably gory history lesson). The Great Central Steam Railway at Rothley is also close.

x children restricted to certain areas
✓ family room
✓ garden
x garden toys
✓ lunchtime meals
✓ evening meals
✓ food lunchtime and evening
✓ children's menu
✓ bottle warming
✓ no smoking area
x accommodation
✓ nearby camping and caravan sites
✓ nappy changing – disabled toilets
x entertainment
✓ high chair
✓ children's certificate
✓ time limit – 9pm

## KEGWORTH

# Red Lion

24 High Street, Kegworth DE74 2DA
**T** 01509 672466  **F** 01509 670987
*Licensee*: Geoff Donoghue
*Opening times*: 11–11; 12–10.30 Sun
*Real ales*: **Adnams Bitter; Banks's Original; Courage Directors; Greene King Abbot**; guest beers

Cartoonist and creator of Kegbuster Bill Tidy used to live in Kegworth which explains why you will find a selection of his cartoons on the wall in this traditional village pub, parts of which date back to the 15th century. The pub's garden makes a good vantage point for any aeronautically-minded kids (and their dads) to watch the planes coming and going at the nearby East Midlands Airport.

Inside, there are four separate rooms with children allowed in the two dining rooms, one of which is no-smoking; these are both designated as family rooms. There is also a skittle alley and two darts rooms. The large secure garden has a play area, while the pub also holds occasional events such as barbecues. Food is served lunchtimes and evenings Monday–Saturday. Please note: no food on Sunday. The **kids' menu** has familiar

choices while smaller portions off the main menu are always available. Choices include sausage, mash and peas, pasta, salad, rolls and jacket potatoes.

There are plenty of walks in the surrounding countryside, while Kegworth Museum is also well worth a look. Further afield, if Formula One has any fans in the family, then the world's largest collection of single-seater racing cars at Donington Grand Prix Collection is a must.

✓ children restricted to certain areas
✓ family room
✓ garden
✓ garden toys
✓ lunchtime meals
✓ evening meals
✓ food lunchtime and evening
✓ children's menu
✓ bottle warming
✓ no smoking area
x accommodation
✓ nearby camping and caravan sites
x nappy changing
x entertainment
x high chair
x children's certificate
✓ time limit – 8.30pm

## OADBY

# Cow & Plough

Stoughton Farm, Gartree Road, Oadby LE2 2FB
**T** 0116 272 0852
www.steamin-billy.co.uk
*Licensee*: Barry Lount
*Opening times*: 12–3 (summer only), 5–10 ; 12–10 Sat; 12–4, 7–10 Sun
*Real ales*: **Fuller's London Pride; Greene King Abbot; Steamin' Billy Bitter**; guest beers
*Directions*: near BUPA hospital

A converted stable and barn on a working farm provides an interesting home to the Cow & Plough, which is also an outlet for Steamin' Billy beers (note however they are not brewed here). There are usually up to four guest beers, usually supplied by micros and Steamin' Billy's own seasonal beers. By the way, the name Steamin' Billy refers to landlord Barry Lount's Jack Russell terrier. The theme inside is total breweriana with the landlord's collection of pub mirrors, interesting bottles and flagons, signs and other beer-related objects all over the place. Note the old Victorian bar-back behind the handpumps with the words Mild and Old emblazoned on the glass.

The pub is split up into the 'vaults', function room and a no-smoking conservatory; the latter is the family room and children are allowed in there. A few traditional pub games such as shove ha'penny, dominoes and table skittles are available. There's a big seated area outside which is fenced off from the farm, but it provides families with an intriguing glimpse into the activities of the farm, including cows going off to milking. There are hopes to open a play area in the summer of 2003 (please call for details). Food is confined to sandwiches at lunchtime, but families have been known to bring their own for younger children and nobody bats an eyelid. A very friendly pub in an unusual situation which suffered badly during the foot and mouth crisis but is now, thankfully, once again in good health. Even though it isn't far from the centre of Leicester, Oadby is a pretty rural area with plenty of good country walks.

✓ children restricted to certain areas
✓ family room
✓ garden
✗ garden toys
✓ lunchtime meals
✗ evening meals
✗ food lunchtime and evening
✗ children's menu
✓ bottle warming
✓ no smoking area
✗ accommodation
✗ nearby camping and caravan sites
✓ nappy changing – disabled toilets
✗ entertainment
✓ high chair
✗ children's certificate
✗ time limit

## LINCOLNSHIRE

### FROGNALL

# Goat

155 Spalding Road, Deeping St James,
Frognall PE6 8SA
T 01778 347629
E goat.frognall@virgin.net
*Licensee*: Peter Wilkins
*Opening times*: 11-2.30, 6–11; 12–3, 6.30–10.30 Sun
*Real ales*: **Elgood's Cambridge Bitter**, guest beers
*Directions*: on the B1525 from Market Deeping

Former alehouse built in the 1640s which has undergone various alterations over the past couple of decades, but the interior still boasts beams and exposed stone walls. Nearly 2000 pumpclips are on display, a sign of the pub's commitment to real ales, which come from both micros and smaller regionals. The Goat also grows its own hops which are used by the local Rockingham Brewery for a beer especially brewed for the pub.

Children under 14 are allowed in the family dining room, where a **kids' menu** with familiar choices is served with chips (no chips served alone though); there is also space in the lobby entrance if you and the kids are just having a drink. Smaller portions off the main menu are served where possible; these include steak and kidney pie, scampi and sandwiches. Roast meals at Sunday lunchtimes (small portions available) alongside the main menus.

Food is served lunchtimes and evenings throughout the week. Outside there's a big garden bordered by leylandii with an action tree, swings and slides; there's also a separate play area for under fives.

Frognall is on the border with Cambridgeshire and nearby attractions include Burghley House where horse trials are held in September and the Nene Valley steam railway just outside Peterborough.

✓ children restricted to certain areas
✗ family room
✓ garden
✓ garden toys
✓ lunchtime meals
✓ evening meals
✓ food lunchtime and evening
✓ children's menu
✓ bottle warming – tinned food only
✓ no smoking area
✗ accommodation
✓ nearby camping and caravan sites
✗ nappy changing
✗ entertainment
✗ children's certificate
✓ highchairs
✗ time limit

## GOSBERTON RISEGATE

# Duke of York

106 Risegate Road, Gosberton Risegate PE11 4EY
**T** 01775 840193
*Licensee*: Susan Anne-Mary Goodenough
*Opening times*: 12(6.30 Mon)–11; 12–4, 7–10 Sun
*Real ales*: **Bateman XB**; **Black Sheep Best Bitter**;
guest beers

Busy village local converted from two
cottages knocked into one during the
Victorian era. One of the pub's more senior
customers remembers his grandfather
being a regular, which gives you a nice
sense of continuity. Inside, there's a main
bar, off which there's a snug which doubles
up as a family room; Friday nights sees it set
aside for darts. There's also a games room
and no-smoking dining room; children are
allowed everywhere apart from the main
bar area. The decor is rustic with old
pictures and wooden beams, while there's a
big secure garden at the back with a
climbing frame, tree house and seesaw. The
pub also holds an annual bonfire night as
well as a Christmas party for local children.

Food is served lunchtimes and evenings
throughout the week apart from Monday
lunchtime. There are the usual kids' choices
with that great, but welcome, rarity,
homemade chips; smaller portions off the
main menu are also served. These include

small steaks, scampi and cod and chips.
There are three roasts available Sunday
lunchtime with small portions served. The
pub is committed to using the very freshest
local produce for its cooking. There are
usually three guest beers, coming from all
over the country with the emphasis on
micros, while the pub supports local efforts
to raise money for charity.

A rural location means that there are
plenty of country walks in the area, while
Boston with its world-famous Stump is a
short drive away.

✗ children restricted to certain areas
✓ family room
✓ garden
✓ garden toys
✓ lunchtime meals
✓ evening meals
✓ food lunchtime and evening
✓ children's menu
✓ bottle warming
✓ no smoking area
✗ accommodation
✓ nearby camping
✓ nappy changing
✗ entertainment
✗ children's certificate
✗ high chairs
✓ time limit – 9pm

## SPALDING

# Birds

108 Halmergate, Spalding PE11 2EL
**T** 01775 723329
*Licensees*: John and Tracy Smith
*Opening times*: 11–11; 12–10.30 Sun
Real Ales: **Greene King IPA, Old Speckled Hen**

The name of this open-planned pub, one of
Greene King's Hungry Horse outlets, comes
from a tale during the war when a load of
birds were killed by aircraft. Some of them
were stuffed and ended up being displayed
in the pub. As the hostelry was built in 1963
(the year when Hitchcock's film *The Birds*
was released) it seems just as likely the
creepy horror film supplied the inspiration
for the name. At the time of writing there
are a couple of the avians left, but come the

summer of 2003 Greene King plan a refurbishment which I'm told will see the demise of these moth-eaten birds.

Whatever the truth behind the tale, Birds is a very family friendly hostelry which allows children anywhere, while the secure garden at the rear can only be entered via the pub. Here there is a slide, climbing frame, bridge and swings. There are also special events held for children of varying ages, including discos, games and treasure hunts. Food is served all day every day, with the **kids' menu** featuring what is termed a 'pick and mix' choice: familiar meals such as mini burgers, hot dogs and turkey shapes, all served with chips, mash or waffles. There are also 'light bites' off the main menu, which include scampi, fish and chips, steak and sausages. Sundays sees a roast (small portions available) alongside the main menus.

During May bank holiday, Spalding is home to the Spalding Flower Parade where the town goes tulip crazy with parades, firework displays and lots of other activities. Keen gardeners should also make for the Bay Tree Garden Centre which is the biggest in Europe – more importantly for children immune to the charms of horticulture, it has a massive play area. Note: the refurbishment is due to take up to a fortnight, when the pub will be closed, so call for details.

- ✘ children restricted to certain areas
- ✘ family room
- ✔ garden
- ✔ garden toys
- ✔ lunchtime meals
- ✔ evening meals
- ✔ food lunchtime and evening
- ✔ children's menu
- ✔ bottle warming
- ✔ no smoking area
- ✘ accommodation
- ✘ nearby camping
- ✔ nappy changing – disabled toilets
- ✔ entertainment
- ✔ children's certificate
- ✔ high chairs
- ✔ time limit – 9pm

## NORTHAMPTONSHIRE

### ASHBY ST LEDGERS

# Olde Coach House Inn

Main Street, Ashby St Ledgers CV23 8UN
**T** 01788 890349    **F** 01788 891922
**E** theoldecoachhouse@traditionalfreehouses.com
*Licensee*: Tony Rose
*Opening times*: 12–11; 12–10.30 Sun
*Real ales*: **Everards Old Original**; **Flowers Original**; guest beers
*Directions*: off A361 north of Daventry

Domesday Book village in whose manor house Guy Fawkes and fellow conspirators apparently hatched the Gunpowder Plot. This is remembered with a massive bonfire which the pub holds in an adjacent field on November 5. Hundreds of people attend and unsurprisingly the pub can get very busy. You can read a bit about the Plot on the walls of the pub as well. Built in the 19th century as a farmhouse, this is a very popular and welcoming establishment with traditional rustic decor inside: beams, wood panelling, books on shelves, agricultural equipment on the walls and high-backed benches. There's a huge long bar which has Sky TV, a snug, games area and restaurant.

Children are allowed everywhere and there are several games for them to play with inside. In the summer the huge beer garden to the side of the pub is popular, while there's a secure play area which includes a climbing frame and slide.

Food is served lunchtimes and evenings all week with the **kids' menu** featuring familiar choices, while sandwiches and baguettes are also available. Smaller portions off the main menu such as scampi can also be served. Roasts (child-sized portions available) are served Sunday lunchtimes alongside the other menus. As well as the regular real ales, up to five guests from local and regional breweries are usually available.

There are plenty of walks in the pleasant countryside surrounding Ashby St Ledgers while Daventry Country Park is a short drive away. Here you will find a massive adventure playground, country walks and a nature club for children.

- ✘ children restricted to certain areas
- ✘ family room
- ✓ garden
- ✓ garden toys
- ✓ lunchtime meals
- ✓ evening meals
- ✓ food lunchtime and evening
- ✓ children's menu
- ✓ bottle warming
- ✘ no smoking area
- ✓ accommodation
- ✘ nearby camping and caravan sites
- ✓ nappy changing – disabled toilets
- ✘ entertainment
- ✘ children's certificate
- ✓ high chairs
- ✘ time limit

## BLISWORTH

# Royal Oak

1 Chapel Lane, Blisworth NN7 3BU
T 01604 858372
*Licensee*: Brian James
*Opening times*: 12–(11 Fri, Sat) 3, 6–11; 12–10.30 Sun
*Real ales*: **Hook Norton Best Bitter**; guest beers
*Directions*: on the old A43

Comfortable 300-year-old pub located in a village lying alongside the Grand Union Canal – hence popular with the narrow-boating fraternity. The nearby Blisworth tunnel is apparently one of the longest tunnels in the English canal system. Inside the Royal Oak, there's a main bar, snug area (which is designated the family room), lounge and no-smoking restaurant. The decor is traditional including an inglenook fireplace and lots of old oak beams.

Children are allowed everywhere and there are a few games for their entertainment, including that perennial favourite Ludo. At the back of the pub you will find a massive, secure garden with a play area which includes swings.

Food is served lunchtimes and evenings throughout the week with the **kids' menu** serving familiar choices. Smaller portions off the main menu can also be served, including small steaks, scampi, fish and chips, pasta and sandwiches. Sunday lunchtimes sees roast meals only; small portions and the kids' menu is also available.

Walk off your lunch with a canalside walk, while Northampton is only a short drive to the north.

- ✘ children restricted to certain areas
- ✓ family room
- ✓ garden
- ✓ garden toys
- ✓ lunchtime meals
- ✓ evening meals
- ✓ food lunchtime and evening
- ✓ children's menu
- ✓ bottle warming
- ✓ no smoking area
- ✘ accommodation
- ✘ nearby camping and caravan sites
- ✓ nappy changing – women's toilets
- ✘ entertainment
- ✓ children's certificate
- ✓ high chairs
- ✓ time limit – 9pm

## STOKE BRUERNE

# Boat Inn

Bridge Road, Stoke Bruerne NN12 7SB
T 01604 862428    F 01604 864314
www.boatinn.co.uk
*Licensee*: Andrew Woodward
*Opening times*: 9–3, 6–11 (9–11 summer); 12–10.30 Sun
*Real ales*: **Adnams Bitter; Banks's Bitter; Frog Island Best Bitter; Marston's Bitter, Pedigree**; guest beer
*Directions*: off A508, opposite Canal Museum

Traditional canalside inn with thatched roof which has been run by the same family since 1877. Until 1921 it was part of the estate of the Duke of Grafton but the Woodwards bought the inn for the princely sum of £1000. At one time, the family had their own on-site butchery and brewery. The oldest parts of the inn are the thatched canalside bars where stone floors and open fires rule.

Children are allowed in the no-smoking bistro and lounge bar, which has a natural timber decor. There's no garden, but as the inn is located alongside the canal this is a wonderful place to sit and watch the boats go by, but it would be wise to keep a very beady eye on the children.

The **kids' menu** has familiar choices, all with chips, while smaller portions of the main menu can be served when possible. These include bar food staples such as steak, scampi and gourgons all with chips; there is also salmon. Food is served from 9am-3pm and 6pm–9pm in the winter and all day Saturday and Sunday; during the summer food is served all day throughout the week. As the inn opens at 9am (not for alcoholic drinks though), this is a good place to have breakfast. Come Sunday there are roasts (smaller portions available) alongside the usual bar and kids' menu.

This is an ideal stop for families on a boating tour, but landlubbers can also find plenty to amuse themselves including plenty of canalside walks, a Canal Museum, boat trips and an open farm with animals about 100 yards away from the inn.

✓ children restricted to certain areas
✗ family room
✗ garden
✗ garden toys
✓ lunchtime meals
✓ evening meals
✓ food lunchtime and evening
✓ children's menu
✓ bottle warming
✓ no smoking area
✗ accommodation
✗ nearby camping and caravan sites
✓ nappy changing – women's toilets
✗ entertainment
✓ children's certificate
✓ high chairs
✓ time limit – 9pm

## WESTON BY WELLAND

# Wheel & Compass

Valley Road, Weston By Welland,
Market Harborough LE16 8ZH
**T** 01858 565864
*Licensee*: David Woolman
*Opening times*: 12–3, 6–11; 12–4, 6–10.30 Sun
*Real ales*: Banks's Bitter; **Greene King Abbot**;

Marston's Bitter, Pedigree; guest beer
*Directions*: off B664 near Sutton Basset

Atmospheric village local set in the middle of farming country. Originally a farm, it is divided into an L-shaped bar and a no-smoking dining room with children allowed everywhere apart from the bar area. The theme inside is rustic with old guns, poachers' paraphernalia and sepia-tinted pictures of the village from yesteryear on the wall while low beams and log fires add to the ambience. There's a huge enclosed garden (with swings and climbing frame) at the back with a view of the surrounding fields. Food is a big draw here, but it's also a great place to unwind with a drink after a bracing walk in the surrounding countryside.

The **kids' menu** has familiar choices with chips, while there is also a £3.50 selection of dishes which is midway between the kids' and full menu. Choices include ploughmans lunch, scampi, fresh fish, sandwiches (lunch only), baked potatoes and salads. Sundays sees a roast dinner plus the main menus; small roasts are always available. Food is served 12pm–2pm Monday–Saturday, 12pm–3pm on Sundays; 6pm–9pm Monday–Thursday during the winter (9.30pm in the summer), 6pm–10pm Friday and Saturday, 6pm–9pm Sundays all year round.

This is beautiful walking, riding and cycling countryside, while the battlefield of Naseby is on the other side of the historic market town of Market Harborough.

✗ children restricted to certain areas
✗ family room
✓ garden
✓ garden toys
✓ lunchtime meals
✓ evening meals
✓ food lunchtime and evening
✓ children's menu
✓ bottle warming
✓ no smoking area
✗ accommodation
✗ nearby camping and caravan sites
✗ nappy changing
✗ entertainment
✗ children's certificate
✓ high chairs
✗ time limit

## NOTTINGHAMSHIRE

# Horse & Groom

Moorgreen, Newthorpe NG16 2FF
**T** 01733 713417
*Licensee*: Mark Allsopp
*Opening times*: 11–11; 12–10.30 Sun
*Real ales*: **Hardys & Hansons Kimberley Best Bitter**;
seasonal beers

Large red-brick country pub which was built
in the 17th century and has a very rustic feel
to the interior with plenty of bric-a-brac and
horse brasses. Inside, it's open-planned with
children allowed anywhere inside as long as
they are eating (each child gets a free
activity book with their meal). Outside,
there's a large garden which opens out onto
the car park so close supervision of younger
children is recommended. There's also a
play area with swings (including a baby
swing) and a climbing frame.

Food is available 12pm–9pm (8pm Sunday)
all through the week with the **kids' menu**
offering soup, burgers, pizzas, cajun chicken,
a small rump steak and lasagne; there's also
a big sweet selection. Smaller portions off
the main menu can be served as well; these
include traditional bar food choices such as
cod or scampi and chips. There are roasts on
Sundays (child-sized ones available) along
with the other menus. Please note: if you
want baby food warming up the pub will
provide you with hot water to do it yourself.

Based in a rural area, the Horse & Groom
is handy for country walks, but Nottingham
with all its various attractions including the
castle, is only about half an hour's drive away.

✓ children restricted to certain areas
✗ family room
✓ garden
✓ garden toys
✓ lunchtime meals
✓ evening meals
✓ food lunchtime and evening
✓ children's menu
✗ bottle warming
✓ no smoking area
✗ accommodation
✗ nearby camping and caravan sites
✗ nappy changing
✗ entertainment
✓ children's certificate
✓ high chairs
✓ time limit – 9pm

# Three Ponds

Nottingham Road, Nuthall NG16 1DP
**T** 0115 9383170
**E** threeponds@hardysandhansons.plc.uk
*Licensee*: Jim Gilchrist
*Opening times*: 11–11; 12–10.30 Sun
*Real ales*: **Hardys & Hansons Kimberley Best Bitter**,
**Ye Olde Trip Ale**; seasonal beers
*Directions*: just off M1 Junction 26

The name of this roadside pub comes from
the three ponds which existed in the gardens
of the Nuthall Temple, an Italian-style
extravagance built in the grounds of Nuthall
Manor in the mid-1700s. The Temple was
knocked down in 1929 and the ruins vanished
when the M1 was built through the village in
the 1960s. If you look carefully to the side of
this imposing 1930s-built Hardys & Hansons
pub, you might see a pillar which marked
the erstwhile entrance to the Manor. As for
the ponds, only one of them still remains.
The interior of the pub was tastefully
refurbished and redesigned several years
back and has a big open-planned bar area
with a lounge and no-smoking restaurant.

Children are allowed everywhere,
though in the summer they will probably
haul you to the large garden at the rear
where there is a sizeable enclosed play area
with swings, slides and frames. Back inside,
activity books are given out with meals.

Food is important here and served
11am–9pm Monday–Saturday, 12pm–8pm
on Sundays. There's a **kids' menu** with
familiar choices, while there are also 'extra
value for money' meals which are smaller

portions off the main menu. These include soup, garlic baguettes, pies, cod and chips and pasta. On Sunday lunchtimes, roasts (including small portions) are available as well as the main menus, but no snacks.

Because of its close proximity to the motorway, the Three Ponds is only a short drive away from the American Adventure theme park at Ilkeston where there are plenty of rides, attractions and lots of other fun (open March-November).

✖ children restricted to certain areas
✖ family room
✓ garden
✓ garden toys
✓ lunchtime meals
✓ evening meals
✓ food lunchtime and evening
✓ children's menu
✓ bottle warming
✓ no smoking area
✖ accommodation
✖ nearby camping and caravan sites
✓ nappy changing – disabled toilets
✖ entertainment
✓ children's certificate
✓ high chairs
✓ time limit – 9pm for non-diners

## SUTTON-IN-ASHfiELD

# King & Miller

Kings Mill Road East, Sutton-in-Ashfield NG17 4JP
T 01623 553290    F 01623 553209
*Licensee*: Tony Pustelnik
*Opening times*: 11–11; 12–10.30 Sun
*Real ales*: **Hardys & Hansons Kimberley Best Bitter**;
seasonal beers

Purpose-built pub/restaurant from the 1990s which is very family-orientated and has an open-planned design. Children are allowed in the separate no-smoking restaurant and family room (in the event of private parties use the restaurant), while there's also an indoor play area with a ball pond and other fun. There's a nappy changing space in the ladies, but men can't get away with their usual excuses as there's also space in the unisex disabled loo. An activity book is given out free with each

children's meal. Outside, there's also a gated play area in the beer garden with swings and a climbing frame.

Food is served 11am-10pm all through the week, changing to midday–9pm on Sundays. The large **kids' menu** has familiar choices with chips, while the kitchen can also offer small gammons and steaks off the main menu. On Sunday lunchtimes, roasts are served (small portions available) alongside the main menu.

A friendly food-led pub based in an old mining town which has the largest sundial in Europe; it is also close to Sherwood Forest with its visitor centre and many woodland walks (tell them the tale of Robin Hood and unleash them on the wild!).

✓ children restricted to certain areas
✓ family room
✓ garden
✓ garden toys
✓ lunchtime meals
✓ evening meals
✓ food lunchtime and evening
✓ children's menu
✓ bottle warming
✓ no smoking area
✖ accommodation
✖ nearby camping and caravan sites
✓ nappy changing – women's and disabled toilets
✖ entertainment
✖ children's certificate
✓ high chairs
✓ time limit – 9pm

# OXFORDSHIRE

## FYFIELD

# White Hart

Main Road, Fyfield OX13 5LW
T 01865 390585    F 01865 390671
*Licensee*: Ian Mintrim
*Opening times*: 12–3, 6–11; 12–3, 6–10.30 Sun
*Real ales*: **Fuller's London Pride; Hook Norton Best**

**Bitter; Theakston Old Peculier; Wadworth 6X;** guest beers
*Directions*: off A420 between Oxford and Swindon

Back in the 1450s, the local lord of the manor built what was to become the White Hart as a chantry house where holy men could pray for his soul. By the middle of the next century it had been bought by one of the Oxford colleges and has been an inn ever since.

Its purpose might have changed but the interior is still a stunning throwback to its medieval origins with the main bar area boasting a high-vaulted, church-like ceiling with original oak beams and a no-smoking minstrels gallery which runs round most of the room; there is also a restaurant which is no smoking. A smaller public bar has an impressive inglenook fireplace and a framed history of the pub hanging on the wall.

Children are allowed everywhere, while the garden outside has swings and a climbing frame, as well as a recently constructed slate-tiled pagoda where barbecues are held in the summer.

Food is served lunchtimes and evenings all week, with the **kids' menu** offering familiar choices. However, smaller portions off the excellent main menu are available and these will include pasta dishes, tuna niçoise and sausage and mash. Sunday lunch sees a roast option (small portions available), alongside the other menus.

Nearby attractions to be visited by car include Oxford, Blenheim Palace and Burford Wildlife Park.

x children restricted to certain areas
x family room
✓ garden
✓ garden toys
✓ lunchtime meals
✓ evening meals
✓ food lunchtime and evening
✓ children's menu
✓ bottle warming
✓ no smoking area
x accommodation
x nearby camping and caravan sites
x nappy changing
x entertainment
x children's certificate
✓ high chairs
✓ time limit – 9pm

# Olde Leatherne Bottel

1 High Street, Lewknor OX9 5TH
T 01844 351482
*Licensee*: Lesley Gordon
*Opening times*: 11–2.30, 6–11; 12–3, 7–10.30 Sun
*Real ales*: **Brakspear Bitter, Special**; guest beer
*Directions*: near M40, Junction 6

Charming old country inn sited in a village on the edge of the Chilterns, formerly owned by the late, lamented Brakspear Brewery – the beers are still available though they are brewed elsewhere. Inside, there's a public bar, lounge and snug, the latter also doubles up as a no-smoking family room. The decor is low beamed ceilings, dark furniture including wooden benches in the snug, and lots of old beer taps and pictures on the wall. There is also a selection of paintings of the pub produced by a local artist.

Children are allowed in the family room and lounge, which doubles up as the main dining area. There's also a large garden boasting a play area with slide, swings and climbing frame which is understandably off-limits in the winter.

Food is served lunchtimes and evenings during the week. The **kids' menu** features familiar choices, but smaller portions off the main menu can also be served. Lunchtimes offer snacks such as filled baguettes alongside traditional bar food such as ham, egg and chips, while there is also a more substantial menu which includes pasta, scampi, homemade curries and ribs; this is also served in the evening. Sunday lunchtimes sees the main menus available as well as an occasional Sunday roast (small portions served).

As the motorway is close this is an ideal stopping spot if you're travelling, while there are plenty of country walks in the immediate vicinity.

✓ children restricted to certain areas
✓ family room
✓ garden
✓ garden toys

- ✓ lunchtime meals
- ✓ evening meals
- ✓ food lunchtime and evening
- ✓ children's menu
- ✓ bottle warming
- ✓ no smoking area
- ✗ accommodation
- ✗ nearby camping and caravan sites
- ✗ nappy changing
- ✗ entertainment
- ✗ children's certificate
- ✗ high chairs
- ✗ time limit

## SONNING EYE

# Flowing Spring

Henley Road, Sonning Eye RG4 9RB
T 0118 969 3207
*Licensee*: Stephen Hunt
*Opening times*: 11.30–11; 12–10.30 Sun
*Real ales*: **Fuller's Chiswick, London Pride, ESB**,
seasonal beers; guest beer (occasional)
*Directions*: on A4155

Fuller's-owned rural local built in 1794 then extended in the 1870s. Recent refurbishments include a balcony which is decorated with hanging flower baskets and has a view over the garden and the Thames Valley beyond. The bar is in the centre of the pub off which there is a public bar, lounge and no-smoking snug. One feature of the decor is the display of old currency, many of which are brought in by the locals. No Euros yet though.

Children are allowed everywhere inside and there are dominoes, draughts and shut-the-box to keep them entertained, while outside there's a huge garden with a slide, climbing frame and swings. It leads onto the car park so keep a beady eye out. There's also an area for impromptu football matches, so bring a ball. The garden is where the local tug-of-war team meet and practice on Wednesday evenings.

Food is served 12pm–3pm every lunchtime daily, 6.30pm–9.30pm Wednesday–Saturday evenings. The **kids' menu** includes familiar choices, while smaller portions off the main menu can be served including pasta, scampi, salads,

chilli and sandwiches. A roast is served Sunday lunchtime alongside the main menus (small roasts available).

Overnight stays permissible for members of the Caravan Club but do contact first. Situated in good rambling country with plenty of walks close to the pub, while Henley is only five miles away.

- ✗ children restricted to certain areas
- ✗ family room
- ✓ garden
- ✓ garden toys
- ✓ lunchtime meals
- ✓ evening meals
- ✓ food lunchtime and evening
- ✓ children's menu
- ✓ bottle warming
- ✓ no smoking area
- ✗ accommodation
- ✓ nearby camping and caravan sites
- ✗ nappy changing
- ✗ entertainment
- ✗ children's certificate
- ✓ high chairs
- ✓ time limit – 8.30pm

## SOUTH MORETON

# Crown Inn

High Street, South Moreton OX11 9AG
T 01235 812262
*Licensees*: Pearl and Malcolm Cook
*Opening times*: 11–3, 5.30–11; 12–3, 7–10.30 Sun
*Real ales*: **Adnams Bitter; Badger Tanglefoot; Wadworth IPA, 6X**

Rustic village pub built in the 19th century which is open-planned and has a selection of curios on the walls, including an ancient fishing rod. The pub is also the place to go if you want to replenish your book collection; locals bring unwanted books which are then sold to help the local hospice.

Children are allowed everywhere though the licensees stipulate that they must be eating. There's also a compact garden at the back. Food is served lunchtimes and evenings throughout the week, with the **kids' menu** including familiar choices. If they want something different some of the main menu can be served in smaller portions.

These include scampi, burgers, sandwiches, jacket potatoes while Sunday lunchtimes offer the main menus alongside a choice of a roast (kids' portions served where possible).

South Moreton is very close to Didcot where the steam train centre is a major attraction.

- ✗ children restricted to certain areas
- ✗ family room
- ✓ garden
- ✗ garden toys
- ✓ lunchtime meals
- ✓ evening meals
- ✓ food lunchtime and evening
- ✓ children's menu
- ✓ bottle warming
- ✗ no smoking area
- ✗ accommodation
- ✗ nearby camping and caravan sites
- ✗ nappy changing
- ✗ entertainment
- ✗ children's certificate
- ✓ high chairs
- ✗ time limit

## STOKE TALMAGE

# Red Lion

Stoke Talmage, Thame OX9 7ES
**T** 01844 281651
*Licensees*: Steve Wilkins
*Opening times*: 6–11; closed Mon; 12–2, 6–11, Fri, Sat; 12–3.30, 7–10.30 Sun
*Real ales*: Beer range varies
*Directions*: turn off A40 at Tetsworth and it's one and a half miles to the village

There is no food sold at this 18th-century pub which is part of a 20-acre livestock farm, but parents are welcome to use the barbecue for a DIY feast which should meet with general approval from most kids. Nevertheless this friendly unchanged local does cater for children with swings and slides out in the safe garden; there is also an Aunt Sally pitch, a pub game which is popular in these parts. Being in the middle of a working farm there is also a poultry and duck corner plus plenty of horses and sheep to be seen.

Inside, children are allowed in the family room, which has comfortable settees, bar billiards, 'hook the fish' and colouring books. It's a very rustic atmosphere everywhere and adults interested in pubs might want to check out the small paralleled bar counter which was installed in 1941 and the old farm pews which are used for seats. There are nappy changing facilities in the disabled toilet.

Three real ales are usually available, one generally from a local micro, and there is a good selection of real cider. Despite the lack of food and restricted opening weekday opening hours, this is a very family-friendly pub – take a picnic and enjoy the great outdoors, or you can even take some food into the family room providing it's not too busy.

Beautiful walking country with the Icknield Way and the Ridgeway very close. There's also the Chilterns where red kites can be spied, while Oxford and Blenheim Palace aren't too far away.

- ✓ children restricted to certain areas
- ✓ family room
- ✓ garden
- ✓ garden toys
- ✗ lunchtime meals
- ✗ evening meals
- ✗ food lunchtime and evening
- ✗ children's menu
- ✗ bottle warming
- ✗ no smoking area
- ✗ accommodation
- ✗ nearby camping and caravan sites
- ✓ nappy changing – disabled toilets
- ✗ entertainment
- ✗ children's certificate
- ✗ high chairs
- ✗ time limit

# SHROPSHIRE

## HEATHTON

# Old Gate Inn

Heathton, Claverley, Shropshire WV5 7EB
**T** 01746 710431    **F** 01746 710131
**E** oldgateinn@aol.com
www.oldgateinn.co.uk
*Licensee*: Jamie Atkins
*Opening times*: 12–2.30, 6.30–11; closed Mon;
12–3, 7–10.30 Sun
*Real ales*: **Enville Ale; Greene King Abbot; Old Swan
Entire; Wells Bombardier**
*Directions*: between B4176 and A458 near
Halfpenny Green

Country inn which has been dispensing
food and drink since the late 17th century.
Located in a rural location on the eastern
edge of Shropshire, it's surrounded by
beautiful countryside, yet a mere 20
minute drive will take you into Bridgnorth.
Inside there are two bars with plenty of
interesting bric-a-brac on display, log fires
in the winter and a welcoming atmosphere;
the lower part of the snug is no-smoking.

Children are allowed everywhere.
Outside there is a large, attractive garden
with a safe play area that includes a
treehouse, sandpit and swings.

Food is important here (there are three
chefs and local produce is used) though it
doesn't detract from the atmosphere of the
pub: 'We're a pub which just happens to serve
excellent food,' insists landlord Jamie Atkins.
The **kids' menu** features familiar selections
alongside some more interesting choices
such as steak and ale pie, lasagne, whole tail
scampi and ham and fries. Smaller portions
can be served off the full menu whenever
that is possible. On Sunday lunchtimes there
is a traditional roast (small-sized roasts
available), alongside the normal menus and
a specials board. Serving times are 12pm–2pm,
6.30pm–9pm Tuesday–Saturday,

12pm–2pm Sunday lunchtime; there is no
food on Monday and Sunday evening.

Well-situated for plenty of country walks
to work off lunch, while aeroplane-spotters
might want to make the trip to nearby
Halfpenny Airport.

✗ children restricted to certain areas
✗ family room
✓ garden
✓ garden toys
✓ lunchtime meals
✓ evening meals
✓ food lunchtime and evening
✓ children's menu
✓ bottle warming
✓ no smoking area
✗ accommodation
✓ nearby camping and caravan sites
✗ nappy changing
✗ entertainment
✗ children's certificate
✓ high chairs
✗ time limit

## LUDLOW

# Church Inn

Buttercross, Ludlow SY8 1AW
**T** 01584 872174    **F** 01584 877146
www.thechurchinn.com
*Licensee*: Graham Wilson-Lloyd
*Opening times*: 11–11; 12–10.30 Sun
*Real ales*: **Brains Bitter; Hobson's Bitter, Mild,
Town Crier; Hook Norton Old Hooky; Wye Valley
Bitter; guest beers**

The oldest pub in Ludlow, the Church Inn
dates right back to the 1440s. You can find it
right in the centre of this beautiful town
which, in the last few years, has been
developing a reputation as the unofficial
foodie capital of the UK. Inside, you will
find a large island bar with two rooms, one
of which is no-smoking. Children are
allowed in both areas and there are
colouring books and pens to amuse them.
The decor is stripped stonework, wooden
pews, loads of pictures of old Ludlow on the
wall and a display of old cameras in a
cabinet. The landlord, a former mayor of
the town, is a great fan of real ale and

usually keeps eight beers on plus a delicious selection of bottled Belgian beers.

Food is served lunchtimes and evenings throughout the whole week. The **kids' menu** has familiar choices though smaller portions can be ordered off the main menu which changes all the time but will probably include pasta dishes and the like; there are also baguettes available. Local produce is used wherever possible. Sunday lunches feature roasts alongside the main menu; small portions are available.

Ludlow is a bustling but traditional market town which has become rather fashionable of late. The castle is great fun for youngsters to run round and has a view over the surrounding countryside, while there are plenty of interesting shops for the older ones.

x children restricted to certain areas
x family room
x garden
x garden toys
✓ lunchtime meals
✓ evening meals
✓ food lunchtime and evening
✓ children's menu
✓ bottle warming
✓ no smoking area
✓ accommodation
x nearby camping and caravan sites
x nappy changing
x entertainment
x children's certificate
✓ high chairs
x time limit

# Dog Inn

Main Street, Worfield WV15 5LF
T 01746 716020
*Licensee*: Vic Pocock
*Opening times*: 12–2.30, 7 (5 Sat)–11; 12–3, 7–10.30 Sun
*Real ales*: **Courage Best Bitter; Highgate Mild; Wadworth 6X; Wells Bombardier**

In the past this family-run 17th-century built pub has been called the Greyhound and the Davenport Arms (which still appears on the sign), but despite these changes of name

locals apparently always called it the Dog. Talking of dogs, the licensees have a Staffordshire Bull terrier called Tosh.

Located next to the village church in an idyllic looking village, the Dog Inn is a solid-looking building which received its first licence to sell beer back in 1790; until recently it was home to the Worfield Brewery who have now moved to Bridgnorth. Inside there are two light and spacious bars with pine furniture and tiled floors; some of the old features which have been retained include oak beams and a large fireplace. Look out for the list of former innkeepers going back to the 1820. Children are allowed everywhere.

In 2001 the pub received the Pub of the Year Good Eating Award from the local council, so it's no surprise that people make their way here from far and near to have a meal. Food is served 12pm–2pm, 7pm–9.30pm throughout the week. The **kids' menu** has the usual choices, but there are smaller portions available off the main menu which includes good warming meals such as faggots and mash, fresh haddock and sausage and mash. There are also a range of snacks at weekends. On Sundays roasts are served alongside the main menus (small roasts available). There is a small secure area for seating at the back.

The historic market town of Bridgnorth is close by and is a stop on the Severn Valley Railway; there is also a funicular railway in the town.

x children restricted to certain areas
x family room
✓ garden
x garden toys
✓ lunchtime meals
✓ evening meals
✓ food lunchtime and evening
✓ children's menu
✓ bottle warming
✓ no smoking area
x accommodation
x nearby camping and caravan sites
x nappy changing
x entertainment
✓ children's certificate
✓ high chairs
x time limit

## UPPER AFFCOT (Church Stretton)

# Travellers Rest Inn

Upper Affcot SY6 6RL
T 01694 781275
www.travellersrestinn.co.uk
*Licensee*: Fraser Allison
*Opening times*: 11–11; 12–10.30 Sun
*Real ales*: **Boddingtons Bitter; Draught Bass; Hobson's Best Bitter; Wood Shropshire Lad**; guest beers
*Directions*: on A49 between Church Stretton and Craven Arms

Former coaching inn in a small Shropshire hills hamlet located on the old Cardiff-Manchester route. Solid-looking stone building which manages to cater to both passing trade and locals; the pub is headquarters for the Pentre tug-of-war team from over the border in Wales. Inside there's a large bar which is divided into several interesting areas including a no-smoking conservatory. The decor includes lots of dark wood, horse brasses and copper.

Children are allowed throughout, while there's a large open-planned garden at the rear with views over the surrounding countryside.

Food is served all day throughout the week, with last orders by 8.30pm. The **kids' menu** has familiar choices though smaller portions off the main grill-based menu are always available if possible; choices include scampi, gammon, small steaks and pasta. The pub provides free bottles of baby food along with a jug of hot water for heating them up. The landlord told me that he puts the onus on parents to heat up their own baby food as the differences in people's microwaves could lead to babies scalding their mouths. This is something I have heard from several landlords, some of whom will not heat up baby food due to a fear of litigious parents if the food is too hot (see page 38 for feature). Sadly it seems that the American practice of suing at the drop of a hat is reaching our pubs.

This is good walking countryside with the Shropshire Hills Discovery Centre at nearby Craven Arms providing a good introduction. It will also make the kids giggle as the

building has a turf roof and looks for all the world like the Teletubbies' house. Weston's draught cider is always available.

- ✗ children restricted to certain areas
- ✗ family room
- ✓ garden
- ✗ garden toys
- ✓ lunchtime meals
- ✓ evening meals
- ✓ food lunchtime and evening
- ✓ children's menu
- ✗ bottle warming
- ✓ no smoking area
- ✓ accommodation
- ✓ nearby camping and caravan sites – camping in the pub's own grounds
- ✓ nappy changing – cloakroom area
- ✗ entertainment
- ✓ children's certificate
- ✓ high chairs
- ✓ time limit – 9.30pm

# STAFFORDSHIRE

## ALSAGERS BANK

# Gresley Arms

High Street, Alsagers Bank ST7 8BQ
T 01782 720297
E carlgresley@aol.com
*Licensee*: Linda Smith
*Opening times*: 12–3, 6–11; 12–10.30 Sun
*Real ales*: Beer range varies
*Directions*: Situated between Newcastle under Lyme and Audley (Junction 16 M6)

Solid looking family run local which has great views over towards Cheshire and Wales – kids (and adults) will be entranced gazing through the handy telescope in the garden. Inside, there's traditional decor (lots of old photographs of the area) with a bar, lounge, dining room and games room. Real ales come from various micros including locals Titanic, Slaters, Beartown and Town House. There is usually one traditional cider on sale.

Children are allowed in the dining room and the games room which doubles up as the family room. Here there are two pool tables, a dart board, cards and other traditional pub games. Parents are welcome to bring games, books or toys for their children. There is also a play area in the garden outside with a large playhouse, slides, see-saw and sandpit. On summer bank holidays the pub organises a bouncy castle.

The **kids' menu** is good value, £1.50 for familiar choices such as fish fingers, sausages and chicken nuggets and chips, while there is also a kids three-course Sunday lunch for £3.50; selections off the main menu are also available then. Food is served from 12pm–2.30pm and 6pm–9.30pm throughout the week, while Sundays sees the kitchen going all day.

Family attractions within easy driving distance include Alton Towers on the other side of Stoke-on-Trent, Trentham Gardens, the entertainment complex Waterworld at Hanley and Amerton Farm, where visitors can see a full working farm.

✓ children restricted to certain areas
✓ family room
✓ garden
✓ garden toys
✓ lunchtime meals
✓ evening meals
✓ food lunchtime and evening
✓ children's menu
✓ bottle warming
✓ no smoking area
✗ accommodation
✗ nearby camping and caravan sites
✗ nappy changing
✓ entertainment
✗ children's certificate
✓ high chairs
✗ time limit

## Hollybush Inn

Ebstree Road, Ebstree WV5 7JE
**T** 01902 895587
*Licensee*: Russ Cocking
*Opening times*: 12–3, 5.30–11; 12–11 Sat; 12–10.30 Sun
*Real ales*: **Taylor Landlord; Tetley Burton Ale;** guest beer

Traditional country pub owned by Punch Taverns, which is half a mile west of the Staffordshire and Worcestershire canal; it is popular with walkers. There are two bars (one of which is no-smoking) with log fires in the winter, while horse brasses and other familiar pub bric-a-brac mingle on the walls.

Children are allowed everywhere, while there's a large secure garden at the back with an adventure playground. During the summer the pub organises several different events including barbecues and a bouncy castle. Even the adults have been known to get in on the fun with a bungee jump in the car park.

Food is served lunchtimes and evenings Monday–Saturday, but on Sundays it is only at lunchtimes. The **kids' menu** has familiar choices with chips, as well as small steaks and gammons, while Sunday lunchtime is roast meals only with kids' portions being served.

Even though Wolverhampton is a short drive away, the Hollybush is located in a very rural area and is handy for canalside walks. Baggeridge Wood is also nearby and full of forest walks.

✗ children restricted to certain areas
✗ family room
✓ garden
✓ garden toys
✓ lunchtime meals
✓ evening meals
✓ food lunchtime and evening
✓ children's menu
✓ bottle warming
✓ no smoking area
✓ accommodation
✗ nearby camping and caravan sites
✗ nappy changing
✓ entertainment
✗ children's certificate
✗ high chairs
✓ time limit – 6pm

## Red Lion

Great Chatwell TS10 9BJ
**T** 01952 691366
**E** mike@theredlion1.freeserve.co.uk
*Licensee*: Paula Smith
*Opening times*: 6 (5 summer)–11; 12–11 Sat; 12–10.30 Sun

*Real ales*: **Everards Beacon, Tiger; Flowers IPA;**
guest beers
*Directions*: two miles east of A41, near Newport

Ivy-clad traditional pub which was once owned by Wem Brewery but is now a popular free house with a good reputation for its food. It was refurbished in the early 1990s when a large lounge was added. Children are allowed in the lounge bar, no-smoking restaurant and games room which is also designated as the family room. This is the place to go if you want to sharpen up your table football skills. Here you will also find pool and several video games. There's a fenced in garden at the back with a secure play area on soft bark; play equipment includes swings and a slide. There is also a large aviary and guinea pigs to which children usually gravitate.

This is more of a pub for the weekend as it doesn't open lunchtimes during the week so food is only available 6pm–9.30pm. However the tables turn at the weekend when food is available all day from midday until 9.30pm (9.00pm Sunday). There are two, age-related, **kids' menus**. Up to age seven there's a familiar menu of chicken nuggets etc with chips while children up to 12 can choose from the likes of grilled chicken, gammon and battered cod. Small portions off the specials board are also served if possible. These might include steaks, mild curries and duck. On Sundays small roasts are available alongside the main menus.

Great Chatwell is a small village located on the eastern edge of Staffordshire and there are plenty of country walks in the vicinity. If you want to drive, then Telford and Shrewsbury aren't too far while other sights to look out for include Shugborough Park and Cosford Aerospace Museum.

✓ children restricted to certain areas
✓ family room
✓ garden
✓ garden toys
✓ lunchtime meals Sat sun only
✓ evening meals
✗ food lunchtime and evening
✓ children's menu
✓ bottle warming

✓ no smoking area
✗ accommodation
✓ nearby camping and caravan sites
✗ nappy changing
✗ entertainment
✗ children's certificate
✓ high chairs
✗ time limit

## ONECOTE

# Jervis Arms

Onecote, near Leek ST13 7RU
**T** 01538 304206
*Licensee*: Peter Hill
*Opening times*: 12–3, 7–11; 12–10.30 Sun
*Real ales*: **Draught Bass**, guest beers
*Directions*: off the A52 on the Leek to Ashbourne road

Seventeenth-century inn which can be found on the southern edge of the Peak District (ideal for good healthy bracing walks) although Alton Towers is only six miles away if you fancy something a bit more stomach-lurching. Named after one of Lord Nelson's admirals, the Jervis Arms has a beautiful riverside location, while inside children are allowed into two family rooms. One of these is no-smoking. There are games, books and toys at hand. Outside, the secure riverside beer garden offers a choice of swings, a tree house and slide. Special events during the year to look out for include a family fun day and an annual duck race. There is also a compact pet area with pygmy goats.

The pub prides itself on having one of the largest menus in Staffordshire – handy if your kids are picky eaters. As well as a **kids' menu** which features small steaks and gammons alongside the usual choices, up to 60% of the main menu can be served in smaller portions if needed. These include sandwiches, baked potatoes and pies. Sundays sees a choice of roast and the main menus, while small roasts are available. Food is served lunchtimes and evenings throughout the week and all day on Sunday.

As well as the Peak District, with its marvellous views and walks especially at Manifold Valley, and Alton Towers, other attractions close by include a couple of farm parks within a few minutes drive.

- ✓ children restricted to certain areas
- ✓ family room
- ✓ garden
- ✓ garden toys
- ✓ lunchtime meals
- ✓ evening meals
- ✓ food lunchtime and evening
- ✓ children's menu
- ✓ bottle warming
- ✓ no smoking area
- ✗ accommodation
- ✓ nearby camping and caravan sites
- ✓ nappy changing – women's toilets
- ✓ entertainment
- ✓ children's certificate
- ✓ high chairs
- ✗ time limit

## WHISTON

## Swan Inn

Whiston, near Penkridge ST19 5QH
**T** 01785 716200
*Licensees*: Jim and Jackie Davies
*Opening times*: 6–11; 12–11 Sat; 12–10.30 Sun
*Real ales*: **Banks's Original; Holden Bitter**; guest beers
*Directions*: Two miles west of Penkridge

Rural freehouse originally built in 1593 with a timber frame. It was rebuilt in 1711 with plenty of exposed beams and quarry tile flooring. Inside there's a traditional bar, with a separate lounge and dining room, all warmed by open fires in the winter.

Children are allowed in the lounge and dining room, the latter is non-smoking. However, in the summer kids race outdoors to the large outdoor play area with an attached obstacle course – including swings, slides, bridges and climbing nets. There's also a five acre field where camping is available.

As well as a wide range of real ales, the food has a good reputation with local produce being used for both the weekend lunchtime bar meals and the more formal courses in the dining room. The **kids' menu** has the usual choices, though smaller portions of the excellent menu can be supplied where possible. Selections include

chicken dishes with various sauces and small steaks. On Sunday lunchtimes there's a roast and the bar menu, with small roasts available for younger customers. Food is served 6pm–9pm Monday–Friday and all day Saturdays and Sundays.

Local family orientated attractions include Ironbridge Gorge Centre, Weston Park, Boscobel House and the Black Country Museum.

- ✓ children restricted to certain areas
- ✗ family room
- ✓ garden
- ✓ garden toys
- ✓ lunchtime meals
- ✓ evening meals
- ✓ food lunchtime and evening – weekends only
- ✓ children's menu
- ✓ bottle warming
- ✓ no smoking area
- ✗ accommodation
- ✓ nearby camping and caravan sites
- ✗ nappy changing
- ✗ entertainment
- ✗ children's certificate
- ✓ high chairs
- ✓ time limit – 9.30pm

# WARWICKSHIRE

## NO MAN'S HEATH

## Four Counties

Ashby Road, No Man's Heath B79 0PB
**T** 01827 830243
*Licensees*: Nicholas and Sandra Pitch
*Opening times*: 11.30–3, 6.30–11; 12–3, 7–10.30 Sun
*Real ales*: **Banks's Original; Everards Original; Marston's Pedigree**; guest beer
*Directions*: on the B5493

The Four Counties is located at the furthest point of north Warwickshire and not surprisingly you can see four counties from the windows. It has belonged to the same family for decades and is unaltered since 1965 according to welcoming landlady Sandra Pitch. In the old days the Four Counties was apparently popular with local highwaymen who used the inn as a bolt hole. Nowadays, this former coaching inn is a very friendly traditional hostelry with one bar divided into two levels. The decor is rustic with lots of brasses and pictures of old Tamworth which is nearby, as well as Toby Jugs.

Children are allowed in the no-smoking area off the bar until 9pm and there's also a secure garden round the back, where the licensees' grandchildren leave their toys which they (very admirably) are happy to share.

Food is served lunchtimes and evenings throughout the week including familiar **kids' menu** choices with chips for the children. Smaller portions off the bar menu can also be ordered; these include homemade steak and kidney pie. Sunday lunchtimes sees roasts only; child-sized portions are available then but no chips.

Located in popular walking country, but it is only seven miles from Tamworth, on the outskirts of which lies Drayton Manor Park.

✓ children restricted to certain areas
✗ family room
✓ garden
✗ garden toys
✓ lunchtime meals
✓ evening meals
✓ food lunchtime and evening
✗ children's menu
✓ bottle warming
✓ no smoking area
✗ accommodation
✗ nearby camping and caravan sites
✗ nappy changing
✗ entertainment
✗ children's certificate
✓ high chairs
✓ time limit – 9pm

## WEST MIDLANDS

### CATHERINE-DE-BARNES

# Boat Inn

222 Hampton Lane, Catherine De Barnes B91 2TJ
T 0121 705 0474
*Licensee:* Nigel Cook
*Opening times:* 11.30–11; 12–10.30 Sun
*Real ales:* **Courage Directors**; **Tetley Bitter**; guest beers

The name of Catherine-de-Barnes apparently originates from the 11th or 12th century. However the village only grew up when the Grand Union Canal was built through it and the waterway also provides the inspiration for the name of this 'Miller's Kitchen' pub and the many old photos of boats and canals on the wall. The Boat is an open-planned pub and, while there's a definite emphasis on food, you won't feel uncomfortable just popping in for a drink.

There are two designated areas for children, one of which is no-smoking, while colouring books and pencils are available to keep younger children busy. It's worth visiting towards the end of October in particular when the pub drapes itself in a Halloween theme every year. There is a big safe garden with a bouncy castle in the summer.

Food is served from midday–9.30pm all week (10pm Friday and Saturday, 9pm Sunday). The **kids' menu** has familiar choices though smaller portions off the main menu can be chosen; these include 'light options' such as scampi, small haddock and 4oz gammon. On Sundays there are small roasts available, alongside the main menus.

Catherine-de-Barnes is situated just north of Solihull, but equally useful for getting to the centre of Birmingham. There are plenty of canal walks in the area which are very popular with families, while the National Motorcycle Museum is a short drive away off Junction 6 of the M42.

✓ children restricted to certain areas
✗ family room
✓ garden
✗ garden toys
✓ lunchtime meals
✓ evening meals
✓ food lunchtime and evening
✓ children's menu
✓ bottle warming
✓ no smoking area
✗ accommodation
✗ nearby camping and caravan sites
✓ nappy changing – disabled toilets
✗ entertainment
✓ children's certificate
✓ high chairs
✗ time limit

## DARLASTON

## Prince of Wales

74 Walsall Road, Darlaston WS10 9JT
**T** 0121 526 6244
*Licensee*: Kathleen Abley
*Opening times*: 12(2 Monday, Tuesday, 1 Thursday) –11; 12–10.30 Sunday
*Real ales*: **Holden's Bitter**, **Golden Glow**, seasonal beers

Children are well looked after in this traditional two-roomed local which is owned by Holden's. Landlady Kathleen Abley organises Easter Egg hunts, a bouncy castle in summer, Halloween parties and even a Christmas party. This is obviously the place that local real ale drinkers and their kids gravitate towards but visiting youngsters are also roped in whenever there's an event going on. Inside the pub, there's a public bar and comfortable cosy lounge/family room with a light and spacious conservatory attached; the conservatory is no-smoking when food is served.

Children are allowed in the latter two spaces, while they also have a large and secure garden at the back to play in, which includes a climbing frame.

Food is served 2pm–7pm Monday, Tuesday, 12pm–7pm Wednesday, Friday, Saturday, 1pm–7pm Thursday and 1pm–5.30pm on Sundays. The **kids' menu** has familiar choices, as well as sandwiches, though if contacted beforehand Kathleen

can produce smaller portions off the main home-cooked menu; these would include liver and onions and pasta dishes. On Sundays there are four roast joints available with small portions served.

Darlaston is a former industrial town close to Walsall and pretty handy for a stop off the M6 (junction 10).

✓ children restricted to certain areas
✓ family room
✓ garden
✓ garden toys
✓ lunchtime meals
✓ evening meals
✓ food lunchtime and evening
✓ children's menu
✓ bottle warming
✓ no smoking area
✗ accommodation
✗ nearby camping and caravan sites
✗ nappy changing
✓ entertainment
✗ children's certificate
✓ high chairs
✗ time limit

## SEDGLEY

## Beacon Hotel

120 Bilston Street, Sedgley DY3 1JE
**T** 01902 883380
*Licensee*: John Hughes
*Opening times*: 12–2.30, 5.30–10.45 (11Fri); 12–3, 6–11 Sat; 12–3, 7–10.30 Sun
*Real ales*: **S**arah Hughes Dark Ruby, Pale Amber, Sedgley Surprise, Snow Flake (seasonal); guest beer

Multi-roomed Victorian pub which has been lovingly restored to its original condition with open fires, tiled floors, mahogany furniture and serving hatches from the central island bar. It's like stepping back into the past and an absolute joy for any real ale fan and lover of traditional pubs. The Beacon also brews its own beers, including the award-winning Ruby Mild which at 6% is stronger than most milds (you can take it home with you in bottle-conditioned form).

Children are allowed in the family room at the back of the pub, where there are a few games such as dominoes. Outside there's a safe garden which has a climbing frame, slide and roundabout.

Beware: food is solely cheese and onion cob rolls at lunchtime so it might not be suitable if your children routinely demand sausage and chips for their lunch. That said, the pub is popular with all ages, especially families taking the stiff walk up to Sedgley Beacon (apparently used to warn of marauding armies in the unruly past).

If you've got the car with you, the Wren's Nest National Nature Reserve is within easy reach and is a stunning showpiece of geological conservation and a must for any child with an interest in fossils, of which there are an abundance in the area.

✓ children restricted to certain areas
✓ family room
✓ garden
✓ garden toys
✗ lunchtime meals
✗ evening meals
✗ food lunchtime and evening
✗ children's menu
✗ bottle warming
✗ no smoking area
✗ accommodation
✗ nearby camping and caravan sites
✗ nappy changing
✗ entertainment
✗ children's certificate
✗ high chairs
✗ time limit

## WORCESTERSHIRE

# King & Castle

Station Approach, Comberton Hill, Kidderminster DY10 1QX
**T** 01562 747505
*Licensee*: Rosemary Hyde
*Opening times*: 11–3, 5-11; 11–11 Sat; 12–10.30 Sun
*Real ales*: **Batham Best Bitter; Highgate Dark; Wyre Piddle Royal Piddle**; guest beers
*Directions*: next to main line station

The Severn Valley Railway is a splendid steam-driven operation which runs between Kidderminster and Bridgnorth and the King & Castle is a faithful recreation of a 1930s station waiting room located on the platform. It is so authentic that you could easily imagine Trevor Howard and Celia Johnson sharing a meat pie and a cup of Rosie Lee there during one of their brief encounters. However, surprisingly, it was only built in the late 1980s. It's a single-room bar with plenty of seating and loads of railway memorabilia on the walls; two guest beers come from all over the country with the emphasis on the smaller brewers.

Children are allowed everywhere apart from at the bar and in the summer you can take your drink with you and sit out on the platform.

Food is served lunchtimes all week long, but evening servings from 6pm–8pm only on Friday, Saturday and Sundays. There's a **kids' menu** with familiar choices, and small roasts are served Sunday lunchtimes during the summer season when the railway is running almost daily; otherwise it's the main menus. The station gets very busy during special rail weekends when the SVR runs with a theme such as the Thomas the Tank or the 1940s, when the pub can seem like an episode out of Dad's Army. It's well worth taking a trip then, or any time really as most kids will love the novelty of this most unusual pub.

Further afield, a visit to the safari park between Kidderminster and Bewdley is much recommended.

✗ children restricted to certain areas
✗ family room
✗ garden
✗ garden toys
✓ lunchtime meals
✓ evening meals
✓ food lunchtime and evening
✓ children's menu
✓ bottle warming ã in station buffet
✗ no smoking area
✗ accommodation
✗ nearby camping and caravan sites
✓ nappy changing out on station platform

- ✗ entertainment
- ✗ children's certificate
- ✗ high chairs
- ✓ time limit – 9pm

## KNIGHTWICK

# Talbot

Knightwick WR6 5PH
T 01886 821235
www.the-talbot.co.uk
*Licensee*: Annie Clift
*Opening times*: 11–11; 12–10.30 Sun
*Real ales*: **Hobson's Best Bitter; Teme Valley T'Other, This, That**, seasonal beer
*Directions*: on B4197, 400 yards from A44 Junction

Excellent food and beer are the twin attractions of this family-owned former coaching inn. It dates back to the Middle Ages but has been changed and added to over the years. Located alongside the Teme, it's also been a farm and ale house, and the Clift family, who have owned it for many years, grow most of the ingredients for the home-cooked food (they also brew their own beer). If they can't grow it themselves, they bring it in from local producers which is a very cheering policy. Inside, there's a public bar, lounge and restaurant, part of which is no-smoking.

Children are allowed in the lounge and restaurant, and food is served lunchtimes and evenings throughout the week. No chicken nuggets and fish fingers here. Children are offered smaller portions off the main menu which changes daily and might include fresh crab blinis, homemade houmus, parsons nose sausages and chips, raised game pie and chicken and tarragon. The prevailing ethos is that you cannot start educating children about good food young enough and I can only agree after watching our four-year-old polish off their delicious sweet potato lasagne. There is a garden adjacent to the car park so keep an eye on roaming toddlers.

Regular farmers' markets take place outside the Talbot, while there are plenty of walks and also worth a visit is the Pig Pen, a working pig farm near Bromyard.

- ✓ children restricted to certain areas
- ✗ family room
- ✓ garden
- ✗ garden toys
- ✓ lunchtime meals
- ✓ evening meals
- ✓ food lunchtime and evening
- ✗ children's menu
- ✓ bottle warming
- ✓ no smoking area
- ✓ accommodation
- ✗ nearby camping and caravan sites
- ✗ nappy changing
- ✗ entertainment
- ✗ children's certificate
- ✗ high chairs
- ✗ time limit

## STONEHALL COMMON

# Fruiterer's Arms

Stonehall Common, near Norton WR5 3QG
T 01905 820462
*Licensee*: Colin Frost
*Opening times*: 12–2, 6–11; 12–10.30 Sun
*Real ales*: Beer range varies
*Directions*: from Norton, first left after garden centre

The name of this old redbrick country pub comes from the days when it was a cider house serving the local hop and fruit pickers. Inside there's a cosy, homely feel to things with an oak-panelled bar, open fires, rustic furnishing as well as a comfy three-piece suite in the bar. There's a light and spacious no-smoking restaurant at the rear which overlooks the garden and children are allowed in here providing they are eating, but the landlord stresses that the pub is very flexible. There's a secure garden at the side of the pub with a climbing frame, slide and a couple of obstacle courses which hopefully will leave you free to sit down and enjoy the views towards the Malverns.

Food is served lunchtimes and evenings daily apart from Sunday when it's an all-day service until 8.30pm. The **kids' menu** has familiar choices with chips, though smaller portions are possible off the main menu including pasta dishes. Sundays sees a choice of roasts only, though there are small roasts and the **kids' menu** available, with the main menu coming on stream in the latter part of the day.

Even though it's only a 10-minute drive from the centre of Worcester the Fruiterer's is based in a very rural area and has lots of country walks to hand (or rather to foot).

✓ children restricted to certain areas
✗ family room
✓ garden
✓ garden toys
✓ lunchtime meals
✓ evening meals
✓ food lunchtime and evening
✓ children's menu
✓ bottle warming
✓ no smoking area
✗ accommodation
✗ nearby camping and caravan sites
✗ nappy changing
✗ entertainment
✗ children's certificate
✗ high chairs
✗ time limit

## WORCESTER

# Salmon's Leap

42 Severn Street, Worcester WR1 2ND
**T** 01905 726260
**E** bernardwalker@thesalmonsleap.freeserve.co.uk
www.thesalmonsleap.co.uk
*Licensee*: Bernard Walker
*Opening times*: 11.30(11 Fri, summer)–3, 5–11;
11–11 Sat; 12–10.30 Sun
*Real ales*: **Taylor Landlord**; guest beers
*Directions*: opposite Worcester porcelain factory

Ansells originally built this free house in 1950 and then, bizarrely, it was knocked down just a few years later only to be rebuilt a few yards away. It was then called the Fountain and has also traded as the Potter's Wheel (due to its proximity to the porcelain factory), until 1999 when the current owners renamed it the Salmon's Leap, taking inspiration from the fact that the river is three minutes away and Severn Street used to be called Fish Street.

'We're aiming to be a good cask ale pub,' says landlady Erica Walker, but that doesn't stop families and their kids from flocking here in the summer to enjoy both the beers and the fenced-in play area adjacent to the pub, where there is a wendy house and climbing frame, as well as a permanent bouncy castle which changes every fortnight during the summer.

Inside, there's a single bar, no-smoking restaurant and pool room. The main beams are plastered with brewery pump clips, evidence of the vast selection of real ales that appear here (there are usually four guest ales). Children are allowed everywhere but because of the compactness of the pub, it must be stressed that this tends to work better in the summer than in the winter, although kids are always welcome.

There's a **kids' menu** during the summer months which includes spaghetti bolognese, meatballs, chips with familiar choices and sandwiches. The licensees made a conscious decision not to have the ubiquitous chicken nuggets but say that it was a hard choice as so many people ask for them. Smaller portions off the main menu are also available throughout the year, with examples including sausage and chips and pasta dishes. Sunday lunch is usually the main menus. There are barbecues on Saturday evenings in the summer when the weather allows it. Food is served lunchtimes and evenings Monday–Thursday and all day the rest of the week.

Ideally placed for Worcester's splendid cathedral as well as the Commandery which has lots of displays and weapons from the English Civil War.

✗ children restricted to certain areas
✗ family room
✓ garden
✓ garden toys
✓ lunchtime meals
✓ evening meals
✓ food lunchtime and evening
✓ children's menu summer only
✓ bottle warming
✓ no smoking area
✗ accommodation
✓ nearby camping and caravan sites
✗ nappy changing
✓ entertainment
✗ children's certificate
✓ high chairs
✓ time limit – 9pm in the winter

# What makes a Child-friendly Pub?

Remember that scene in the film *American Werewolf in London* where they walk into a remote country pub? The entire place freezes and stares with slack jaws and overt horror. Ten to one, if you're a parent, you'll recognise that scene all too well. If you want to replicate it, all you need do is to walk into any number of pubs (or restaurants, or cafes for that matter) with a child (or, even worse, several).

Let's face it, Britain is not a child-friendly country. We treat children like unexploded bombs or nasty smells. Contrast that with the continent where children are not just accepted but welcomed with open arms, and you can understand why many families head abroad for their holidays.

The problem is that we're caught in a Catch 22 situation. Going into a pub with children can be such an unpleasant experience that many parents twitch at the very memory and swear they would rather walk over burning coals than do it again. So they pack themselves off to the likes of the Charlie Chalk theme pubs where their children can run amuck (while they sit wistfully dreaming of Adnams Broadside or Oakham's JHB with ear-plugs firmly in place). The children think it's great fun and figure that standard behaviour in a public eating place is to chase each other at full pelt into ball pits and scream for ice cream. Give them a few years of this and they can never be taken into civilised company again. If this sort of child does find its way into a pub, it will probably convince the landlord that children are an unholy menace and drive the poor devil to find any way he can to avoid ever having another of the beasts in the place.

So what can be done? Plenty, if both parents and landlords play their part. Parental discipline seems to be an unfashionable policy nowadays, but as parents we simply cannot allow our children to run riot in pubs (or any other establishments). First rule: be prepared, as the scouts say. Taking a small bag of favourite (quiet) toys and books (or Gameboys for older children) with which you can ease the habitual "I'm bored" syndrome. Few landlords would object to you bringing a bag of snacks to offset the burning hunger children develop when the kitchen is running late. Second rule: be considerate. If a baby starts yelling or a toddler tantrums, the same etiquette applies as in church. If it's clear and obvious (ie someone has said so) that the landlord and your fellow drinkers truly don't give a toss, then let them go for it. Otherwise, quietly pick up said infant, march out and wait until sanity returns. Common sense really, isn't it?

On the other side, there are so many things a pub can do to make children happy and put their parents in seventh heaven. We don't demand ball ponds and bouncy castles; we're not asking for clowns on tap or Norland nannies. Truly you don't have to turn your beautiful olde worlde pub into ye olde crèche. Yes, the odd slide or swing is a bonus, but we don't expect it. Most of the things that convince us to come back again and again are really very simple – and ludicrously cheap to implement. A box of toys in a corner is lovely. A pot or two of crayons and some scrap paper (or cheap colouring books) are bliss. A high-chair (that works and isn't covered in grime) is wildly helpful (tip to landlords – there are some excellent versions that clip onto normal chairs so they don't litter your lounge). A changing mat in both sets of loos shows willing. A no-smoking room protects small delicate lungs – and a lot of adult punters would be grateful too. A little flexibility from the kitchen would be beyond wonderful. I clearly remember a bar in Ireland where our (then) three-year-old clambered onto a bar stool. We leapt to remove him but the barman brushed us aside and addressed James. "So, what would you like, sir?" he asked. And James, feeling very grown-up and proud, politely ordered an orange juice and some sausages. "Of course, sir," winked the barman. Sausages weren't on the menu but nobody batted an eyelid and they duly arrived. We gulped in amazement and gave that bar our solid patronage for the entire fortnight's holiday.

Above and beyond everything, you see, it's the attitude of the pub that is all-important. Children are like little psychic sponges – put them in a tense environment (where they know you're scrutinising every move and are primed to leap, Ninja-like, if they make the merest move towards the china) and they'll play up. On the other hand, put them in a relaxed, easy-going atmosphere and everyone has a good time.

Children and pubs are not incompatible. All it takes is a little consideration and a large dose of being grown-up – from the adults, that is.

# North East

Durham
Northumbria
Tyne & Wear

*Travellers Rest*
WITTON GILBERT, DURHAM

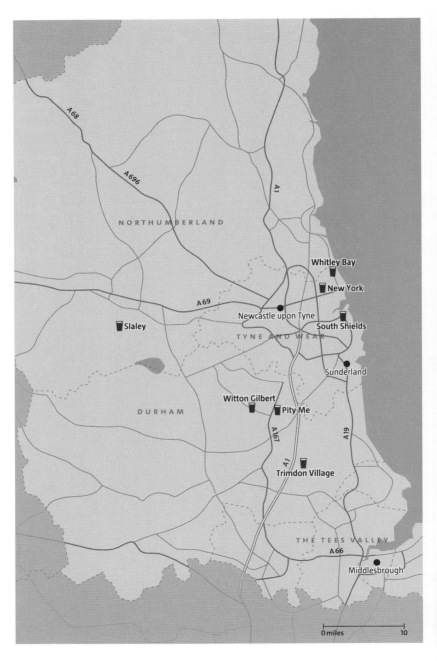

Whitley Bay
New York
Newcastle upon Tyne
South Shields
Slaley
Sunderland
Witton Gilbert
Pity Me
Trimdon Village
Middlesbrough

NORTHUMBERLAND
TYNE AND WEAR
DURHAM
THE TEES VALLEY

A68
A696
A1
A69
A167
A1
A19
A66

0 miles 10

Drop the stereotypes. There's more to this region than cheeky Geordies drinking 'Newkey Brown' or rampaging around in Newcastle United shirts. For a start, the dynamic city of Newcastle is well worth a visit, especially for Life Interactive World with its thrilling motion rides. Furthermore, the area is also home to Mordue Brewery whose Workie Ticket beer was judged to be Beer of the Year several years ago at CAMRA's annual beer festival at Olympia.

For a start, the county of Northumbria has more than a hint of the wilderness about it. Bordered in the south by the remnants of Hadrian's Wall and shoved up in the north against the Scottish border it was once a lawless place where border raids were a part of life and remains pretty untamed today. Take a trip to Hexham where the Museum of Border History looks back at those troubled times. The scenery is impressive, especially in the Northumberland National Park. The coast is equally imposing, with Holy Island (or Lindisfarne) which is the historic centre of early English Christianity.

Further south, Durham cathedral is a jewel of a building, with its origins going back to the Normans. However, smaller children are more likely to wail to go to Langley Park just outside the city where there is the adventure park Diggerland – yes, they will get to learn how to drive a JCB!

## DURHAM

### PITY ME

# Lambton Hounds

62 Front Street, Pity Me DH1 5DE
T 0191 386 4742   F 0191 375 0805
*Licensee*: Alan Sabin
*Opening times*: 11–11; 12–10.30 Sun
*Real ales*: **Black Sheep Best Bitter; Caledonian Deuchars IPA**; guest beer (summer)
*Directions*: off A167 roundabout, two miles north of Durham

Old coaching inn owned by Enterprise Inns which used to take up one entire side of the street. As for the intriguing name of the village (several others are similarly titled in the North-east), there are theories that it originates from the Norman–French *petit mere*, or small lake, which was probably a long vanished local feature. Given the antique antecedents of such village names, the Lambton is a youngster having only appeared a mere 250 years ago.

Inside there's a main bar area to one side and a lounge on the other which leads to the snug and no-smoking restaurant. The bar itself comes from luxury liner the *Olympic*, sister ship to the *Titanic*. Pictures of horses and dogs line the walls.

Children are allowed in the restaurant and snug which doubles up as the designated family room; colouring books are supplied. There's a beer garden at the back linked by an archway entrance to the car park.

Food is served lunchtimes and evenings throughout the week apart from Sunday evening when the kitchen has a rest. The **kids' menu** features familiar choices, while sandwiches, salads and jacket potatoes can also be ordered. Sunday lunch sees a choice of roast (kids' roasts available), alongside the main menus.

As the village is located on the northern outskirts of Durham this is an ideal stopping place before or after visiting the historic city and its beautiful cathedral.

✓ children restricted to certain areas
✓ family room
✓ garden
✗ garden toys
✓ lunchtime meals
✓ evening meals
✓ food lunchtime and evening
✓ children's menu
✓ bottle warming
✓ no smoking area
✗ accommodation
✓ nearby camping and caravan sites
✗ nappy changing
✗ entertainment
✗ children's certificate
✓ high chairs
✓ time limit – 9.30pm

### TRIMDON VILLAGE

# Bird In Hand

Salters Lane, Trimdon Village TS29 6SQ
T 01429 880391
*Licensee*: Nicholas Steggall
*Opening times*: 12–4, 7–11; 12–11 Fri, Sat; 12–10.30 Sun
*Real ales*: **Black Sheep Best Bitter**; guest beers

Comfortable local pub built in the 1950s, located in a small former mining village. As Sedgefield is only three miles away it is also part of Tony Blair's constituency, so you never know you might be enjoying a quiet pint with the kids just as the PM pops in to slum it (with accompanying camera crew). There's a light and airy conservatory at the front which doubles up as a dining space and leads into the lounge which is where children are allowed; this is designated as the family room. There is regular live entertainment including monthly meetings of the local folk club; up to six guest real ales are available. Outside there's a secure beer garden which, according to the landlord, seems to be getting bigger every year.

Food is served lunchtimes and evenings throughout the week apart from Monday when there's nothing all day. The **kids' menu** features familiar choices, while smaller portions off the main menu can also be served, these include chicken dishes and scampi. There's a choice of roasts at Sunday lunchtime (small portions available), alongside the main menus.

As this is a rural area, there is a good selection of country walks very close by, while Hardwick Hall Country Park with its nature trails, picnic areas and wildlife sites is a short drive away in the direction of Sedgefield.

✓ children restricted to certain areas
✓ family room
✓ garden
✗ garden toys
✓ lunchtime meals
✓ evening meals
✓ food lunchtime and evening
✓ children's menu
✓ bottle warming
✓ no smoking area
✗ accommodation
✗ nearby camping and caravan sites
✗ nappy changing
✗ entertainment
✗ children's certificate
✓ high chairs
✓ time limit – 9pm

## WITTON GILBERT

# Travellers Rest

Front Street, Witton Gilbert DH7 6TQ
**T** 0191 371 0458    **F** 0191 371 1051
*Licensee*: Paul Stabler
*Opening times*: 11.30–3, 5.30–11; 11.30–11 Sat; 12–10.30 Sun
*Real ales*: **Theakston Best Bitter**; guest beers
*Directions*: off A691, Consett Road, two miles from Durham City Centre

Recently refurbished open-planned pub which was converted from old stables. Inside there are different sections including a conservatory, the 'green room' (which is no longer green!) and a restaurant – all no-smoking. Children are allowed everywhere apart from the main bar area. Dominoes and backgammon are available from behind the bar, while CAMRA historians can ask to peruse the old editions of the *Good Beer Guide* which are also kept in the pub. Outside there's a beer garden. There are

usually five real ales on, with at least one coming from the local Durham Brewery.

Food is served lunchtimes and evenings throughout the week and there's a massive menu. The **kids' menu** features familiar choices, as well as mince and dumplings (good for warming up a winter's day!). On the main menu, some of the choices can be served in smaller portions, these include pasta dishes, omelettes and scampi, as well as sandwiches and jacket potatoes.

Langley Park is just a short drive away where you will find Diggerland, an adventure park with a profusion of JCB diggers and dumpers with rides, drives, static displays and play areas.

✗ children restricted to certain areas
✗ family room
✓ garden
✗ garden toys
✓ lunchtime meals
✓ evening meals
✓ food lunchtime and evening
✓ children's menu
✓ bottle warming
✓ no smoking area
✗ accommodation
✗ nearby camping and caravan sites
✗ nappy changing
✗ entertainment
✓ children's certificate
✓ high chairs
✗ time limit

# NORTHUMBERLAND

## SLALEY

# Travellers Rest

Slaley, NE46 1TT
**T** 01434 673231    **F** 01434 673906
**E** enquiries@travellersrest.sagehost.co.uk
www.travellersrest.sagesite.co.uk
*Licensee*: Jed Irving
*Opening times*: 12–11; 12–10.30 Sun
*Real ales*: **Black Sheep Best Bitter**; guest beers
*Directions*: on B6306, one mile north of village

Former farmhouse which was built in the 16th century and has been an inn for over 100 years. Inside the decor is traditionally rustic with slate floors, an open log fire and church pews. The main open-planned bar area has several separate areas, while there's also a comfortable no-smoking restaurant.

Children are allowed everywhere, but during the summer months they'll probably want to make their way out to the safe adventure playground at the bottom end of the beer garden; here they will find swings, a slide and an aerial runway.

Food is served lunchtimes and evenings throughout the week, except for Sunday evenings. The **kids' menu** includes familiar choices, while half portions off the main menu can be served where possible. These include Cumberland sausage in a baguette, tortilla wraps and scampi from the lunchtime menu, and sausage and mash, rosti potatoes in a tomato sauce, pasta and stir fries from the evening menu which has more à la carte style choices. Sunday lunch sees a choice of roast (kids' half portions available) plus vegetarian options, as well as sandwiches, baguettes and the standard kids' menu.

Slaley is in the heart of Hexhamshire, a traditional agricultural area with plenty of rural charm; it's also a short drive from the town of Hexham, where there is the Museum of Border History which details the troubled times of the area when border raids were a common part of life around here.

- ✘ children restricted to certain areas
- ✘ family room
- ✔ garden
- ✔ garden toys
- ✔ lunchtime meals
- ✔ evening meals
- ✔ food lunchtime and evening
- ✔ children's menu
- ✔ bottle warming
- ✔ no smoking area
- ✔ accommodation
- ✘ nearby camping and caravan sites
- ✔ nappy changing – women's toilets
- ✘ entertainment
- ✔ children's certificate
- ✔ high chairs
- ✘ time limit

## TYNE & WEAR

### NEW YORK

# Shiremoor House Farm

Middle Engine Lane, Shiremoor, New York NE29 8DZ
**T** 0191 2576302    **F** 0191 257 8602
*Licensee*: Bill Kerridge
*Opening times*: 11–11; 12–10.30 Sun
*Real ales*: **Mordue Workie Ticket**; **Taylor Landlord**; guest beers

Award-winning conversion of a former farm which has been a popular eating and drinking place for the past 14 years. Inside the decor offers stripped stone walls, wooden beams and lots of farming implements hanging up. There's an open-planned bar, dining area and the granary (the latter two no-smoking), which is designated as the family room. However, children are allowed anywhere, as long as it's not in the main bar area. Outside there's a beer garden and terrace.

Food is served midday–10pm every day throughout the week, with the **kids' menu** having familiar choices. Sunday lunchtimes sees a choice of roasts (small portions available) and the kids' menu.

If you're travelling on the A1, this is a relaxing and friendly detour to enjoy a drink and a meal with the family. Attractions in the area include the Stephenson Railway Museum which is a short drive away and has a collection of engines, including George Stephenson's world-famous Rocket; you can also take a journey on a real steam train.

- ✘ children restricted to certain areas
- ✔ family room
- ✔ garden
- ✘ garden toys
- ✔ lunchtime meals
- ✔ evening meals
- ✔ food lunchtime and evening
- ✔ children's menu
- ✔ bottle warming

✓ no smoking area
✗ accommodation
✗ nearby camping and caravan sites
✓ nappy changing – main toilets
✗ entertainment
✗ children's certificate
✓ high chairs
✗ time limit

## SOUTH SHIELDS

# Bamburgh

175 Bamburgh Avenue, South Shields NE34 6SS
**T** 0191 4541899
*Licensee*: Shelley Paulter
*Opening times*: 11–11, 12–11 Sat; 12–10.30 Sun
*Real ales*: **Flowers Original**; **Greene King Abbot**,
**Old Speckled Hen**; guest beers

Popular 60s-built pub which is very close to the finishing line of the Great North Run. As you can imagine, it gets incredibly busy when said event is on, as spectators probably drown their guilty consciences while they watch the superfit runners trundle in.

Children are allowed everywhere, including the no-smoking lounge, while there is an area at the back of the pub which is designated as the family space. Here you'll find colouring books on tap. No garden, but there's a patio which would be ideal for summer drinking with older children.

Food is served midday–3pm, 5–8pm Monday to Thursday, midday–8pm Friday, Saturday and midday–4pm on Sundays. The **kids' menu** has familiar choices, while 'light bites' off the main menu can be ordered if their appetite is for something a little more substantial. Choices include traditional bar snacks such as sandwiches, fish and chips and burgers. There's a choice of roast at Sunday lunchtime (small roasts available), alongside the main menus.

As well as the Great North Run, this is very handy for South Shields' Marine Park where there is a playground and fairground-style amusements.

✗ children restricted to certain areas
✓ family room
✗ garden

✗ garden toys
✓ lunchtime meals
✓ evening meals
✓ food lunchtime and evening
✓ children's menu
✓ bottle warming
✓ no smoking area
✗ accommodation
✓ nearby camping and caravan sites
✓ nappy changing – disabled toilets
✗ entertainment
✗ children's certificate
✓ high chairs
✓ time limit – 8.30pm

## WHITLEY BAY

# Briar Dene

71 The Links, Whitley Bay NE26 1UE
**T** 0191 2520926
**E** briardene@sjf.co.uk
*Licensee*: Susan Gibson
*Opening times*: 11–11; 12–10.30 Sun
*Real ales*: beer range varies

Large pub, part of the Sir John Fitzgerald chain, which enjoys magnificent views over the sea and St Mary's Lighthouse. Its name is taken from an adjoining stream. Even though Whitley Bay is a popular and busy seaside resort, the Briar Dene's location in lush green surroundings, a mile or so from the town centre, makes it a haven from the raucous fun of the seaside.

Popular with walkers, cyclists, visitors and locals, the pub has an open-planned interior with two bars and a no-smoking family space at the back, where children are allowed. There are lots of old pictures and other pub bric-a-brac on the walls. The beer garden and patio at the front is probably better for older kids. The range of real ale varies, with the pub adopting the slogan 'every day is a beer festival'. Real ales available have included ones from **Caledonian**, **Mordue**, **Black Sheep** and **Greene King** amongst others.

Food is served lunchtimes and evenings Monday to Saturday and midday–4pm only on Sundays. The **kids' menu** has familiar choices with smaller portions off the main menu also available; these include fish and chips, a daily roast and sandwiches. Sunday lunchtime sees a choice of roasts only, with small portions available.

There's plenty to do during the summer in Whitley Bay, but if you're after quieter pleasures, take a visit to St Mary's Lighthouse which has spectacular views; there's also a nearby nature reserve.

✓ children restricted to certain areas
✓ family room
✓ garden
✗ garden toys
✓ lunchtime meals
✓ evening meals
✓ food lunchtime and evening
✓ children's menu
✓ bottle warming
✓ no smoking area
✗ accommodation
✓ nearby camping and caravan sites
✓ nappy changing – disabled toilets
✗ entertainment
✓ children's certificate
✓ high chairs
✓ time limit – 9.30pm

# North West

Cheshire
Lancashire and Cumbria
Merseyside
Greater Manchester

*Watermill Inn*
INGS, CUMBRIA

The cliché used to be 'it's grim up north', but you'd sound a bit foolish trotting that out nowadays. The NORTH WEST is a thriving region which is proud of its industrial heritage but also keen to show visitors that there's more to it than clogs and cogwheels. Bounded in the east by the Pennine Chain and in the west by the Irish Sea, it offers a contrast of beautiful rugged countryside, alluring forest walks, narrow-boating on the old industrial canals, theme parks, bustling city centres and even a few peculiar museums. Of course there are also some splendid pubs selling superb beers from a variety of regional brewers such as Robinson's and Thwaites, as well as dedicated craft brewers.

Cheshire stretches from the Welsh border, with its history of bloody raids and counter-raids, to the foothills of the Peak District and it possesses some particularly beautiful stretches of countryside, such as Delamare Forest. Check out the Goshawk which is right on the outskirts of this compact swathe of greenery.

If that sounds all too rustic, how about Cheshire Oaks near Ellesmere Port, which is Europe's biggest designer shopping outlet? However, if you're looking for something a little bit offbeat to intrigue the kids there's a perfectly preserved nuclear bunker to visit not far from the Combermere Arms at Burleydam. There are also haunted pubs, canalside ones and even one which features go-karts as its family attraction.

Liverpool and Manchester have always been great cities but in recent years they have regenerated to a point where they can rival most others. They are bustling and exhilarating, full of great shops, restaurants, sports, culture and nightlife. You'd have to be a very picky family not to find something for everyone here. However the city centre pubs can be disappointing – either fake and lacking in real ale, or distinctly chilly towards children. Cast your net a little further afield and you'll find the outer areas provide a selection of excellent pubs which cater for

Kirk Michael

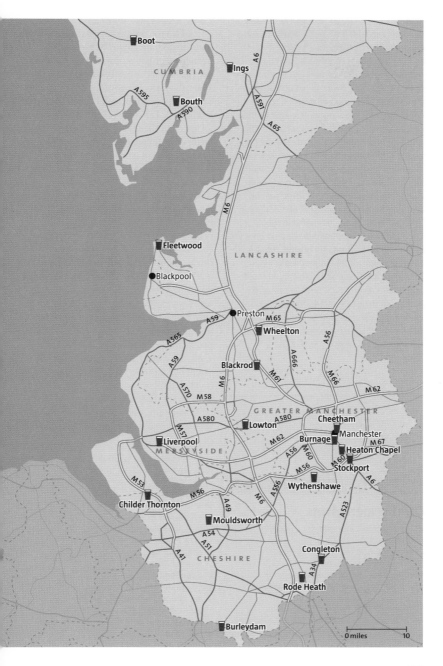

families without losing their soul. If you've spent a tiring morning tramping round a museum or the Albert Docks, the likes of the Allerton Hall (Pub in the Park) and the Queen's Arms will restore weary souls. Other attractions in the area include an Arthurian theme park and canalside walks.

Moving on we find the proud county of Lancashire, home of crumbly cheese, friendly homebrew pubs, Morecombe Bay's potted shrimps and Blackpool Tower. There's an abundance of seaside resorts along the coastline. The grand esplanade at Fleetwood promises a sweeping view of Morecombe Bay and the Lake District. Further inland there is the beautiful rural haven of the Forest of Bowland and the Ribble Valley.

Finally, if in Cumbria sample the Cumberland sausage but do also try to work off the excess pounds tramping along some of the gorgeous and rugged walks of the Lake District. There are also steam trains and boat trips to keep the kids occupied before it's time to visit the likes of the Watermill Inn at Ings, which can boast up to 16 real ales at a time. Put your feet up and sip a pint or two – you deserve it.

## CHESHIRE

# Combermere Arms

Whitchurch Road, Burleydam SY13 4AT
**T** 01948 871223
*Licensee*: Dave Sutton
*Opening times*: 12–11; 12–10.30 Sun
*Real ales*: **Draught Bass**; guest beer
*Directions*: A525, five miles west of Audlern

Friendly, family-run 16th-century establishment which won South Cheshire CAMRA Pub of the Year in 2001. Ghost-busting children will itch to make their way to this 450-year-old former coaching inn as it is supposedly haunted by the ghost of a monk from a nearby abbey. Apparently, he fell in love with a barmaid and used to take a tunnel to the inn for his romantic meetings. Sadly, the tunnel, one of several in the area, collapsed and the monk was no more. Typically, no trace can be found of this subway of love but it makes a good yarn and one which landlord Dave Sutton relishes in repeating.

Inside the decor comprises original beams and cheery open fires in the winter. There's a unique semi-circular bar, two separate serving areas plus a no-smoking restaurant. Children are allowed everywhere but the big attraction for them has to be the indoor play-ball splash pool where they can monkey about to their heart's content. In the summer there's a courtyard which is used for outdoor drinking but it does lead onto the car park.

Food is served lunchtimes and evenings during the week and all day at the weekend (until 9.30pm Saturday, 9pm Sunday). The **kids' menu** has familiar choices while half portions can also be ordered off the main menu; these include pasta, salads and sandwiches (the latter lunchtime only). There's also a child's roast every day.

The Combermere is in a very rural spot with lots of walks aroundabouts. A nearby – if offbeat – attraction is a nuclear bunker which was once top secret and is now open to the public.

- x children restricted to certain areas
- x family room
- ✓ garden
- x garden toys
- ✓ lunchtime meals
- ✓ evening meals
- ✓ food lunchtime and evening
- ✓ children's menu
- ✓ bottle warming
- ✓ no smoking area
- ✓ accommodation
- x nearby camping and caravan sites
- ✓ nappy changing – women's toilets
- x entertainment
- x children's certificate
- ✓ high chairs
- ✓ time limit – 9.30pm

# White Lion

New Road, Childer Thornton CH66 5PU
**T** 0151 339 3402
*Licensee*: Peter Dalton
*Opening times*: 11.30–11; 12–10.30 Sun
*Real ales*: **Thwaites Bitter, Lancaster Bomber, Mild**
*Directions*: off A41

Award-winning village pub which can be found on the outskirts of Ellesmere Port. Over 300 years old, it's a traditional rural hostelry with two small rooms and a bar area. Children are allowed in the compact parlour which doubles up as a family room, but in the summer families tend to relax in the garden or the covered eating area to the side of the building. There's a secure playing space in the garden, with swings, a climbing frame and slide to hand.

Food is served lunchtimes only (no food Sundays), with the **kids' menu** including such favourites as sausage, egg and bacon or scampi with chips; small portions of the home-made chicken tikka can be served as well. There are also sandwiches. This is a very friendly pub which is at its best in the summer. It's also ideal for recuperation after a morning spent shopping and chasing the kids at the nearby Cheshire Oaks shopping outlet, one of the largest in Europe.

✓ children restricted to certain areas
✓ family room
✓ garden
✓ garden toys
✓ lunchtime meals
✗ evening meals
✗ food lunchtime and evening
✓ children's menu
✓ bottle warming
✗ no smoking area
✗ accommodation
✗ nearby camping and caravan sites
✗ nappy changing
✗ entertainment
✗ children's certificate
✗ high chairs
✓ time limit – 8.30pm

# Wharf

121 Canal Road, Congleton CW12 3AP
**T** 01260 272809   **F** 01260 273472
*Licensee*: Mike Pickering
Opening hours: 12–3 (11 Fri, Sat), 5–11; 12–10.30 Sun
*Real ales*: **Cains Dark Mild; Greenalls Bitter;** guest beer
*Directions*: near Dog Lane aquaduct

The Cheshire Ring Canal is about 50 yards from the Wharf and so this former bonded wine cellar is very popular with narrow-boating fans – there are moorings close by. Canalside walkers and local families also enjoy its friendly atmosphere and smart interiors. Children are well catered for with a range of activities including a wooden fort, slide and swings in the large gated garden. To make things go even more with a bang in the summer, the Wharf also holds Fundays on relevant bank holidays with bouncy castle and barbecues (call for details).

Until the early 1990s the pub used to be, in the words of the landlord, 'a bit spit and sawdust'. Nowadays, it's all one spacious bar which is divided up into three distinct spaces; there's also an eating area. On the walls hang old pictures of Congleton, which was recorded in the Domesday Book and was once a busy mill town. Children are allowed in the lounge and a no-smoking eating area, the latter being built in the early 1990s with french windows leading out to the garden. Toys are always on hand to entertain toddlers. Food is served lunchtimes and evenings all week. The **kids' menu** includes familiar choices, while smaller portions off the main menu can be served if possible. These include pasta, scampi and curries. On Sundays roast lunches are also available (small portions served). As for local attractions, there are bracing canalside walks, while further afield Alton Towers is a 30-minute drive away.

✓ children restricted to certain areas
✗ family room
✓ garden

✓ garden toys
✓ lunchtime meals
✓ evening meals
✓ food lunchtime and evening
✓ children's menu
✓ bottle warming
✓ no smoking area
✗ accommodation
✗ nearby camping and caravan sites
✗ nappy changing
✓ entertainment
✓ children's certificate
✓ high chairs
✓ time limit – 9pm

## MOULDSWORTH

## Goshawk

Station Road, Mouldsworth CH3 8AJ
**T** 01928 740900   **F** 01928 740965
*Licensee*: Duncan Falconer
*Opening times*: 11.30–3 (11 Fri, Sat), 5.30–11;
closed Mon; 12–10.30 Sun
*Real ales*: **Adnams Bitter**; **Taylor Landlord**; guest
beer

Former coach-house on the outskirts of
Delaware Forest which has recently been
refurbished. Inside there is a restaurant, a
lounge area, public bar and another eating
space at the back of the pub which is called
the 'Library' and is usually no smoking.
It's a very homely atmosphere with comfy
armchairs and sofas.

Children are allowed everywhere –
though if the pub is busy on Sundays you
may be requested to stick to the designated
family area. Outside in the fenced-off garden
there's a kids' play area with plenty of swings,
a slide and climbing frame; there's also a
bowling green which is not for children.

Food is served lunchtimes and evenings
Tuesday–Thursday and all day Friday,
Saturday and Sunday throughout the year.
The **kids' menu** has familiar choices, while
smaller portions off the main menu can be
served. These include chicken breast,
sausage and mash, fish cakes and a
vegetarian pasta dish, while Sundays see
roast lunches (small portions available) as
well as the main menus.

Even though it is very small, Delamere
Forest is full of walks and cycle paths, while
the Mouldsworth Motor Museum has to be
a must for any child fascinated by the
internal combustion engine.

✗ children restricted to certain areas
✗ family room
✓ garden
✓ garden toys
✓ lunchtime meals
✓ evening meals
✓ food lunchtime and evening
✓ children's menu
✓ bottle warming
✓ no smoking area
✓ accommodation
✗ nearby camping and caravan sites
✗ nappy changing
✗ entertainment
✓ children's certificate
✓ high chairs
✓ time limit – 6.30pm

## RODE HEATH

## Royal Oak

41 Sandbach Road, Rode Heath ST7 3RW
**T** 01270 875670
*Licensee*: Christopher Forester
*Opening times*: 12–11; 12–10.30 Sun
*Real ales*: **Adnams Broadside**; **Draught Bass**; **Greene
King Abbot**; **Tetley Bitter**, **Dark Mild**; **Titanic Premium**

Very family-friendly pub which was built in
the 19th century. Inside there's one big bar
area, a separate no-smoking dining room,
lounge and games room. Children are
allowed everywhere though it would be hard
for them to resist the large, gated and fenced
garden where there's a big play area including
swings, a slide and even go-karts. Further
family fun occurs during the two regular
beer festivals which are held over the Easter
weekend and August bank holiday. As well
as a goodly selection of real ales for mum
and dad, there is usually a bouncy castle
and a magician for the kids. The interior is
traditional in design (exposed beams, old
pictures on the wall) but colouring books
are kept behind the bar. There are also a
couple of large satellite TV screens.

The pub is renowned for its food with the **kids' menu** featuring familiar choices which come with a free ice cream – good value for £2.25. Smaller portions off the main bar menu are also available, these include sandwiches, mini mixed grills and scampi. On Sundays there are roasts of suitable size for children available alongside the kids' menu. There are also pensioners' specials from Monday–Friday. Food is served 12pm–9pm every day. Based in good walking country, especially alongside the Trent-Mersey canal which is nearby.

- ✘ children restricted to certain areas
- ✘ family room
- ✓ garden
- ✓ garden toys
- ✓ lunchtime meals
- ✓ evening meals
- ✓ food lunchtime and evening
- ✓ children's menu
- ✓ bottle warming
- ✓ no smoking area
- ✘ accommodation
- ✘ nearby camping and caravan sites
- ✓ nappy changing – women's toilets
- ✓ entertainment
- ✘ children's certificate
- ✓ high chairs
- ✓ time limit – 9pm

## CUMBRIA

### BOOT

# Brook House Inn

Boot CA19 1TG
**T** 019467 23288   **F** 019467 23160
**E** stay@brookhouseinn.co.uk
www.brookhouseinn.co.uk
*Licensees*: Gary and Sarah Thornley
*Opening times*: 11–11; 12–10.30 Sun
*Real ales*: **Taylor Landlord; Theakston Best Bitter**; guest beers
*Directions*: A595 to Eskdale then on to Boot, or from Ambleside over the Hardknott Pass

Family-run inn and restaurant in the Lake District National Park which also offers rooms and has an annual beer festival in the late spring. It's in the heart of beautiful scenery with high peaks, woodlands and the River Esk all to hand. Children are allowed everywhere. There is no family room as such but the pub recommends the use of the snug which is a no smoking area. There is also a restaurant which opens in the evening. Outside, there's a patio area but the pub asks parents to keep an eye on their charges.

The **kids' menu** features familiar choices, while smaller portions can be served off the main menu – these include beef and beer pie, Cumberland sausage with mash or chips and pasta dishes. Sunday lunchtime sees the full menu and a roast, which is also available as a children's choice. Food is served all day from 11am–8.30pm.

Eskdale Valley is popular with tourists so, as you'd expect, there's plenty to do for families including the Ravenglass and Eskdale Railway, otherwise known as La'al Ratty, Muncaster Castle, the Roman Hardknott Fort (up an excitingly perilous – as far as kids are concerned – twisting road), an owl centre and for the more physically inclined lots of opportunities for walking, mountain biking and climbing.

- ✘ children restricted to certain areas
- ✘ family room
- ✘ garden
- ✘ garden toys
- ✓ lunchtime meals
- ✓ evening meals
- ✓ food lunchtime and evening
- ✓ children's menu
- ✓ bottle warming
- ✓ no smoking area
- ✓ accommodation
- ✓ nearby camping and caravan sites
- ✓ nappy changing – separate toilets
- ✘ entertainment
- ✓ children's certificate
- ✓ high chairs
- ✓ time limit – 9.30pm

## BOUTH

# White Hart Inn

Bouth LA12 8JB
**T** 01229 861229
**E** nigelwhitehart@aol.co.uk
www.whitehartbouth.co.uk
*Licensees*: Nigel and Peter Barton
*Opening times*: 12–2 (not Mon, Tues), 6–11;
12–11, 12–10.30
*Real ales*: **Black Sheep Best Bitter; Jennings
Cumberland Ale; Tetley Bitter**; guest beers
*Directions*: off A590, 6 miles NE of Ulverston

Coaching inn based in the Lake District
National Park. Dating from the 1600s it was
built when Bouth was on the main Ireleth
to Kendal road and consequently was kept
pretty busy with passing traffic and
farmers' hiring fairs. After the building of a
'new' road in the 1800s (it later became the
A590), Bouth became a sleepy backwater
almost overnight. Surrounded by fields and
fells, the White Hart Inn has ancient
agricultural implements and old village
photos on the wall, low wooden beams and
two real fires.

Children are allowed everywhere, but
the games room is designated as the family
room; here you'll find pool, darts, bar
football, video games, pinball and a TV,
plus some children's games, books and toys.
No restrictions apart from children to be
out of the bar before 9pm. Outside there's a
west-facing beer patio with gorgeous views
of surrounding woods; patio heaters can
be switched on when the sun sinks behind
Colton Fell. No play area in the pub, but
there's a village playground close by with
slide, swings and an adventure trail.
Food is served from midday to 2pm, except
on Mondays and Tuesdays when the pub
is closed at lunchtime; in the evening it is
served 6pm–8.45pm. The **kids' menu** (for
under-12s only) has familiar choices such as
fish fingers, chips and beans and chicken
nuggets, as well as pasta Siciliana, while
small portions can be served off the main
menu where possible; these include
Cumberland sausage, salads and scampi.

On Sundays roasts are served alongside the
main menu; there is also a children's roast.
There's plenty to do in the area, including
country walks in Grizedale Forest,
Haverthwaite Steam Train Railway, the
Laurel and Hardy Museum at Ulverston and
the South Lakes Wild Animal Park at
Dalton-in-Furness.

✘ children restricted to certain areas
✓ family room
✘ garden
✘ garden toys
✓ lunchtime meals
✓ evening meals
✓ food lunchtime and evening
✓ children's menu
✓ bottle warming
✘ no smoking area
✓ accommodation
✓ nearby camping and caravan sites
✓ nappy changing – foyer before women's toilets
✘ entertainment
✓ children's certificate
✓ high chairs
✓ time limit – 9pm

## INGS

# Watermill Inn

Ings, near Staveley LA8 9PY
**T** 01539 821309
**E** all@watermill.co.uk
www.watermillinn.co.uk
*Licensees*: Alan and Brian Coulthwaite
*Opening times*: 12–11; 12–10.30 Sun
*Real ales*: **Black Sheep Best Bitter, Special;
Coniston Bluebird; Hawkshead Bitter; Jennings
Cumberland Ale; Lees Moonraker; Theakston
Best, Old Peculier**; guest beers
*Directions*: Off the A591, two miles east of
Windermere

Former lumber mill and guesthouse built
from local stone, which was converted into
a cosy and traditional Lakeland pub in 1990.
Inside, brewery pumpclips, jugs and CAMRA
awards are evidence of the popularity of this
award-winning, family-run establishment,
which can boast up to 16 real ales on at any
time. There is also a selection of bottled
Belgian beers. The bar is made from church
pews, while the onetime residents' bar was

converted into a lounge which also doubles up as the family room. Children are allowed in here. There's another impressive bar in here made from wood also reclaimed from a church and a warming log stove (watch out for toddlers). Children's games, toys and books are available. In the summer families gravitate to the large and secure paved beer garden. There is no play area, but after lunch you can stroll 30 yards to a local one with swings.

The **kids' menu** features the usual choices, but smaller portions of the good homecooked food are also available where possible. Choices include beef and ale pie, lasagne and Cumberland sausages; there's also a specials board which features such choices as Thai fishcakes with a Thai-style marinade and scrumpy braised pork casserole. Sundays sees a choice of roasts alongside the full menu; small roasts are available. Food is served from 12pm–4.30pm and 5pm–9pm every day.

This is a wonderful haven in the middle of beautiful scenery with plenty of nearby walks and cycle ways. Other attractions include the World of Beatrix Potter at Bowness-on-Windermere and cruises on Lake Windermere.

✓ children restricted to certain areas
✓ family room
✓ garden
✗ garden toys
✓ lunchtime meals
✓ evening meals
✓ food lunchtime and evening
✓ children's menu
✗ bottle warming
✓ no smoking area
✓ accommodation
✓ nearby camping and caravan sites
✓ nappy changing – disabled toilet
✗ entertainment
✓ children's certificate
✓ high chairs
✗ time limit

# GREATER MANCHESTER

## BLACKROD

## Thatch & Thistle

Chorley Road, Blackrod BL6 5LA
T 01257 474044    F 01257 474026
*Licensee*: Peter Haynes
*Opening times*: 12–11; 12–10.30 Sun
*Real ales*: **Bank Top Bitter**; guest beers

Thatch-roofed single-storey pub which can be found off the A6 in the pleasant countryside outside Bolton. It used to be a cafe and has had several names including the Pavilion and Drunken Duck. Now it is noted for its good food, which means that weekends can be very busy. Inside there's a single bar with an attached restaurant; there's also a spacious conservatory at the far end of the bar which is no smoking. There are pleasant views of the local beauty spot Rivington Pike, while inside the decor is dark wood, real fires in the winter and old photos on the wall. The whole effect makes for a cosy atmosphere.

Children are allowed everywhere but families tend to make for the conservatory. Outside there's a beer garden which has an adjoining secure play area with swings and climbing frame. Food is served 12pm–2.30pm, 6pm–9pm Monday–Saturday and all day until 7.30pm on Sundays. The interesting **kids' menu** includes a soup, potato wedges with garlic pitta bread, bangers and mash, sausages and chips and salads, while smaller portions off the main menu can also be served where possible. These include scampi, chicken tikka and sandwiches; but the licensees are very helpful so ask if there is anything else you would like your child to have. On Sundays there's a kids' roast alongside the main children's menu.

Even though to the unfamiliar traveller Bolton would conjure up images of relentless urban sprawl, there is in fact lots of beautiful countryside with plenty of opportunities for walking and cycling. Other attractions in the area include Camelot, an Arthurian theme park.

- ✗ children restricted to certain areas
- ✗ family room
- ✓ garden
- ✓ garden toys
- ✓ lunchtime meals
- ✓ evening meals
- ✓ food lunchtime and evening
- ✓ children's menu
- ✓ bottle warming
- ✓ no smoking area
- ✗ accommodation
- ✗ nearby camping and caravan sites
- ✓ nappy changing – disabled toilets
- ✗ entertainment
- ✗ children's certificate
- ✓ high chairs
- ✓ time limit – 8.30pm

## BURNAGE

## Rising Sun

Burnage Lane, Burnage M19 2HZ
**T** 0161 2256721
*Licensee*: Karen Keenan
*Opening times*: 12–11; 12–10.30 Sun
*Real ales*: **Banks Original; Marston's Bitter, Pedigree**

Recently refurbished open-planned pub which apparently was built on the site of an old petrol station. When it was called the Milestone it was the site of the first gig from a band which included a couple of brothers who lived around the corner. They were Liam and Noel Gallagher who of course went on to form Oasis. This early incarnation of their rock'n'roll style was actually videoed by one of the pub's locals who won't part with the recording for love nor money.

This friendly community pub is owned by Wolverhampton & Dudley who carried out the sympathetic renovation producing a well-lit and spacious one-room lounge with an L-shaped bar. Children are allowed everywhere but have to leave by 8pm. To keep them entertained there are colouring

books available. Good affordable food is sold from opening time until 8pm and includes a **kids' menu** with familiar choices, while smaller portions off the large main menu can also be ordered; examples include scampi, sausage, egg and chips, sandwiches and salads.

The Rising Sun is close to Parrswood Leisure Complex which offers a cinema as well as activities such as bowling.

- ✗ children restricted to certain areas
- ✗ family room
- ✗ garden
- ✗ garden toys
- ✓ lunchtime meals
- ✓ evening meals
- ✓ food lunchtime and evening
- ✓ children's menu
- ✓ bottle warming
- ✓ no smoking area
- ✗ accommodation
- ✗ nearby camping and caravan sites
- ✓ nappy changing – women's toilets
- ✗ entertainment
- ✓ children's certificate
- ✓ high chairs
- ✓ time limit – 8pm

## CHEETHAM

## Queen's Arms

6 Honey Street, Cheetham M8 8RG
**T** 0161 834 4239
*Licensee*: David Price
*Opening times*: 12–11; 12–10.30 Sun
*Real ales*: **Phoenix Bantam; Taylor Landlord;** guest beers
*Directions*: off A665, half a mile north of Victoria Station

Well-established free house which sits a brisk 10-minute uphill walk from the city centre – but it's well worth a bit of puffing and panting to get there. The well-preserved tiled facade recalls onetime owners the Empress Brewery, who were based at Old Trafford and stopped brewing at the end of the 1920s. Children are allowed throughout the two-roomed pub. There are pub games, including pinball, backgammon and devil-among-the-tailors.

Outside, there is a secure back garden with slide, swings and a climbing frame, as well as pet rabbits belonging to the licensees' son; barbecues are held here in the summer. The garden also looks down on Victoria Station and the city centre.

Food is served at lunchtimes and evenings during the week and from 12pm–8pm at weekends. There is no kids' menu but smaller portions off the main menu are available; these include familiar bar food favourites such as chips with sausage, burgers, scampi and chicken nuggets; other more interesting selections include lasagne, coronation chicken, casseroles and vegetarian options.

As well as a good choice of real ales, there's a real cider usually available as well as a selection of Belgian bottled beers and even the rare delight of a wheat beer on draught. A friendly and relaxed pub which is very close to Manchester's many attractions including the city's museum, the Lowry arts complex and plenty of shopping.

- ✗ children restricted to certain areas
- ✗ family room
- ✓ garden
- ✓ garden toys
- ✓ lunchtime meals
- ✓ evening meals
- ✓ food lunchtime and evening
- ✗ children's menu
- ✗ bottle warming
- ✗ no smoking area
- ✗ accommodation
- ✗ nearby camping and caravan sites
- ✗ nappy changing
- ✗ entertainment
- ✓ children's certificate
- ✗ high chairs
- ✓ time limit – 8pm

## HEATON CHAPEL

# Ash

232 Manchester Road, Heaton Chapel, Stockport SK4 1NN
**T** 0161 476 0399
*Licensee*: Jayne Hall
*Opening times*: 12–11; 12–10.30 Sun
*Real ales*: **Boddingtons Bitter**; guest beer

The Ash was rebuilt close to the site of an older and derelict structure in 1901 and nowadays it is a large imposing pub with its original stone window frames still in place. Also look out for the name Ash Hotel etched in stone – a reminder that Victorian builders thought their works would last for a long time. Over the years, the building has been extensively refurbished and is now a friendly and thriving pub with a dining room and traditional vault area which allows children in the eating area of the pub up until 8pm. Outside there is a large patio, safe garden and extensive children's play area which includes climbing equipment.

A **kids' menu** offers familiar choices with chips while smaller portions of the large main menu can be ordered where possible; these include scampi and pasta. Food is served between 12pm–7pm Sunday–Friday, while Saturday is 12pm–9pm.

Located just a mile outside Stockport, attractions for the family include the Museum of Hatting which recalls the local industry and wartime air-raid shelters. You'll need to book to see the latter – it's well worth it as they are perfectly preserved and a great insight into how the locals survived the bombings of 1940/41. Manchester and all its attractions are also not too far away.

- ✓ children restricted to certain areas
- ✗ family room
- ✓ garden
- ✓ garden toys
- ✓ lunchtime meals
- ✓ evening meals
- ✓ food lunchtime and evening
- ✓ children's menu
- ✓ bottle warming
- ✗ no smoking area
- ✗ accommodation
- ✗ nearby camping and caravan sites
- ✗ nappy changing
- ✗ entertainment
- ✗ children's certificate
- ✓ high chairs
- ✓ time limit – 8pm

## LOWTON (St Lukes)

# Hare & Hounds

1 Golborne Road, Lowton WA3 2DP
**T** 01942 728387
*Licensee*: Colin Cox
*Opening times*: 11–11, 12–10.30 Sun
*Real ales*: **Greene King Abbot; Tetley Bitter; Wadworth's 6X**

Former farmers' inn which was popular in the old days when they used to go to market in Wigan. Nowadays, it's a solid, popular local with one main horse-shoe shaped bar-room split into four areas. Children are allowed in the dining room and the no-smoking area which can be found at the back of the pub. The dining room doubles up as the family room and includes a small TV, colouring books and games, while off the room is a play area which includes a climbing frame and ladder plus punch bags. Outside, adjacent to the car park, there is a large gated garden with a safe playing area including climbing frame and Wendy House.

Food is served 11am–9.30pm every day with the **kids' menu** including familiar choices such as sausage and mash, pizza, burgers and spaghetti. Older children can pick from the main menu choices under the title of 'lite bites' and 'weight watchers', which feature the likes of half a chicken breast, 8oz rump steaks and lasagne. On Sundays there's a lunchtime roast alongside the main menu (small roasts served). As for nearby family attractions how about a short drive to Warrington where you will find the Gulliver's World theme park which is located in a lakeland setting?

✓ children restricted to certain areas
✓ family room
✓ garden
✓ garden toys
✓ lunchtime meals
✓ evening meals
✓ food lunchtime and evening
✓ children's menu
✓ bottle warming
✓ no smoking area
✗ accommodation

✗ nearby camping and caravan sites
✓ nappy changing – disabled toilets
✗ entertainment
✓ children's certificate
✓ high chairs
✓ time limit – 9pm

## STOCKPORT

# Royal Oak Inn

Buxton Road, High Lane, Stockport SK6 8AY
**T** 01663 762380
*Licensees*: Peter and Susan Abell
*Opening times*: 12–3, 6–11 (12–11 Sat, bank holidays); 12–10.30 Sun
*Real ales*: **Burtonwood Bitter**; guest beer
*Directions*: follow A6 towards Buxton

Cream-painted traditional community pub which can be found on the western edge of Stockport en route to the Peak District National Park. Inside the one-roomed bar, the decor is rustic with oak beams. Children are allowed everywhere, but they do have to be out of the pub by 9pm. There are games, toys and books provided while outside in the secure garden there's a bouncy castle in a covered area throughout the year, plus a covered play area for younger children.

Food is familiar **kids' menu** choices, while smaller portions are available off the extensive main menu. These include sandwiches, soups, salads and home-cooked specials such as Thai chicken curry and chicken and onion pie. On Sundays children can choose a small roast lunch along with food from the other menus. Food is served lunchtimes and evenings daily during the week and all day at weekends.

The Peak District National Park with all its opportunities for walking and outdoor pursuits is a short drive away, while nearer to hand there is the National Trust owned Lyme Park where *Pride and Prejudice* was filmed.

✗ children restricted to certain areas
✗ family room
✓ garden
✓ garden toys
✓ lunchtime meals
✓ evening meals

✓ food lunchtime and evening
✓ children's menu
✓ bottle warming
✗ no smoking area
✗ accommodation
✓ nearby camping and caravan sites
✗ nappy changing
✗ entertainment
✗ children's certificate
✓ high chairs
✓ time limit – 9pm

✓ garden toys
✓ lunchtime meals
✓ evening meals
✓ food lunchtime and evening
✓ children's menu
✗ bottle warming
✗ no smoking area
✓ accommodation
✗ nearby camping and caravan sites
✓ nappy changing
✗ entertainment
✓ children's certificate
✗ high chairs
✓ time limit – 9pm

## WYTHENSHAWE

## Airport Hotel

Ringway Road, Wythenshawe, Manchester M22 5WH
**T** 0161 437 2551
**E** airporthotel@aol.com
*Licensee*: Pamela Shotton
*Opening times*: 11–11; 12–10.30 Sun
*Real ales*: **Robinson's Best Bitter, Hartley's XB, Hatters Mild**

Recently refurbished pre-war hotel/pub owned by Robinson's which can be found at the end of Manchester Airport's runway. A major attraction of the pub is that the garden is just 100 yards from the runway, which is even closer than the official viewing park. This makes it mesmerising for all ages.

Children are allowed in the 'runway room' which is modern and spacious. There are aviation photos on the walls and teletext details of flights and arrivals, while comfy settles add to the air of relaxation. Access to the garden and playing area is only through the lounge. In the garden there is an activity play area and in the summer there are bouncy castles and magicians laid on.

Food starts at 7.30am with breakfast (no alcohol until normal opening times), and is served all the way until 10.30pm. The **kids' menu** has familiar choices, but there are also sandwiches and other bar snacks available. A friendly pub which puts a major emphasis on welcoming families, whether they are travelling or visiting the airport as part of a day out.

✓ children restricted to certain areas
✓ family room
✓ garden

## *LANCASHIRE*

## FLEETWOOD

## North Euston Hotel

Esplanade, Fleetwood FY7 6BN
**T** 01253 876525
**E** admin@northeustonhotel.co.uk
www.northeustonhotel.co.uk
*Licensees*: Philip Cassidy and Victoria Cawpe
*Opening times*: 11–11; 12–10.30 Sun
*Real ales*: **Moorhouse's Black Cat; Webster's Yorkshire Bitter**; guest beers

Imposing Victorian seafront hotel with a unique semi-circular frontage. Built by Decimus Burton who was responsible for planning Fleetwood during the 1840s. The name is a link with London's Euston station which serves the north-west. Inside, children are allowed in a separate family room at the side of the bar; this is no-smoking all day until 7.30pm which is also the time children have to be out by. Wonderful views can be had from here of the wide sweep of Morecambe Bay and the Wyre estuary with a constant parade of ferries, fishing boats and private yachts passing by; the Lake District can also be seen. On the walls, there are old photos of the town and ancient adverts for long-gone products.

Food is served lunchtimes only from Monday–Saturday. The **kids' menu** includes familiar choices while smaller portions can be had from the main menu where possible. These include fish and chips (a hotel speciality), steak pudding and chips, soup, salads and sandwiches. Please note: there is no food on Sundays.

Well worth a visit if you are in the area and afterwards take a walk along the seafront with its bracing air. Along this way, there are bowling greens, pitch and putt, the largest model yacht lake in the UK and other child-friendly attractions. Blackpool is also a 20-minute drive away.

✓ children restricted to certain areas
✓ family room
✗ garden
✗ garden toys
✓ lunchtime meals
✗ evening meals
✗ food lunchtime and evening
✓ children's menu
✓ bottle warming
✓ no smoking area
✓ accommodation
✓ nearby camping and caravan sites
✓ nappy changing – women's toilets
✗ entertainment
✗ children's certificate
✓ high chairs
✓ time limit – 7.30pm

## WHEELTON

# Dressers Arms

Briers Brow, Wheelton PR6 8HD
T 01254 830041
E dressers.arms@virgin.net
*Licensee*: Steven Turner
*Opening times*: 11–11; 12–10.30 Sun
*Real ales*: **Boddingtons Bitter; Old Wheelton Big, Frank's Bitter, Milk of Amnesia; Taylor Landlord; Tetley Bitter; Worthington Bitter**; guest beers
*Directions*: near A674

Multi-roomed pub which was originally a quartet of terraced cottages built in the late 17th century to house workers from the local quarry. It's a solid-looking establishment with an exterior of dressed stone, while inside the decor offers wooden beams, a log fire in winter and lots of bric-a-brac. There is a no-smoking lounge, games room and snug. Children are allowed anywhere except the immediate bar area while there is a small garden at the front where parents are advised to keep an eye on children.

A small two-barrel brewery, the Old Wheelton brewery, operates from the pub as well, which means a large selection of real ales (usually eight). An intriguing aspect of the pub is the authentic Cantonese restaurant which opens upstairs in the evening; they have a small **kids' menu** but it is a real draw for those youngsters who like Chinese food. Back in the pub, more standard fare is served lunchtimes and evenings during the week and all day at the weekend. The children's menu includes familiar choices, while smaller portions off the main bar menu can be served, including scampi and curries. On Sundays there is a roast lunch (smaller portions available) alongside the main menus.

The local CAMRA branch Pub of the Year for 2002–03, this is a short drive from the Arthurian theme park Camelot, which can be found at Charnock Richard. Here you will find plenty of rides, activities and shows designed to keep children occupied for hours.

✗ children restricted to certain areas
✗ family room
✓ garden
✗ garden toys
✓ lunchtime meals
✓ evening meals
✓ food lunchtime and evening
✓ children's menu
✓ bottle warming
✓ no smoking area
✗ accommodation
✗ nearby camping and caravan sites
✗ nappy changing
✗ entertainment
✗ children's certificate
✓ high chairs
✗ time limit

## MERSEYSIDE

# Allerton Hall (Pub in the Park)

Springwood Avenue, Clarke Gardens,
Liverpool L25 7UN
**T** 0151 494 2664   **F** 0151 427 3021
*Licensee*: Sarah Bowen
*Opening times*: 11.30–11; 12–10.30 Sun
*Real ales*: **Cains Bitter; Marston's Pedigree**; guest beers

Grade II listed former old mansion house found in the grounds of Clarke's Gardens, an ideal picnic place which is also home to a small collection of goats, geese, ponies and rabbits. The Hall is a pub and restaurant which was badly damaged by a fire six years ago and has been renovated very much in the style of its original interior. That means plenty of plasterwork ceilings, columns and wooden panelling.

Children are allowed in the two family dining rooms which lead out onto the secure outside play area in the back garden. One of the rooms is no smoking and colouring books and crayons are provided. In the summer there are occasional Fundays when, weather permitting, there's a bouncy castle, lots of games and a kids' disco.

The **kids' menu** has familiar selections, while there's also the option of 'lighter bites', which can include gammon, fish dishes and vegetarian choices. On Sundays the general menu and a specials board are available along with roast lunches (small roasts available). Food is served all day every day.

This is a spacious family-friendly hostelry which is ideal for regrouping after a trip to Liverpool city centre which is seven miles away. Nearer to hand there's the National Trust property of Speke Hall.

✓ children restricted to certain areas
✓ family room
✓ garden
✓ garden toys
✓ lunchtime meals
✓ evening meals
✓ food lunchtime and evening
✓ children's menu
✓ bottle warming
✓ no smoking area
✗ accommodation
✗ nearby camping and caravan sites
✓ nappy changing – disabled toilet
✓ entertainment
✗ children's certificate
✓ high chairs
✗ time limit

## ISLE OF MAN

# Mitre Hotel

Main Road, Kirk Michael IM6 1AJ
**T** 01624 878244
*Licensee*: Tony Carter
*Opening times*: 12–2.30 (12 Fri), 4.30–11; 12–12 Sat; 12–3.30, 7–11 Sun
*Real ales*: **Okells Bitter**; guest beers
*Directions*: on the A3

When the French were revolting in 1789 this pub was built, making it the oldest such establishment on the Isle of Man. It's the only pub in Kirk Michael but it does lie on the circuit of the June TT races when it (along with the entire village) can get very busy. Inside there's a lounge and public bar decorated in what can only be described as 'olde worlde', with plenty of sepia-tinted pictures of the village in days gone by.

Children are allowed in a group of tables towards the end of the lounge and also in the compact family room; both these spaces are no-smoking. There's a large beer garden to the front and at the back, where there is also a secure play area; a climbing frame and slides.

Food is served both lunchtimes and evenings all through the week with the **kids' menu** offering familiar choices. There are roast lunches as well as the other menus on Sundays with small roast dinners available.

As well as the excitement generated by the TT Races, the Isle of Man is a beautiful holiday location with stunning coastal scenes, relaxed towns and villages and several excellent local breweries.

✓ children restricted to certain areas
✓ family room
✓ garden
✓ garden toys
✓ lunchtime meals
✓ evening meals
✓ food lunchtime and evening
✓ children's menu
✓ bottle warming
✓ no smoking area
✗ accommodation
✓ nearby camping and caravan sites
✗ nappy changing
✗ entertainment
✓ children's certificate
✓ high chairs
✓ time limit – 9pm

# The South

Berkshire
Buckinghamshire
Hampshire
Hertfordshire
Isle of Wight
Jersey *(Channel Isles)*
Kent
Surrey
Sussex

*Moulin de Lecq*
ST OUEN, JERSEY

From the hubbub of sophisticated metropolitan life in London you can shift gear in tucked-away villages where the loudest noise you'll hear is the dawn chorus. The countryside varies from downland and weald to stunning coastlines. Seaside resorts are diverse too – from brash and breezy to trendy and stylish.

To the south of London, Hampshire, Kent, Sussex and Surrey offer plenty of country walks, wildlife parks, family-friendly attractions and fascinating towns such as the Cinque Port New Romney, Canterbury and Lewes (visit the latter for Bonfire Night when stupendous bonfire celebrations occur). Hampshire has the magical New Forest – ideal for picnics presided over by curious wild ponies. Kent, nicknamed the Garden of England, may be bisected by the Eurostar line but the hop fields still remain and harvest time brings the heavenly scent of freshly-picked hops. If you're stumped for something to do after lunch, why not have a go at Bat and Trap? It's a local Kentish pastime which is related to cricket and can be played at the Rose & Crown in Perry Wood.

Island life always sounds appealing and the Channel Isles offer island living at its most civilised (and family friendly). The French nickname for the islanders – Toads – has inspired the Tipsy Toad brew pub. Even though France is just a few miles away the accent is on traditional pubs rather than bars. On the islands you will find beautiful beaches and family-friendly attractions such as the Living Legend village which uses special-effects to tell the history of Jersey. The Isle of Wight is also very popular and has its own pace of life. There are glorious beaches, plenty of coastline walks, a children's amusement park and a model village amongst the varied attractions.

North and west of London we find Berkshire and Buckinghamshire, beautiful countryside right on the doorstep of London. This area includes the historic Thames

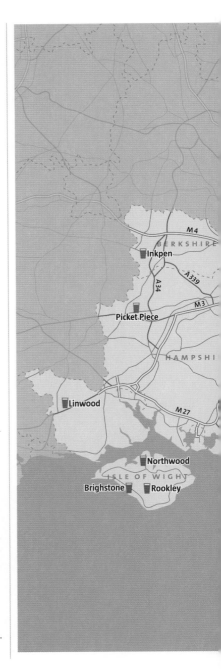

M1
Hanslope
A5
Aston
Chearsley
A41
HERTFORDSHIRE
A10
BUCKINGHAMSHIRE
Aldenham
West Wycombe
M40
M4
Hurst
M3
Windlesham
A3
M25
A23
M20
Stansted
Long Sutton
A2
M25
M26
M20
M2
A299
Wrecclesham
SURREY
Perry Wood
A2
Witley
Coldharbour
M23
KENT
Bossingham
A3
A259
Maplehurst
A21
A23
WEST SUSSEX
EAST SUSSEX
Oving
East Chiltington
Chiddingly
Brighton
Firle
A27
A259
Angmering
A27

CHANNEL ISLES

St Ouen
St Martin
St Peter

0 miles          10

Valley along which so much history and heritage has flowed. There are pretty villages, busy and lively towns and plenty of riverside and country walks. Take a boat along the Thames or go shopping in Reading, but don't forget Windsor Great Park or Legoland (paradise for young children). Walkers will be thrilled by the Chilterns or the Ridgeway which stretches back into antiquity. Hertfordshire is also close to London, but maintains its own identity. Places to visit include the historic city of St Albans (also the home of the Campaign For Real Ale!) and Watford, where the massive Harlequin Shopping Centre can be found.

familiar choices with chips, while smaller portions off the main menu can be served where possible – spicy examples include beef chilli and cajun chicken. The pub describes its food as 'English cuisine with a touch of Mediterranean thrown in', so this is a good place to attempt to persuade children to try more adventurous flavours. Sunday lunchtime sees a choice of roasts (small portions available), alongside the main menus and a selection of specials.

Ideally placed for taking the air at the California Country Park at Finchampstead, where there are 100 acres of rare ancient bogland and lowland heath. Just don't let on that Legoland is within kicking distance or younger children will scream the pub down – fair play, it *is* an excellent theme park.

- ✗ family room
- ✓ garden
- ✓ garden toys
- ✓ lunchtime meals
- ✓ evening meals
- ✓ food lunchtime and evening
- ✓ children's menu
- ✓ bottle warming
- ✓ no smoking area
- ✗ accommodation
- ✗ nearby camping and caravan sites
- ✗ nappy changing
- ✗ entertainment
- ✓ children's certificate
- ✗ highchairs
- ✓ time limit – 8.30pm

## BERKSHIRE

### HURST

## Green Man

Hinton Road, Hurst RG10 0BP
**T** 0118 934 2599
**E** info@thegreenman.uk.com
www.thegreenman.uk.com
*Licensees*: Simon and Gordon Guile
*Opening times*: 11–3, 5.30–11; 12–3, 6–10.30 Sun
*Real ales*: **Brakspear Best Bitter, Special**
*Directions*: off A321, next to cricket pitch in Hurst

Comfortable village local which was built as an ale-house back in the 17th century using timbers from retired warships in Portsmouth. Several refurbishments later have seen the addition of further seating and dining areas, some of which are no-smoking.

Inside, children are allowed everywhere while the pretty garden boasts good views of the surrounding countryside and a well-stocked play area with a low-level climbing frame, slides, monkey rings and stepping stones.

Food is served lunchtimes and evenings throughout the week. The **kids' menu** has

### INKPEN

## Crown & Garter

Inkpen Common, Inkpen RG17 9QR
**T** 01488 668325
www.crownandgarter.com
*Licensee*: Gillian Hern
*Opening times*: 12–3 (not Mon or Tue); 6.30 (6 Fri, Sat)–1; 12–3, 7–10.30 Sun
*Real ales*: **West Berkshire Gold Old Boy, Mr Chubbs Lunchtime Bitter**; guest beer
*Directions*: signed from A4 at Kintbury

Traditional 16th-century inn renowned for its food and located in a beautiful rural setting. Inside, it's open-planned with a horseshoe-shaped bar and lots of photos on the walls and dried hops festooning the old beams.

Children are allowed everywhere and colouring books, crayons and games are supplied to keep them amused. Outside, to the side of the pub, there's a secure garden with a slide and swings.

Food is served lunchtimes and evenings Wednesday–Sunday (no food Monday, Tuesday or Sunday unless you are staying there). The **kids' menu** offers the usual choices with chips, though small portions of the excellent main menu can be served where possible. Examples include sausage and mash, pasta dishes, chillis and homemade burgers. Sunday lunchtime sees a roast choice, alongside the main menus.

There are plenty of walks in the surrounding countryside, while Legoland is a short drive away.

- ✗ family room
- ✓ garden
- ✓ garden toys
- ✓ lunchtime meals
- ✓ evening meals
- ✓ food lunchtime and evening
- ✓ children's menu
- ✓ bottle warming
- ✗ no smoking area
- ✓ accommodation
- ✗ nearby camping and caravan sites
- ✗ nappy changing
- ✗ entertainment
- ✗ children's certificate
- ✓ highchairs
- ✗ time limit

# BUCKINGHAMSHIRE

## CHEARSLEY

# Bell

The Green, Chearsley HP18 0DJ
**T** 01844 208077
*Licensee*: Peter Grimsdell

*Opening times*: 12–2.30 (not Mon), 6–11 (12–11 Sat in summer); 12–2.30, 7–10.30 (12–10.30 summer) Sun
*Real ales*: **Fuller's Chiswick, London Pride**; seasonal beers

Four hundred years ago the Bell was built as a hostelry for the workers who were casting the village's church bell, hence the name. Overlooking the village green, it's very traditional with a thatched roof, while inside the one-bar pub there are wooden beams, pewter and brass hanging up and a large inglenook fireplace.

Children are allowed everywhere and games and books are available for them, while at the rear of the pub there's a fenced in garden with a climbing frame, slide and ride-on toys; there are also chickens and rabbits for them to look at.

Food is served lunchtimes and evenings all week when the pub is open. The **kids' menu** has familiar choices as well as sandwiches, while selected dishes off the main menu can be served in small portions; examples include ham, egg and chips, casseroles and lasagne. On Sundays there's the main menus and a specials board.

In 1998 and 2000 the Bell was the winner of Aylesbury Vale Council's Best Village Pub award. Local attractions for the family include the Quainton Railway Centre, which is a short drive away over the A41 and has regular Thomas the Tank days.

- ✗ children restricted to certain areas
- ✗ family room
- ✓ garden
- ✓ garden toys
- ✓ lunchtime meals
- ✓ evening meals
- ✓ food lunchtime and evening
- ✓ children's menu
- ✓ bottle warming
- ✗ no smoking area
- ✗ accommodation
- ✗ nearby camping and caravan sites
- ✗ nappy changing
- ✗ entertainment
- ✗ children's certificate
- ✓ highchairs
- ✗ time limit

## HANSLOPE

# Globe

50 Hartwell Road, Longstreet, Hanslope MK19 7BZ
**T** 01908 510336
*Licensee*: Stephen Castree
*Opening times*: 12–3 (closed Tues lunchtime),
6–11; 12–3.30, 7–10.30 Sun
*Real ales*: **Banks's Bitter**, guest beer (occasional)
*Directions*: Longstreet Village between Hanslope
and Hartwell on unclassified road

Rural pub dating from the 17th century
which reputedly has a ghost. Inside the decor
is rustic with old beams, a quarry tile floor
and lots of brass. Children are allowed in the
lounge bar (designated as the family room),
games room and the no-smoking restaurant
(eating only here and booking advisable).
To the rear of the pub there's a secure
garden with a climbing frame and slide.

Food is served lunchtimes and evenings
throughout the week; no food all day
Tuesday and Sunday evening. The **kids'
menu** serves familiar choices such as
burgers, sausages, fish cakes and chips,
while smaller portions off the main menu
can be served where possible. These include
small gammons and steaks, battered cod
and home-made beef and onion pie, while
on Sunday lunchtimes small roasts are
available alongside the main menus.

Hanslope is a few miles from Milton
Keynes where the X-scape leisure complex
can be found, while for more pastoral
pleasures try Salcey Forest just over the
border in Northamptonshire which has a
network of woodland walks and children's
play area.

✓ children restricted to certain areas
✓ family room
✓ garden
✓ garden toys
✓ lunchtime meals
✓ evening meals
✓ food lunchtime and evening
✓ children's menu
✓ bottle warming
✓ no smoking area
✗ accommodation
✗ nearby camping and caravan sites
✗ nappy changing

✗ entertainment
✓ children's certificate
✗ highchairs
✓ time limit – 9.30pm for under 14s

## WEST WYCOMBE

# George & Dragon Hotel

High Street, West Wycombe HP14 3AB
**T** 01494 464414
**E** enq@george-and-dragon.co.uk
www.george-and-dragon.co.uk
*Licensee*: Phillip Todd
*Opening times*: 11–2.30, 5.30–11; 12–3,
7–10.30 Sun
*Real ales*: **Courage Best Bitter**; **Wells Bombardier**;
guest beers
*Directions*: on A40

National Trust-owned 18th-century
coaching inn which is reputedly haunted by
the ghost of a beautiful young woman who
once worked at the inn as a servant.
According to the story, her beauty was her
undoing. After she had set out wooing a
rich young man from afar, three jealous
local lads lured her to a meeting place at
night pretending that her well-off lover
would be there. When she discovered it was
all a trick, a fight developed between her
and the lads and she was accidentally killed.
Other strange things have been known to
happen with objects going missing and
turning up in other parts of the building.
As you can imagine with all this going on,
the interior is comfortingly traditional with
low wooden beams, log fires, flagstone
floors and plenty of 'olde worlde' character.

Children are allowed in the no-smoking
compact family room which doubles up as
a dining area; there is also a fenced play
area outside which includes a climbing
frame and swing tyres.

Food is served lunchtimes and evenings
throughout the week and the **kids' menu**
hearteningly avoids going down the chips
and nuggets route. Choices include lamb
burgers in pastry, sausage and beans,
homemade pizzas, spaghetti bolognese and
a daily special. If that's not enough there are
smaller portions off the main menu

available where possible, including casseroles and curries. Sunday lunch sees a roast (small portions available) alongside the main menus.

The village of West Wycombe is mainly owned by the National Trust and its High Street has been carefully repaired to reflect a ranging of building styles which span several centuries. Close by are the West Wycombe caves which were the meeting place of the 18th-century Hellfire Club and are well worth taking the kids along to; incidentally, it was once thought that a secret tunnel ran from the inn to the caves.

✓ children restricted to certain areas
✓ family room
✓ garden
✓ garden toys
✓ lunchtime meals
✓ evening meals
✓ food lunchtime and evening
✓ children's menu
✓ bottle warming
✓ no smoking area
✓ accommodation
✗ nearby camping and caravan sites
✗ nappy changing
✗ entertainment
✗ children's certificate
✓ highchairs
✗ time limit

## HAMPSHIRE

# Red Shoot Inn

Toms Lane, Linwood BH24 7QT
T 01425 475792
*Licensees*: Paul and Margo Adams
*Opening times*: 11–3, 6–11; 11–11 Sat; 12–10.30 Sun
*Real ales*: **Red Shoot Forest Gold, Tom's Tiddler; Wadworth Henry's Original IPA, 6X,** seasonal beers
*Directions*: three miles east of Ellingham Cross on the A338

The Red Shoot can be found in the middle of the New Forest and takes its name from the wood across the road. It has only been a pub since 1963 and was once a garage and a private club. Even though it's owned by Wadworth and sells their beers, it also has its own small brewery which produces beers for the pub; the kit can be seen from the bar; there are two beer festivals throughout the year. Inside there's an L-shaped, open-planned bar with old furniture, pictures of animals, a couple of stuffed grey squirrels having a game of cricket and the odd stuffed fox's head.

Children are allowed in the raised family area off the bar which leads out onto the compact but secure garden with an adventure playground. Inside there are also a couple of games (Connect 4, pack of cards) to help entertain the kids on wet days.

Food is served every day, lunchtimes and evenings, with familiar choices served with chips on the **kids' menu**. Smaller portions off the main menu which are available include lasagne, chilli and small steaks. Sunday lunch sees a selection of roasts, specials and the kids' menu; small roasts are available.

There is a large camp site and caravan park next to the pub. As this is in such a rural location, it is an ideal watering hole to start or end a vigorous country walk.

✓ children restricted to certain areas
✓ family room
✓ garden
✓ garden toys
✓ lunchtime meals
✓ evening meals
✓ food lunchtime and evening
✓ children's menu
✓ bottle warming
✗ no smoking area
✗ accommodation
✓ nearby camping and caravan sites
✓ nappy changing – disabled toilets
✗ entertainment
✗ children's certificate
✓ highchairs
✗ time limit

## LONG SUTTON

# Four Horseshoes

The Street, Long Sutton RG29 1TA
**T** 01256 862488
www.fourhorseshoes.com
*Licensee*: Tony Brookes
*Opening times*: 12–2.30, 6.30–11; 12–3,
7–10.30 Sun
*Real ales*: **Fuller's London Pride**; **Gale's Butser**,
**HSB**; guest beers
*Directions*: four miles from Junction 5 of the M3
and situated next to the Lord Wandsworth School

Two centuries have passed since this handsome country inn was built, though its site is much older. Apparently, the pub stands on an ancient trackway and landlord Tony Brookes uncovered Iron Age remains when he was putting down the pétanque pitch. Inside, the bar is open-planned and features log fires in the winter, rustic beams and plenty of horses brasses; there's also a bright and airy conservatory where children are allowed. In the warmer months, the garden is a magnet for children and their parents. There are attractive views across the surrounding countryside, while the play equipment includes a climbing frame, swings, slide and other goodies.

The food has a good reputation and is served lunchtimes and evenings throughout the week. The **kids' menu** has familiar choices but smaller portions off the main menu are served where possible. These include pasta, homemade pies and scampi. Sunday lunchtimes sees a carvery with small portions available for the kids. There are usually two guest beers with one of them frequently a mild, which is a favourite of the landlord. Camping at the pub by arrangement.

Set in the middle of the beautiful North Hampshire countryside, this is an ideal base if you're walking or cycling in the area. Also worth visiting is Milestones in Basingstoke, which is described as Hampshire's Living History Museum and has a network of streets and buildings based on those found in the county from the Victorian era to the 1930s.

✓ children restricted to certain areas
✗ family room
✓ garden
✓ garden toys
✓ lunchtime meals
✓ evening meals
✓ food lunchtime and evening
✓ children's menu
✓ bottle warming
✗ no smoking area
✓ accommodation
✓ nearby camping and caravan sites
✗ nappy changing
✗ entertainment
✗ children's certificate
✓ highchairs
✗ time limit

## PICKET PIECE

# Wyke Down Country Pub & Restaurant

Picket Piece, Andover SP11 6LX
**T** 01264 352048   **F** 01264 324661
www.wykedown.co.uk
*Licensee*: William Read
*Opening times*: 12–3, 6–11; 12–3, 7–10.30 Sun
*Real ales*: **Exmoor Ale**: guest beers
*Directions*: follow signs for Wyke Down from A303

Family-run business on the edge of Andover which includes a small working farm and camping and caravan site; it has also done time as a petrol station. The bar is in a converted barn and has all sorts of agricultural relics hanging on the wall, while children are allowed in the light and airy conservatory where there is pool and a snakes-and-ladder table. They are also welcome in the no-smoking restaurant (Friday, Saturday, Sunday evenings excepted). Outside there's a children's play area attached to the camp site which they are welcome to use.

Food is served lunchtimes and evenings throughout the week with the **kids' menu** having the usual choices. Children can also pick smaller portions off the main menu including lasagne, cottage pie, scampi, pasta bake, as well as choose some of the starters such as salmon and broccoli fishcake (one way of getting them to eat vegetables!). Sunday lunchtimes sees a choice of roasts only (small portions available) plus the kids' menu. Ask for hot water if you want to warm food or bottles.

The camping and caravan site also has a golf driving range and swimming pool. Handy for a stop off the A303, while very close by Finkley Down farm park can be found.

✓ children restricted to certain areas
✗ family room
✓ garden
✓ garden toys
✓ lunchtime meals
✓ evening meals
✓ food lunchtime and evening
✓ children's menu
✗ bottle warming
✓ no smoking area
✗ accommodation
✓ nearby camping and caravan sites
✗ nappy changing
✗ entertainment
✗ children's certificate
✓ highchairs – booster chairs
✗ time limit

## HERTFORDSHIRE

### ALDENHAM

## Roundbush

Roundbush Lane, Aldenham WD25 8BG
T 01923 855532
*Licensee*: Lorraine McCarthy
*Opening times*: 12–11; 12–10.30 Sun
*Real ales*: **Greene King Abbot, IPA; Marston's Pedigree; Tetley Bitter**

Even though the Roundbush is on the eastern fringes of Watford, just over the M1, it manages to be a friendly and relaxed country local. Inside it's all olde worlde with wooden beams, old photos on the walls and an open fire in the winter, while outside there's a secluded garden to the back with a play area which is well suited for young

children. There's also a garden at the front. Inside, kids are allowed in the no-smoking restaurant, providing they are eating.

Food is served 12pm–3pm and 6pm–8pm (no food Monday or Tuesday evening), with food on Sundays being served midday–4pm only. The **kids' menu** features familiar choices and there are also salads and sandwiches at lunchtime, while Sunday sees a roast (small portions available) as well as the kids' menu.

Family-orientated attractions in the area include Aldenham Park with its collection of animals, country walks and picnic sites. Further afield in the direction of St Albans there is an intriguing museum devoted to the World War Two fighter plane the Mosquito.

✓ children restricted to certain areas
✗ family room
✓ garden
✓ garden toys
✓ lunchtime meals
✓ evening meals
✓ food lunchtime and evening
✓ children's menu
✓ bottle warming
✓ no smoking area
✗ accommodation
✗ nearby camping and caravan sites
✓ nappy changing – disabled toilets
✗ entertainment
✗ children's certificate
✗ highchairs
✓ time limit – 9pm

### ASTON

## Rose & Crown

10 Benington Road, Aston SG2 7DX
T 01438 880243
*Licensee*: Denis Clifton
*Opening times*: 11–3, 5.30–11 Mon–Thur (summer 11–11); 11–11 Fri, Sat; 12–4 (summer 12–10.30), 7–10.30 Sun
*Real ales*: **Draught Bass; McMullen AK, County;** guest beer
*Directions*: off A602

There's been a pub on this site for nearly 500 years, and not surprisingly it is apparently haunted. However the ghost in question is a relatively recent acquisition – thought to be a former licensee called Mary who ruled the roost between 1903 and 1926. Her picture can be seen on the wall. Spectral apparitions notwithstanding, this is a friendly two-bar pub with a cosy saloon lounge and a public bar which boasts a leather chesterfield; the original oak beams and old photos of the pub on the wall add to the atmosphere.

To the rear there's an acre of fenced in garden with climbing frame, slides and see-saws. The first Sunday of July sees the village having a special fun day with a fete and stalls. At the time of writing I am told that this year the Rose & Crown is hoping to host a living history exhibit of Native Americans complete with tepees – sounds like good fun.

Children are allowed everywhere in the pub which serves food midday–2pm Mon-Sat, 1pm–3pm on Sundays, and every evening except for Sunday night. There are familiar choices on the **kids' menu**, while smaller portions can be ordered off the main menu including egg and chips, sausage and mash, jacket potatoes and half-baguettes. Sundays sees roast lunches (small portions available) only; however a selection of bar snacks will be available if the roast runs out.

Aston is not far from Stevenage which is good for shopping, but for a more genteel trip there's the beautiful gardens at nearby Benington Lordship which also has an animal quiz trail for children.

✗ children restricted to certain areas
✗ family room
✓ garden
✓ garden toys
✓ lunchtime meals
✓ evening meals
✓ food lunchtime and evening
✓ children's menu
✓ bottle warming
✗ no smoking area
✗ accommodation
✗ nearby camping and caravan sites
✗ nappy changing
✓ entertainment
✗ children's certificate
✗ highchairs
✓ time limit – 9pm

# ISLE OF WIGHT

## BRIGHSTONE

## Countryman

Limerstone Road, Brighstone PO30 4AE
**T** 01983 740616
*Licensees* Roy and Jane Priest
*Opening times*: 11–3, 5.30–11; 12–3, 6–10.30 Sun
*Real ales*: **Badger K&B Sussex, Best, Tanglefoot,** guest beer

Very friendly one-bar pub which was originally built as a garage in the early years of the 20th century. Run by a local family, there's a lot of farming implements, teapots and cameras hanging from the wooden beams, while the secure gardens have lovely views over the fields towards the south coast of the island. As well as the main bar area there's a cosy no-smoking snug.

Children are allowed everywhere and there are books and games available behind the bar, as well as toys for the younger ones.

Food is served lunchtimes and evenings every day with the **kids' menu** featuring familiar choices as well as spaghetti bolognese. Smaller portions off the main menu can be served including lasagne, scampi, jacket potatoes and sandwiches. Sunday lunchtime sees a roast (small portions available) alongside the main menus.

Brighstone is within a very short drive of Brighstone Bay with its glorious beaches. Further fun can be found four miles away where you will find Blackgang Chine, a popular children's amusement park.

✗ children restricted to certain areas
✗ family room
✓ garden
✗ garden toys
✓ lunchtime meals
✓ evening meals
✓ food lunchtime and evening
✓ children's menu
✓ bottle warming

- ✓ no smoking area
- ✗ accommodation
- ✓ nearby camping and caravan sites
- ✗ nappy changing
- ✗ entertainment
- ✗ children's certificate
- ✓ highchairs
- ✓ time limit – 9pm

# Travellers Joy

85 Pallance Road, Northwood PO31 8LS
**T** 01983 298024
**E** tjoy@globalnet.co.uk
www.tjoy.co.uk
*Licensee*: Derek Smith
*Opening times*: 11–2.30, 5–11; 11–11 Fri, Sat; 12–3, 7–10.30 Sun
*Real ales*: **Goddards Special Bitter**; guest beers
*Directions*: main road Cowes to Yarmouth

Old country inn which dates back to the 1700s and has been much renovated over the years. Featuring up to eight real ales, it's very popular with drinkers on the Isle of Wight and has been voted Pub of the Year by the local CAMRA branch five times. There are apparently a couple of ghosts, an old man in a flat cap and a woman in period dress who oddly enough only materialises when decorating is carried out.

Inside there's the main bar area, a lounge, conservatory (designated as the family room) and pool room. Children are allowed everywhere away from the bar area. Outside there's a large secure garden with play area and pets' corner.

Food is served lunchtimes and evenings throughout the week. The **kids' menu** includes familiar dishes with chips and beans, while smaller portions off the main menu are also possible including steak and kidney pie, scampi, ham, egg and chips and steak. A roast is also served midweek and Sunday lunchtimes (small portions available), along with the main menus.

Northwood is close to Cowes and also Parkhurst Forest where there are picnic spots and woodland walks.

- ✗ children restricted to certain areas
- ✓ family room
- ✓ garden
- ✓ garden toys
- ✓ lunchtime meals
- ✓ evening meals
- ✓ food lunchtime and evening
- ✓ children's menu
- ✓ bottle warming
- ✓ no smoking area
- ✗ accommodation
- ✓ nearby camping and caravan sites
- ✗ nappy changing
- ✗ entertainment
- ✗ children's certificate
- ✓ highchairs
- ✗ time limit

# Chequers Inn

Niton Road, Rookley PO38 3NZ
**T** 01983 840314
*Licensee*: Richard Holmes
*Opening times*: 11–11; 12–10.30 Sun
*Real ales*: **Courage Best Bitter**; **Greene King Old Speckled Hen**; guest beers
*Directions*: off A3020

Back in the 1700s because this building was on the only road between Newport and Shanklin it was ideally placed to stop smugglers and so the Customs and Excise had it as one of their houses. It became a pub in 1799 when it was known as the Star. By 1988 Whitbread were the owners and decided it wasn't viable anymore and so shut the doors and sold it to the present owners who have turned things around and made it a very popular and busy family-friendly pub. Inside, there's a lounge bar, public bar with flagstoned floor, family room and by the summer of 2003 there will be also a new conservatory.

Children are allowed in the no-smoking family room (and the conservatory when it is built), where there is a Lego table and colouring books. Outside in the secure garden there's plenty of stuff for the kids to do, including a log cabin, tree house, climbing frame, monkey bars, rope nets, swings and play area for the smaller kids.

Food is served all day throughout the whole week, with familiar choices on the **kids' menu**, as well as small steaks and jacket potatoes. Smaller selections off the main menu include gammon, salads, some of the à la carte dishes and sandwiches. Sundays sees a carvery (served in the family room) with small portions for children; the main menus are also available. A Braille menu is available. Situated in the centre of the island, this is well placed for country walks, while there's a model village several miles down the A3020 at Godshill.

✓ children restricted to certain areas
✓ family room
✓ garden
✓ garden toys
✓ lunchtime meals
✓ evening meals
✓ food lunchtime and evening
✓ children's menu
✓ bottle warming
✓ no smoking area
✗ accommodation
✓ nearby camping and caravan sites
✓ nappy changing – disabled toilets
✓ entertainment
✗ children's certificate
✓ highchairs
✗ time limit

## JERSEY (Channel Isles)

### ST MARTIN

## Royal Hotel

La Grande Route de Faldouet, St Martin JE3 6UG
**T** 01534 856289
*Licensee*: John Barker
*Opening times*: 9.30–11.30; 11–11.30 Sun
*Real ales*: **Courage Directors; Draught Bass**

Friendly and popular traditional pub which can be found in the old part of this village. Children are allowed in the bright and well-designed dining area (with designated no-smoking areas) and games room where there's pool and table football. Outside there's a large and secure garden with a play area which includes swings and a seesaw.

Food is served lunchtimes and evenings throughout the week, though there's no service on Sunday evenings in the winter. There's a **kids' menu** with familiar choices, while smaller selections can be had off the main menu including pasta, curries and pies; there's also an all-you-can-eat salad bar (handy for picky eaters – and a rare beacon of healthy eating amidst the chips). Sunday lunchtimes sees a choice of a roast (small portions available) alongside the main menu.

An ideal place to visit after a morning spent at one of the nearby excellent beaches.

✓ children restricted to certain areas
✗ family room
✓ garden
✓ garden toys
✓ lunchtime meals
✓ evening meals
✓ food lunchtime and evening
✓ children's menu
✓ bottle warming
✓ no smoking area
✗ accommodation
✓ nearby camping and caravan sites
✓ nappy changing – disabled toilets
✗ entertainment
✗ children's certificate
✓ highchairs
✓ time limit – 9pm

### ST OUEN

## Moulin de Lecq

Grève de Lecq, St Ouen JE3 2DT
**T** 01534 482818
*Licensee*: Caroline Byrne
*Real ales*: **Greene King IPA, Old Speckled Hen; Guernsey Sunbeam; Ringwood Old Thumper**
*Opening times*: 11–11 (11–2, 5–11 winter); 11–11 Sun

Picturesque country pub which was converted from a Middle Ages water mill; there is a water wheel behind the bar which still works and has been known to surprise unwary drinkers when it starts moving. During the Second World War rumour has it that the occupying Germans used it to recharge their searchlight batteries. Inside, it's open-planned with a single bar and a no-smoking dining room upstairs; cosy log fires in the winter.

Children are allowed everywhere, though the upstairs room is designated as a family area. There are also games for the children kept behind the bar. At the back there's a fenced-in garden with a play area that includes swings and slides. In the summer there's often a bouncy castle to hand (or rather foot).

Food is served lunchtimes and evenings through the week with the **kids' menu** offering familiar choices with chips. Smaller portions off the main menu are also available where possible; these might include sandwiches, jacket potatoes, and salad. Sunday lunchtimes sees a choice of roast (small ones available) alongside the kids' menu.

A very friendly pub which is near the lovely sheltered beach of Grève de Lecq.

- ✗ children restricted to certain areas
- ✓ family room
- ✓ garden
- ✓ garden toys
- ✓ lunchtime meals
- ✓ evening meals
- ✓ food lunchtime and evening
- ✓ children's menu
- ✓ bottle warming
- ✓ no smoking area
- ✗ accommodation
- ✓ nearby camping and caravan sites
- ✗ nappy changing
- ✗ entertainment
- ✗ children's certificate
- ✓ highchairs
- ✓ time limit – 9pm

## ST PETER

# Star & Tipsy Toad Brewery

La Route de Beaumont, St Peter JE3 7BQ
**T** 01534 485556
*Licensee*: John Dryhurst
*Opening times*: 10–11; 11–11.30 Sun
*Real ales*: **Jimmy's Bitter, Tipsy Toad Ale, Horny Toad**

Very friendly brew pub and the only one of its sort on Jersey; apparently the brewery name derives from the French nickname for islanders – toads. It was refurbished in 2000 and there are several drinking and eating areas leading off from the single main bar; including a parlour with a sunken floor and snug.

Children are allowed in the games room (pool and video games) and the spacious family room and bright and airy conservatory which is connected to an outside drinking patio and kids' play area. There is also a view of the award-winning brewery from the family room. Outside in the play area there is a climbing frame, slide and so forth.

Food is served lunchtimes and evenings Monday–Saturday (no food Monday evenings in the winter); no food on Sundays. The **kids' menu** has familiar choices and a free ice cream is thrown in, while smaller portions off the main menu are also available including scampi and chicken curry.

Family attractions close by include Jersey Zoo and the Living Legend Village which uses state-of-the-art special effects to recreate the history of the Channel Islands, as well as having plenty of activities such as adventure golf and other children's activities.

- ✓ children restricted to certain areas
- ✓ family room
- ✓ garden
- ✓ garden toys
- ✓ lunchtime meals
- ✓ evening meals
- ✓ food lunchtime and evening
- ✓ children's menu
- ✓ bottle warming
- ✗ no smoking area
- ✗ accommodation
- ✗ nearby camping and caravan sites
- ✓ nappy changing – disabled toilets
- ✗ entertainment
- ✗ children's certificate
- ✓ highchairs
- ✗ time limit

# *KENT*

## BOSSINGHAM

# Hop Pocket

The Street, Bossingham CT4 6DX
**T** 01227 709866
*Licensee*: Paul Forgan
*Opening times*: 12–3, 7–11; 12–3, 7–10.30 Sun
*Real ales*: **Shepherd Neame Masterbrew; guest beers**

Very traditional pub in a rural part of Kent. Built in the 19th century but the cellar is reckoned to be 300 years old and is reputedly haunted. Inside, it's rustic through and through with low ceilings, wooden beams, garlands of dried hops and a wooden floor. There are usually three real ales on with local Canterbury-based brewers Hopdaemon featuring regularly.

There's a bar area and a modern no-smoking conservatory which attracts families and diners. Children are allowed everywhere apart from at the bar of course; there are dominoes and board games such as snakes and ladders for their entertainment. Outside there's a beer garden with a slide and further on after the car park there's another kids' playing area.

Food is served lunchtimes and evenings throughout the week, with familiar choices on the **kids' menu**. Smaller portions off the main menu are available when possible; these include chicken dishes as well as Mexican-style enchiladas. Sunday sees a choice of roasts (kids' portions always available), plus several specials, the bar menu and the kids' choices.

The pub's beautiful countryside location means that there are plenty of good walks in the area.

✗ children restricted to certain areas
✗ family room
✓ garden
✓ garden toys
✓ lunchtime meals
✓ evening meals
✓ food lunchtime and evening
✓ children's menu
✓ bottle warming
✓ no smoking area
✗ accommodation
✓ nearby camping and caravan sites
✗ nappy changing
✗ entertainment
✗ children's certificate
✓ highchairs
✗ time limit

## PERRY WOOD

# Rose & Crown

Perry Wood, Selling ME13 9RY
**T** 01227 752214
*Licensees*: Richard and Jocelyn Prebble
*Opening times*: 11–3, 6.30–11; 12–3, 7–10.30 Sun
*Real ales*: **Adnams Bitter; Goacher's Mild; Harveys BB; guest beer**
*Directions*: one mile south of Selling

Cosy pub which was converted from three 16th century cottages, one of which was a woodcutter's home. Located in the middle of the 150-acre Perry Wood, this is a great place to go to after doing one of the many walks in the area; it's also close to local hop- and apple-growing areas and consequently there's a lovely scent of hops on the air when they're being picked.

Inside there's a main bar, family room and no-smoking restaurant with children allowed in the latter two places. Keep an eye out for the unique collection of corn dollies; strings of local hops hang above the bar, while the family room has hand-stencils of woodland animals on the wall. The award-winning garden is full of flowers in the spring and summer months and there is a wood-chipped play area; there is also a bat and trap pitch, a Kentish game which is from the same family as cricket and involves hitting a ball after you've made it spring out of a trap; ask if you can have a go.

Food is served midday–2pm and 7pm–9.30pm throughout the week apart from Sunday and Monday evenings. The **kids' menu** features familiar choices with chips, while smaller portions off the main menu can be served where possible; these include spaghetti bolognese and jacket potatoes. Sunday lunchtimes sees a choice of roast (small portions available), alongside a specials board and the kids' menu.

If a country walk is not to your liking, Faversham, Canterbury and Whitstable are all close by car.

✓ children restricted to certain areas
✓ family room
✓ garden
✓ garden toys
✓ lunchtime meals
✓ evening meals
✓ food lunchtime and evening
✓ children's menu
✓ bottle warming
✓ no smoking area
✗ accommodation
✓ nearby camping and caravan sites
✗ nappy changing
✗ entertainment
✗ children's certificate
✗ highchairs
✗ time limit

## STANSTED

# Black Horse

Humblefield Road, Stansted TN15 7PR
**T** 01732 822355
*Licensee*: Ian Duncan
*Opening times*: 11–11; 12–10.30 Sun
*Real ales*: **Larkins Traditional; Millis' Capall Dubh Bitter**; guest beers
*Directions*: one mile north of the A20

Back in the 1850s, the Black Horse was built as a hotel to deal with the anticipated crowds of passengers who would be using the Chatham to London line which seemed to be on the verge of being built. Sadly, it didn't materialise until years later, so that's why this secluded village has a stern and imposing building slightly out of character with the rest of the village which is mainly flint exteriors.

Inside there's a bar area, no-smoking restaurant and a back room which is called the garden room (children allowed in the latter two areas); this connects to the large secure garden which has a climbing frame, slide and swings. It's a busy pub. During the second week in July the pub hosts a Kent week, where Kentish beers, food and cider are promoted (ring for details). On the Sunday of that week there's usually a vintage motor rally, barbecue and jazz; monthly Irish music days also take place throughout the year with musicians coming from all over.

Food is served lunchtimes and evenings throughout the week with familiar choices on the **kids' menu** and smaller portions off the main menu also available; these include scampi, sausage and pasta. The upstairs restaurant serves Thai cuisine Tuesday–Saturday evenings, but there is no kids' menu up there during this time. Bibbenden real cider is available.

Even though the M20 isn't too far away, Stansted is in an enviable Downland location with plenty of country walks, while Brands Hatch and the Vigo Country Park are within a short driving distance.

✓ children restricted to certain areas
✗ family room
✓ garden
✓ garden toys
✓ lunchtime meals
✓ evening meals
✓ food lunchtime and evening
✓ children's menu
✓ bottle warming
✓ no smoking area
✓ accommodation
✓ nearby camping and caravan sites
✗ nappy changing
✗ entertainment
✗ children's certificate
✓ highchairs
✓ time limit – 8pm

## SURREY

### COLDHARBOUR

# Plough Inn

Coldharbour Lane, Coldharbour RH5 6HD
**T** 01306 711793
*Licensees*: Richard and Anna Abrehart
*Opening times*: 11.30–3, 6–11; 11.30–11 Sat;
12–10.30 Sun
*Real ales*: **Leith Hill Crooked Furrow, Tallywhacker;
Ringwood Old Thumper; Taylor Landlord**; guest
beers
*Directions*: Leith Hill-Dorking road

Traditional rural pub with its own two-barrel brewery. It dates back to the 1640s when it was originally two cottages and a forge. Inside, there's lot of stained beams and brass rubbings and it gets very busy with families out walking during the weekend.

Children are allowed in designated areas at the bar and at weekends there's a heated barn which is opened for families; tables can be booked for meals. There's also a large back garden.

Food is served lunchtimes and evenings through the week and the **kids' menu** has familiar choices, while smaller portions off the main menu are available where possible. These include cottage pie, lasagne, ploughman's and baked potatoes. Sunday lunch includes a choice of roasts (small portions available) as well as the usual menus. Bibbenden cider is also served on handpump. Located amidst attractive National Trust-owned countryside, this is an ideal watering hole after a walk to nearby Leith Hill which is crowned by a 64 foot tower which officially makes the Hill a mountain; there are wonderful views and on clear days you can see all the way to the English Channel.

✓ children restricted to certain areas
✗ family room
✓ garden
✗ garden toys
✓ lunchtime meals

✓ evening meals
✓ food lunchtime and evening
✓ children's menu
✓ bottle warming
✗ no smoking area
✓ accommodation
✗ nearby camping and caravan sites
✗ nappy changing
✗ entertainment
✗ children's certificate
✗ highchairs
✗ time limit

### WINDLESHAM

# Bee

School Road, Windlesham GU20 6PD
**T** 01276 479244
**E** tj205@compuserve.com
*Licensee*: Timothy Jones
*Opening times*: 12–11; 12–10.30 Sun
*Real ales*: **Brakspear Bitter; Courage Best Bitter;
Hop Back Summer Lightning; Shepherd Neame
Spitfire**; guest beer
*Directions*: off the A30

Mid-Victorian village local with a single bar. From the outside, it looks small but there's a Tardis-like quality about the space inside. Decor is traditional with old photos and lots of brass.

Children are allowed everywhere while there's a huge garden at the back which has barbecues, a bouncy castle and live jazz during the summer. There is also a play area with climbing frames and swings.

Food is served lunchtimes and evenings throughout the week (all day Monday and Sunday evening excepted). The **kids' menu** has familiar choices, but the landlord says that the kitchen is flexible and if young customers just want chips and beans then that's no problem. Smaller portions off the main menu can include sausage or ham, egg and chips and filled baguettes. Sundays sees a choice of roast, including a vegetarian option (small roasts available).

Ideal for Legoland and Windsor Great Park.

✗ children restricted to certain areas
✗ family room
✓ garden
✓ garden toys

✓ lunchtime meals
✓ evening meals
✓ food lunchtime and evening
✓ children's menu
✓ bottle warming
✗ no smoking area
✗ accommodation
✗ nearby camping and caravan sites
✗ nappy changing
✓ entertainment
✗ children's certificate
✓ highchairs
✓ time limit – 9pm

## WITLEY

## Star

Petworth Road, Witley GU8 5LU
T 01428 684656
E thestarph@aol.com
*Licensee*: Charles Pilcher
*Opening times*: 12–2.30, 4.30–11; 11.30–11, Fri,
Sat; 12–3, 7–10.30 Sun
*Real ales*: **Greene King IPA; Jennings Cumberland
Ale**; guest beer

Former 17th-century mill which became an
ale house during the 1850s when it was
bought by a local brewery. Now it's Grade II
listed with an interior full of low ceilings, oak
beams, stone fireplaces, wonky stone walls
and lots of old photos of the area on the wall.

There's a public bar, lounge and dining area
/conservatory which is where children are
allowed and is designated as the family room.
There are a few games available behind the bar
such as Connect 4. Outside there's a walled
and gated garden with swings, climbing
frame and a slide; barbecues are often held
in good weather during the summer. Food is
served lunchtimes and evenings throughout
the week with the **kids' menu** featuring
familiar choices with chips and baked beans
or salad. Smaller portions off the main menu
can be served including lasagne, curries,
sausage and mash and scampi. Older children
with an appetite will also love the homemade
pizzas, which are the pub's speciality.

There are plenty of walks in the area,
including the National Trust-owned Witley
Common while Winkworth Arboretum is
also close.

✓ children restricted to certain areas
✓ family room
✓ garden
✓ garden toys
✓ lunchtime meals
✓ evening meals
✓ food lunchtime and evening
✓ children's menu
✓ bottle warming
✗ no smoking area
✗ accommodation
✗ nearby camping and caravan sites
✗ nappy changing
✗ entertainment
✗ children's certificate
✓ highchairs
✗ time limit

## WRECCLESHAM

## Bat & Ball

15 Bat and Ball Lane, Boundstone (via Upper
Bourne Lane), Wrecclesham DU10 4RA
T 01252 792108
E pub@batandball.fsnet.co.uk
*Licensee*: Andy Bujok
*Opening times*: 12–3, 5.30–11; 12–11 Fri, Sat;
12–10.30 Sun
*Real ales*: **Fuller's London Pride; Triple fff Alton's
Pride; Young's Ordinary**; guest beers

Traditional free house which dates back to
1820 or earlier and is thought to have been
popular with workers in the hop fields
which once dominated the area. As for the
name, there are suspicions that it has
something to do with cricket but no one is
too sure. Even though a residential area is
close, the pub has a cosy isolated feel and is
best approached on foot along the Bourne
stream, while if you are going by car be
prepared for a few head-scratching
moments, but it is worth it. Inside it's cosy
and traditional with wooden settles, while
hops and mugs hang over the bar; there is
also the usual pub bric-a-brac including
brasses plus a few old sporting prints.

Children are allowed in the family room
at the front of the pub and the no-smoking
restaurant. There's a large garden at the
front with a Wendy house, while in the
summer the Aunt Sally pub game is

brought out and children are encouraged to be involved.

Food is served lunchtimes and evenings all week apart from Sunday night. The **kids' menu** has familiar choices, while smaller portions off the main menu can be served including sausage and mash, lasagne and sandwiches (lunchtimes only). Sunday lunch is a choice of roast (small portions available) alongside the main menus and a specials board.

Located on the edge of the North Downs Wrecclesham has plenty of country walks in the area, while Birdworld, which is Britain's largest bird park and gardens, is only a short drive away.

✓ children restricted to certain areas
✓ family room
✓ garden
✓ garden toys
✓ lunchtime meals
✓ evening meals
✓ food lunchtime and evening
✓ children's menu
✓ bottle warming
✓ no smoking area
✗ accommodation
✗ nearby camping and caravan sites
✗ nappy changing
✗ entertainment
✗ children's certificate
✓ highchairs
✓ time limit – 8.30pm

## EAST SUSSEX

## Six Bells

Chiddingly BN8 6HE
**T** 01825 872227
*Licensees*: Paul and Jacquie Newman
*Opening times*: 12–3, 6–11; 12–11 Sat; 12–10.30 Sun
*Real ales*: **Courage Directors**; **Harveys BB**; guest beer
*Directions*: off A22

Built in the 1700s, this former coaching inn was the scene of the trial of Sara French in 1852 who was accused of murdering her husband with an onion pie laced with arsenic. The jury apparently sat in session in the pub and promptly found her guilty and she was strung up at Lewes. Not surprisingly, a ghost has been known to haunt the pub. From the outside, the Six Bells is almost cottage-like in style, with hanging baskets and window boxes bursting with colour in the summer. Inside there's a main bar and family room with rustic decor throughout including an inglenook fireplace, stripped brick walls, assorted pub bric-a-brac and antiques; there's also a pianola, the early 20th-century's version of karaoke where a roll of sheet music was fed into the music which then played the tune all on its own. Sadly, I'm told that it works very badly so chances of hearing it are slim. More up-to-date music is important here though with jazz sessions on Sundays, folk club meetings and other assorted bands during the week.

Children are allowed in the family room, while there's a garden to the rear with a netted fishpond; during the summer there are occasional barbecues and meets of the Sunbeam owners motorcycle club.

Food is served lunchtimes and evenings during the week, and all day at the weekends. No kids' menu but smaller portions off the main menu are served including leek and mushroom bake, stilton and walnut pie, lasagne and salads. Instead of chips there are fried new potatoes.

A very friendly pub which is popular with walkers doing the Weald and Vanguard Ways. Further afield Beachy Head and the south coast are a short drive away.

✓ children restricted to certain areas
✓ family room
✓ garden
✗ garden toys
✓ lunchtime meals
✓ evening meals
✓ food lunchtime and evening
✗ children's menu
✓ bottle warming

x no smoking area
x accommodation
✓ nearby camping and caravan sites
x nappy changing
x entertainment
x children's certificate
x highchairs
x time limit

## EAST CHILTINGTON

# Jolly Sportsmans

Chapel Lane, East Chiltington BN7 3BA
T 01273 890400
E jollysportsman@mistral.co.uk
www.thejollysportsman.com
*Licensee*: Bruce Wass
*Opening times*: 12–2.30; 6–11 (closed Mondays); 12–4 (closed evenings) Sun
*Real ales*: **Horsham Best Bitter**; guest beer
*Directions*: near Plumpton

Upmarket food-orientated pub in a pretty village not too far from Lewes. Inside there's one open-planned bar with a second no-smoking area to the back. The decor is rustic with oak tables and an open fire, while the walls have a constantly changing exhibition of local artists' work on the walls, many of which are for sale.

Children are allowed everywhere and foodie families will be delighted to know that this is a chicken nugget and chip-free zone, with smaller portions off the main menu available rather than the usual kids' choices. These can include freshly cooked, homemade pasta with sauces as well as salads.

Food is served 12pm–2pm, 7pm–9pm (10pm Sat) and 12.30pm–3pm Sundays throughout the week and I would suspect that the pub gets very busy and so it is worth booking a table. Games such as snakes and ladders, Scrabble and colouring books are thoughtfully available. There's a garden to the front and back, though it's recommended that the back is more suitable for the young. A climbing frame is available.

There are country walks in the area, while Lewes is also close by – don't forget

that the town hosts a particularly mad Bonfire Night in November.

✓ children restricted to certain areas
x family room
✓ garden
✓ garden toys
✓ lunchtime meals
✓ evening meals
✓ food lunchtime and evening
x children's menu
✓ bottle warming
✓ no smoking area
x accommodation
x nearby camping and caravan sites
x nappy changing
x entertainment
✓ children's certificate
✓ highchairs
x time limit

## FIRLE

# Ram Inn

The Street, Firle BN8 6NS
T 01273 858222
ww.raminnfirle.net
*Licensees*: Keith and Nicola Wooller
*Opening times*: 11.30–11; 12–10.30 Sun
*Real ales*: **Harveys BB**; guest beers
*Directions*: half mile off the A27

The picturesque village of Firle nestles at the foot of the South Downs and the Ram Inn is a cosy 16th-century coaching inn which is popular with families; the licensees have their own children and know what is expected. There's nappy changing in the ladies and the gents (so no excuses!) and tins of baby food are sold; there are even emergency nappies available. Inside, there are three main rooms, two of which are no-smoking.

Children are allowed throughout though most families make for the designated family room where there are toys, games and a microwave where parents can warm up baby food and bottles. Outside there are two gardens, including a large secure one with a play area that has swings, monkey bars, a slide and a climbing frame; there is also a resident goose called Gertie.

Food is served midday–9pm every day and the **kids' menu** comes in three different sizes: toddler size; child size and hungry kids; familiar choices are served with chips, mash or smiley faces alongside peas or beans. Smaller portions can also be served off the main menu including chicken and ham pie and quiches. Sunday lunchtime sees a choice of Sunday roast (small portions available) alongside the main menus. Real cider is also served; Mole's Black Rat or a local one from a nearby farm.

Plenty of walks in the area, while Lewes and its castle are a short drive away.

✗ children restricted to certain areas
✓ family room
✓ garden
✓ garden toys
✓ lunchtime meals
✓ evening meals
✓ food lunchtime and evening
✓ children's menu
✓ bottle warming
✓ no smoking area
✗ accommodation
✗ nearby camping and caravan sites
✓ nappy changing – women's and men's toilets
✗ entertainment
✓ children's certificate
✓ highchairs
✓ time limit – 9pm in the main bar

*WEST SUSSEX*

## Spotted Cow

High Street, Angmering BN16 4AW
T 01903 783919
*Licensees*: Michael Collins and Paul Moore
*Opening times*: 10.30–3, 5–11; 10.30–11 Sat; 12–10.30 Sun
*Real ales*: **Fuller's London Pride; Greene King Old Speckled Hen; Harveys BB**; guest beers
*Directions*: 100 yards off B2225

Traditional 18th-century pub which was when it was popular with local smugglers, but these days it caters to villagers and walkers who have been plodding across the nearby Downs. Inside, it's a wealth of old beams, open fireplaces and cartoons of spotted cows on the walls; there's also an old spinning jenny in the saloon bar.

Children are allowed in the dining area and the no-smoking conservatory as long as they are eating, though there is a safe garden where they can wear themselves out with a climbing frame; in the summer there are barbecues, hog roasts, visits by Morris Men on Midsummer's Day and a conker competition in the second week of October in which old and young take part.

Food is served lunchtimes and evenings throughout the week, with the **kids' menu** featuring familiar choices. Smaller portions available off the main menu include scampi, macaroni cheese and jacket potatoes. Sunday lunchtime sees a selection of roasts and a fish dish with half portions for children.

Angmering is an ideal launching pad for a walk to Highdown Hill, where legend has it that a mill-stone once rolled down the hill before striking an unfortunate man on the Worthing Road. Another attraction is Arundel and its castle which is only a short drive away.

✓ children restricted to certain areas
✗ family room
✓ garden
✓ garden toys
✓ lunchtime meals
✓ evening meals
✓ food lunchtime and evening
✓ children's menu
✓ bottle warming
✓ no smoking area
✗ accommodation
✗ nearby camping and caravan sites
✗ nappy changing
✗ entertainment
✗ children's certificate
✓ highchairs
✗ time limit

## MAPLEHURST

# White Horse

Park Lane, Maplehurst RH13 6LL
T 01403 891208
*Licensee*: Simon Johnson
*Opening times*: 12–2.30 (11.30–3 Sat), 6–11;
12–3, 7–10.30 Sun
*Real ales*: **Harveys BB; Weltons Pride & Joy**; guest
beers
*Directions*: midway between A281 and A272

The White Horse is supposed to have the widest bar counter in Sussex which means there's plenty of room when you're being served. Situated in a small community south of Mannings Heath and Nuthurst, this is a very friendly country pub with a traditional rustic interior and which is a regular meeting place for the local gardening club on Saturday mornings. The pub has also won awards from the local CAMRA branch.

Inside, children are allowed in the back bar and the light and airy conservatory which is no-smoking at lunchtimes. There are various pub games with which to entertain children, while outside in the lovely open garden (beautiful views of the surrounding countryside) there's a climbing net and platforms, parallel bars and swings; there is also half an acre of open field where the really energetic ones can let off steam.

Food is served lunchtimes and evenings throughout the week; the **kids' menu** has familiar choices while smaller portions off the main menu can be served. These include scampi, breaded prawns and chilli. The normal bar menus are available on Sunday lunchtimes.

As this is set in the Sussex Weald there are plenty of country walks.

✓ children restricted to certain areas
✗ family room
✓ garden
✓ garden toys
✓ lunchtime meals
✓ evening meals
✓ food lunchtime and evening
✓ children's menu

✓ bottle warming
✓ no smoking area
✗ accommodation
✓ nearby camping and caravan sites
✗ nappy changing
✗ entertainment
✓ children's certificate
✓ highchairs
✓ time limit – 9.30pm

## OVING

# Gribble Inn

Gribble Lane, Oving PO20 2BP
T 01243 786893   F 01243 788841
E brianelderfield@hotmail.com
*Licensee*: Brian Elderfield
*Opening times*: 11–3, 5.30–11 (11–11 Sat in
summer); 12–3, 7–10.30 (12–10.30 summer) Sun
*Real ales*: **Gribble Fursty Ferret, Gribble Ale, Reg's
Tipple, Plucking Pheasant, Pig's Ear**, seasonal beers

Thatched country pub which dates from the 16th century and has been the home of the Gribble Brewery for a couple of decades; even though now owned by Badger Brewery, the Gribble is given a free hand to produce its own real ales as well as a couple of King & Barnes ones for Badger. The interior is traditional rustic with settles, pews, low beams, bare stonework and some of the largest log fires to be found anywhere in the county.

Children are allowed in the no-smoking family room which has a toy box and a guard over the log fire. In the summer you can sit out in the delightful large garden which is home to a variety of ancient apple trees.

Food is served lunchtimes and evenings throughout the week; the **kids' menu** has familiar choices all served with potatoes, chips, beans, salad or vegetables and some of the dishes off the main menu can be served in smaller portions; these include sandwiches, sausage and mash, liver and bacon, curries and pasta. Sundays sees a selection of roasts (small portions available) alongside the kids' menu and a limited main menu.

With both Brighton and Portsmouth within easy driving distance there is much to do, while in the immediate vicinity of the pub there is a good country walk, though as part of it is along a country lane, do take care.

✓ children restricted to certain areas
✓ family room
✓ garden
✗ garden toys
✓ lunchtime meals
✓ evening meals
✓ food lunchtime and evening
✓ children's menu
✓ bottle warming
✓ no smoking area
✗ accommodation
✗ nearby camping and caravan sites
✗ nappy changing
✗ entertainment
✗ children's certificate
✓ highchairs
✗ time limit

# The South West & West Country

Cornwall
Devon
Dorset
Gloucestershire & Bristol
Somerset
Wiltshire

*Jamaica Inn*
BOLVENTOR, CORNWALL

From the beautiful villages of the Cotswolds, down to the stunning coastlines of Dorset, Devon and Cornwall, taking in the high moors of Dartmoor and Exmoor and the gentle rolling downs of Wiltshire, and not forgetting the urban charms of Bristol, Bath and Exeter, the South West is a popular holiday destination for many families.

Whether it's bucket, spades and surfboards for the many sandy beaches, trusty walking boots to traipse across the spectacular countryside or a day at a zoo, wildlife park, tank museum or specially-designed play area in the middle of a town, there is something for all families.

And thanks to the profusion of free houses and small breweries, the South West is also home to a goodly number of family friendly pubs, where children are welcomed with open arms. These pubs have their own menus, safe and secure gardens with play areas and even the odd bouncy castle in the summer. The real ale is pretty excellent.

Cornwall and Devon are the counties of fair weather and lots of light, granite tors and dramatic seascapes. There are pubs hidden away down small rural lanes near ruined castles and countryside walks; or you might opt for unusually sited pubs like one which can be found on the beach at Perranporth. Attractions near this selection of pubs include the wondrous Eden Project at St Austell, Paradise Park at Hayle (plus attached brewpub), the Lost Gardens of Heligan, Crealy Park outside Exeter, the National Aquarium at Plymouth and Big Sheep at Bideford (which also has its own brewery).

There's more beautiful, if gentler, countryside in Somerset and Dorset, with Exmoor, the Somerset Levels, the Blackdown Hills and the Blackmore Vale, all splendid for walking off pub lunches. If you don't fancy a perambulation, how about a ride on the West Somerset Railway, which puffs its way out of Minehead along some spectacular coastline. The call of the sea is not far away either with beaches at Burnham-on-Sea, Weymouth and Bournemouth. Animal loving kids will want to visit Tropiquarium just outside Watchet, which has a massive lifesize pirate ship, or Monkey World at Wareham.

The rolling downs of Wiltshire eventually raise their way northwards to the picture-book attractiveness of Gloucestershire and the Cotswolds. On the way there are plenty of prehistoric diversions such as Stonehenge, Silbury Hill and Avebury. The New Forest is also near enough for a spot of pony-watching while Longleat and Beaulieu are also to hand. After all this, you'll be in need of a decent pub to rest in!

## CORNWALL

### BLISLAND

## Blisland Inn

The Green, Blisland PL30 4JF
**T** 01208 850739
*Licensees*: Gary and Margaret Marshall
*Opening times*: 11.30–11; 12–10.30 Sun
*Real ales*: Beer range varies
*Directions*: village is signed from the A30

East of Bodmin, down a couple of miles of narrow country roads off the A30 you will find the award-winning Blisland Arms opposite the only village green in Cornwall. From the outside, it's a stern, granite building constructed at the end of the Victorian era, while a massive Cornish flag fluttering on a pole declares the pub's allegiance. Inside, the welcome is warm and genuine, with log fires, plenty of brewery artifacts on the wall, and hundreds of pump clips festooned everywhere. Children are allowed in the family room at the back where Dino the green iguana keeps a watchful eye on things. In fact, Dino is so popular that he gets fan mail from across the world. There are also drawing materials available.

This was CAMRA National Pub of the year 2001, but it is not just a place for great real ales (there are usually between six and nine available, from all over the country, including a lot of local ones). It also has the feel of a pub for all ages and tastes, with local food being used for the home-cooked meals and local wines and meads being stocked. There is no kids' menu, as Margaret Marshall, who runs the kitchen, is a champion of children eating the same food as their parents, so smaller portions of the main menu include pies, casseroles, sausages in Yorkshire pudding, veggie options, lasagne. Chips are served. It is strongly recommended that you book for Sunday lunchtime roasts (smaller portions also available), bar food such as scampi is also served then. Food is available 12pm–2.15pm, 6.30pm–9.30pm (7.30pm–9.30pm, Sundays). There is seating at the front which is open onto the road though; there is a patio and pond but it was closed after parents ignored warnings not to leave their children alone there.

A good place to replenish the soul after walking on Bodmin Moor. Other nearby attractions include the Bodmin and Wenford Steam Railway and Bodmin Jail Museum.

✓ children restricted to certain areas
✓ family room
✗ garden
✗ garden toys
✓ lunchtime meals
✓ evening meals
✓ food lunchtime and evenings
✗ children's menu
✓ bottle warming
✓ no smoking area
✗ accommodation
✗ nearby camping or caravan
✗ nappy changing
✗ entertainment
✗ children's certificate
✓ high chairs
✓ time limit

## BOLVENTOR

## Jamaica Inn

Bolventor, Launceston PL15 7TS
**T** 01566 86250   **F** 01566 86177
**E** enquiry@jamaicainn.co.uk
www.jamaicainn.co.uk
*Licensees*: Martin Watts and Glen Swan
Opening Times: 11–10.30 (11 summer);
12–10.30 Sun
*Real ales*: **Wadworth's 6X**, guest beers
*Directions*: sign posted off A30 east of Bodmin

Hardy stone-built, slate-roofed coaching inn which was made famous in the Daphne du Maurier novel of the same name after she'd spent time there writing the book; it was also acclaimed for the parrot which lived in the pub. However, Percy is now in his sixties and been pensioned off and lives at the home of a member of staff. Even though there's a cafe, a Museum of Curiosity (for sale at time of writing) and gift shop complex attached which is a mecca for coach parties, it's easy to go into the pub with its granite fireplace, oak settles and tables and get all atmospheric about how bleak the windswept Bodmin Moor must get in the winter.

Children are confined to their own no-smoking room which can be found at the end of the bar and this is also atmospheric, described as an olde worlde hideaway with child-sized rustic furniture. Families visiting in the summer can also spend time in the walled garden which has a boat, tractor and swings for active little ones.

Food is served from midday to 9pm all year round. The **kids' menu** includes favourites such as chicken animal shapes, pork sausages and fishy whales, all served with chips or potato nuggets. Small portions can be had off the main lunchtime menu where possible, including pasta, curries and pies; on Sundays kid-sized roasts are served. In the evenings children are confined to their own menu. The house beer, Jamaica Inn, is rebadged St Austell's Tinners.

An ideal base from where to explore Bodmin's legendary sites such as Dozmary Pool with its Arthurian legends; there is also Colliford Lake Park, a theme and adventure park at Dobwalls off the A38, while the Eden Project is about 20 minutes away by car.

✓ children restricted to certain areas
✓ family room
✓ garden
✓ garden toys
✓ lunchtime meals
✓ evening meals
✓ food lunchtime and evenings
✓ children's menu
✓ bottle warming
✓ no smoking area
✓ accommodation
✓ nearby camping and caravan sites
✓ nappy changing – disabled toilet
✗ entertainment
✗ children's certificate
✓ high chairs
✗ time limit

## FALMOUTH

## Boathouse

Trevethan Hill, Falmouth TR11 2AG
**T** 01326 315425
*Licensee*: Sue Fergus
*Opening times*: 12–3, 6–11; 11–11 Fri–Sat;
12–10.30 Sun
*Real ales*: **Greene King Abbot, Fuller's London Pride**

As the name suggests there's a nautical theme to this large family-orientated pub, located on the edge of the town centre not too far from the bus station. The interior is decorated with all sorts of boating paraphernalia, including rudders, oars and displays of knots, while the wooden decked balcony on the second floor, which overlooks the river, boasts a large sail.

The pub is split into two levels with the bar on the ground floor where children are not allowed; upstairs on the second floor balcony is where families congregate and there are pencils, crayons and paper available. There's also a secure play area to the side of the pub, which includes a slide, playhouse and chairs.

Food is traditional pub grub with fishy shapes, chicken nuggets, sausages and pizza shapes all served with chips on the **kids' menu**. Smaller portions of the main menu can also be served where possible – these include lasagne, sausage and mash, roast chicken, salads, sandwiches and paninis. A kids' portion of the Sunday roast is also available, and there's a vegetarian option. Food is served every lunchtime and evening apart from Sunday evenings.

This is very much a busy town pub which is very easy-going and an ideal stop-off if you're visiting the historic port of Falmouth. There's plenty to see in Falmouth including the National Maritime Museum and the Fox Rosehill Gardens, while outside the town attractions include St Mawes Castle, Pendennis Castle, Penjerrick Gardens and the National Seal Sanctuary a few miles drive away at Gweek.

✓ children restricted to certain areas
✓ family room
✗ garden
✗ garden toys
✓ lunchtime meals
✓ evening meals
✓ food lunchtime and evenings
✓ children's menu
✓ bottle warming
✗ no smoking area
✗ accommodation
✗ nearby camping and caravan sites
✗ nappy changing
✗ entertainment
✗ children's certificate
✓ high chairs
✓ time limit – 6.30pm for younger children

## LISKEARD

# Old Stag

Station Road, Liskeard PL14 4DA
**T** 01579 342280
*Licensee*: Paul Schofield
*Opening times*: 11(12 Mon)–11; 12–10.30 Sun
*Real ales*: **Bishops Tipple**; **Sharp's Doom Bar**

Family-friendly Victorian pub on the edge of town and handily situated opposite the railway station. Inside there are two bar areas and a separate no-smoking room is guarded by a wrought iron gate structure

and contains a dartboard, TV and cosy sofa; this is designated as the family room. There's also a games room with a pool table. Outside, the large and secure beer garden has swings and slides, plus a 'pets corner' with goats, chickens and ducks. Children are allowed everywhere apart from the bars themselves.

Homecooked food is served 11am–8pm in the summer and 11am–3pm and 5pm–8pm during the winter with the **kids' menu** featuring familiar choices not only with chips, but also salads. Smaller portions off the mainly pub grub orientated menu are available and an all-day breakfast is served. Sunday lunchtimes see a choice of roasts (small portions available) alongside the main menus. No nappy changing facilities as such but the pub says that there is ample room in the ladies. A very welcoming pub which is well placed for visiting Dobwalls Adventure Park, just outside Liskeard.

✗ children restricted to certain areas
✓ family room
✓ garden
✓ garden toys
✓ lunchtime meals
✓ evening meals
✓ food lunchtime and evening
✓ children's menu
✓ bottle warming
✓ no smoking area
✗ accommodation
✗ nearby camping and caravan sites
✗ nappy changing
✗ entertainment
✗ children's certificate
✓ high chairs
✗ time limit

## MARAZION

# Godolphin Arms

West End, Marazion, Cornwall TR17 0EN
**T** 01736 710202   **F** 01736 710171
**E** reception@godolphinarms.co.uk
www.godolphinarms.co.uk
*Licensees*: Martin Britten and Jonathan Bray
*Opening times*: 11–11; 12–10.30 Sun
*Real ales*: **Sharp's Eden Ale**, guest beer

Children are not allowed in the bar of this solid-looking, Georgian-style squarish hotel-pub but they probably won't care when they feast their young eyes on the 'Pirate Ship' ball-pool in the family area. 'Wow' is the word I would predict our four-year-old would utter. The ingenious folks who run the Godolphin have mocked up a small part of the pub as a pirate ship, which acts as a front for the sort of ball-pool that most kids love. Parents can relax with a drink at tables and chairs nearby while their young ones go hunting for lost treasure. The ball-pool closes at 8pm as it can get quite noisy for the evening drinkers. Children are also allowed in the restaurant, which like the ball-pool area is no smoking. And when the weather is nice and the buccaneering spirit is weary, there is also a secure terraced beer garden which has a stupendous view of the beach and St Michael's Mount just across the water. Penzance also shimmers away to the right.

As for food, there's a well-priced **kids' menu** serving chips with familiar choices, but the pub will also produce half portions of anything off the menu. This includes pasta dishes, salads and sandwiches. There's a carvery on Sunday and if your children don't want a 'kids roast', they can have something off the bar menu. Food is served lunchtimes and evenings all through the week. The guest beers are usually from a Cornish brewer.

When it comes to things to do, the words 'spoilt for choice' spring to mind. St Michael's Mount is accessible across a cobbled causeway at low tide, then there's Land's End, which despite its rampant commercialisation is still worth a visit, the Lost Gardens of Heligan, Hayle Paradise Park and many facilities for horse riding and bird watching.

✓ children restricted to certain areas
✓ family room
✗ garden
✗ garden toys
✓ lunchtime meals
✓ evening meals

✓ food lunchtime and evenings
✓ children's menu
✓ bottle warming
✓ no smoking area
✓ accommodation
✓ nearby camping and caravan sites
✓ nappy changing – disabled toilet
✗ entertainment
✗ children's certificate
✓ high chairs
✓ time limit – 8pm

## PERRANPORTH

# Watering Hole

The Beach, Perranporth, Cornwall TR6 0BQ
**T** 01872 572888
www.the-wateringhole.co.uk
*Licensee*: Graham Job
*Opening times*: 11–11 (closed Mon-Thu October to March); 12–10.30 Sun
*Real ales*: **Skinner's Spriggan Ale, Blonde**, guest beers
*Directions*: On the beach, east side

Continental-style bar-cafe and restaurant which can be found amongst the sand dunes on one of the best surfing beaches in Europe. It is the only bar in the UK which is on a beach. Does the tide ever come into the building I asked. 'Only once,' came the reply, 'we look the other way most times.' Built on the concrete foundations of an old tearoom, it sees itself as totally family friendly, especially in the summer when giant slides, trampolines, a bouncy castle, volleyball and even a mini-bungie jump are permanently on tap. If the weather is grey, the spacy, light and airy interior has plenty of room for the family with children being allowed pretty much anywhere. Food is served all day and night.

There's the usual **kids' menu** staples, but small portions can also be served from the main menu: this includes fresh fish, pasta, chillies, Tex-Mex, salads and potato wedges. There's a carvery on Sundays, with half portions, while breakfast is also served every day. Barbecues are held Mondays and Thursdays throughout the summer. The beach is just outside the bar so this is an ideal, er, watering hole to turn to for a day by the sea.

If you want to tear yourself away from the beach, nearby days out include Flambards theme park, Paradise Bird Park at Hayle, the Eden Project, the Lost Gardens of Heligan and the Blue Reef Aquarium at Newquay.

✘ children restricted to certain areas
✘ family room
✘ garden
✘ garden toys
✔ lunchtime meals
✔ evening meals
✔ food lunchtime and evenings
✔ children's menu
✔ bottle warming
✘ no smoking area
✘ accommodation
✔ nearby camping and caravan sites
✘ nappy changing
✔ entertainment
✘ children's certificate
✔ high chairs
✘ time limit

## POLGOOTH

# Polgooth Inn

Ricketts Lane, Polgooth, St Austell PL26 7DA
**T** 01726 74089
*Licensees*: Peter and Marlene Pagan
*Opening times*: 12–3, 6–11; 12–3, 6–10.30 Sun
*Real ales*: **St Austell Tinners, HSD**, seasonal beer

The secluded village of Polgooth can be found In a quiet valley between the china clay capital of St Austell and the former pilchard port of Megavissey. The large, sympathetically modernised local is both popular with village folk and visiting families. For the summer months there's an outside playground. Built from local stone several hundred years ago, the Polgooth once belonged to the local tin mine and some of the timbers were recycled after being used underground.

Children are allowed in the compact but cosy family room, the large garden and the play area, but not in the w-shaped bar. There is also a restaurant, open to over-eights.

The family room is comfortable and has old historical pictures on the wall as well as other artifacts. There is also booth-style seating.

Food is served from 12pm–2pm and 6pm–10pm, with the **kids' menu** including burgers, sausages and chicken nuggets all served with chips, there is also beans on toast. Smaller portions can be served from the main menu, which includes pies, quiches, salads, vegetarian options, fish and scampi. Sunday lunch is confined to roasts (half portions for the young ones), but there is a limited bar menu including salads and sandwiches. Sunday evening sees a return to the full menu. The outside play area is to the side of the pub, but is fenced in; it has a tree house, slide, swing, seesaw and climbing frame.

Nearby attractions include the Eden Project, the Lost Gardens of Heligan, Ben's Playworld at Par and Kids Kingdom at St Austell.

✔ children restricted to certain areas
✔ family room
✔ garden
✔ garden toys
✔ lunchtime meals
✔ evening meals
✔ food lunchtime and evenings
✔ children's menu
✔ bottle warming
✔ no smoking area
✘ accommodation
✔ nearby camping and caravan sites
✘ nappy changing
✘ entertainment
✘ children's certificate
✘ high chairs
✘ time limit

## POLMEAR

# Ship Inn

Polmear Hill, Polmear, Par PL24 2AR
**T** 01726 812540
www.theshipinnpar.com
*Licensees*: Nicholas James Moore and Christopher Giles
*Opening times*: 11.30–3, 6–11 (11–11 summer); 12–10.30 Sun

*Real ales*: **Draught Bass, Marston's Pedigree, Sharp's Doom Bar,** guest beer
*Directions*: on the main road through the village which lies to the west of Fowey on the A3082

Cosy free house dating from the 18th century which is ideal for the sandy expanses of Par Beach. Exposed beams, stone floors and a working Cornish range give the interior plenty of charm and character; also note the boat shell which props up the bar.

Children are allowed in the compact no-smoking family room, to be found off the bar area. It also has its own separate outside door. Over tens are allowed in the no-smoking restaurant (picturesque views over Par sand) and over 14s in the bar, which also has a no-smoking area. Outside, to the side and rear there's a large beer garden with under-cover seating plus a bandstand, from where there's regular live entertainment in the summer, as well as a play area which includes a swing, tree house and slide.

There's a well-priced **kids' menu** which includes sausage and mash, a pasta dish, omelettes and other old favourites, all served with chips. Small portions can also be served from the main menu where possible and children's roasts are also available on Sundays, along with the main menu and specials. Food is served in the bar and family room from 12pm–2pm and 6.15pm–9pm all week, while the restaurant is open Tuesday to Saturday and Sunday lunchtime.

The pub has its own caravan site, while there is also a log cabin available on a weekly rental during the summer. There's plenty to see and do in the area, including Par Sands, the Eden Project, Ben's Playworld, Kids Kingdom and the Land of Legend and Model Village at Polperro.

✓ children restricted to certain areas
✓ family room
✓ garden
✓ garden toys
✓ lunchtime meals
✓ evening meals
✓ food lunchtime and evenings
✓ children's menu

✓ bottle warming
✓ no smoking area
✗ accommodation
✓ nearby camping and caravan sites
✗ nappy changing
✗ entertainment
✗ children's certificate
✓ high chairs
✗ time limit

## ST ERTH

## Star Inn

1 Church Street, St Erth, Cornwall TR27 6HP
**T** 01736 752068
*Licensees*: Paul Drinkwater and Chris Hosken
*Opening times*: 11–11; 12.10.30 Sun
*Real ales*: **Draught Bass, Sharp's Doom Bar,** guest beers

Even though it's only a small village, there's a lot going on in St Erth. For a start there's St Erth Animal Farm where visitors can feed the animals, a pitch and putt golf course and a go-karting track for both adults and children, while the picturesque River Hayle is within 100 yards of the pub. Recently awarded National Family Pub of the Year, this is a very traditional inn which was built back in 1647. Inside the characterful interior (low beams, log fires), there are plenty of antiques and bric-a-brac, while the history of the village is told in pictures dotted around the walls. There's also a smugglers look out from the days when some locals made their living from contraband brandy.

There is no dedicated family room, but children are allowed in the main bar and both restaurants (one of which is no-smoking), though not at the bar itself, and they have to be out by 9pm unless they are dining. They are not allowed to use the pool table after 9pm either. A varied selection of games, books and toys are available. There's a big beer garden outside (seating for 30) which is exceptionally childproof, being fenced all round and entered by a gate with a spring hinge. There's no play area as such, but the boules area is often used as a sandpit by youngsters.

The **kids' menu** has all the regular favourites, as well as child-sized sirloin steak and scampi, all served with chips. Smaller portions of the main menu, which uses fresh local produce, will also be served where possible. Sunday lunchtimes sees a roast, along with a blackboard menu of specials, plus salads, sandwiches and vegetarian options. Food is served 11am–2.30pm and 6.30pm–9.30pm (12pm–8pm Sundays in the à la carte restaurant). Up to four real ales can be available during busy periods.

As well as attractions within the village, others close by include Paradise Park at Hayle (with its own brewpub), Merlin's Magic Land and Paradise Railway.

- ✗ children restricted to certain areas
- ✗ family room
- ✓ garden
- ✗ garden toys
- ✓ lunchtime meals
- ✓ evening meals
- ✓ food lunchtime and evenings
- ✓ children's menu
- ✓ bottle warming
- ✗ no smoking area
- ✗ accommodation
- ✓ nearby camping and caravan sites
- ✓ nappy changing – women's toilets
- ✗ entertainment
- ✗ children's certificate
- ✓ high chairs
- ✓ time limit – 9pm

## SOUTH PETHERWIN

# Winds Of Change

South Petherwin, Launceston, Cornwall PL15 7LP
**T** 01566 776988
www.thewindsofchange.co.uk
*Licensees*: Val and Mike Ratcliff
*Opening times*: 11–3, 6.30–11; 12–3.30,
6.30–10.30 Sun
*Real ales*: **Draught Bass, Worthington's 1744**

Pub and restaurant which was only built back in 1989. Situated in a quiet village south of Launceston, it has wonderful views of Dartmoor to the east. Inside, there's plenty of room with a restaurant, games room and a family room with a child-sized

pool table; the beams over the stone-built bar are plastered with paper currencies from all over the world.

Children are allowed in most places, but have to keep away from the bar. Outside, there's a garden for children to work off their excess energy. Sometimes the licensees' children are out playing football or cricket and customers' children have been known to join in the fun. A well-priced **kids' menu** (£1.75–£3) includes sausages, chicken nuggets and burgers with chips; children's roasts are also produced every day. Smaller portions off the main menu can also be served if possible; these will include pasta dishes, omelettes and bar food staples such as ham, egg and chips. On Sundays there is a set meal in the restaurant while bar food is available. Food is served from 12pm–2pm and 7pm–9pm, seven days a week.

In the summer the pub is also a focus for vintage vehicles, with the landlord, who used to be a haulier, very proud of his old Bedford OB. There is also room for two to three motor homes, though the pub would welcome prior notice. Nearby attractions include Launceston Steam Railway, Tamar Otter Sanctuary at North Petherwin, Hidden Valley Nature World and Dingles Steam Village over the border in Devon.

- ✗ children restricted to certain areas
- ✓ family room
- ✓ garden
- ✗ garden toys
- ✓ lunchtime meals
- ✓ evening meals
- ✓ food lunchtime and evenings
- ✓ children's menu
- ✓ bottle warming
- ✓ no smoking area
- ✗ accommodation
- ✗ nearby camping and caravan sites
- ✓ nappy changing – women's toilets
- ✗ entertainment
- ✗ children's certificate
- ✓ high chairs
- ✗ time limit

## WIDEMOUTH BAY

# Bay View Inn

Marine Drive, Widemouth Bay, Bude EX23 0AW
T 01288 361273
*Licensee*: Dave Kitchener
*Opening times*: 11–3, 6–11 (11–11 summer);
12–3, 6–10.30 (12–10.30 summer) Sun
*Real ales*: **Sharp's Doom Bar, Own**, guest beers

Three miles south of the bustling family resort of Bude, the Bay View Inn overlooks the golden sands of Widemouth Bay and the Atlantic Ocean beyond, so this is the place for the dedicated beach-going family. It's a welcoming hotel with the family room situated in the non-smoking Atlantic Room which runs the whole length of the sea-facing side – there are superb views of the sea and the new wild bird lake opposite. Kids' games are also available. Children are also allowed in the dining room (non-smoking), but not in the bar which seems to be taken over by a growing variety of beer mats, bar towels and pumpclips, as well as frogs! There are currently no nappy changing facilities, but it is hoped to rectify that by the time this book is out. The garden can be found to the side of the inn and has a castle, rope ladder, seesaw and tyre swings. This is enclosed and within view of the terrace and family room.

There's a standard **kids' menu**, all served with chips, and smaller portions of the main menu can also be served where possible. This includes lasagne, salads, sandwiches, Cornish pasties, baguettes etc. Roasts and the full menu are available on Sundays, and where possible children's portions of the roast will be served. Food is served 12pm–2.30pm, 6pm–9pm all week. The house beer, Kitch's Klassic, is named after the owner. This is supplied by Skinner's of Truro.

Widemouth Beach is one of the UK's top surfing beaches, but if you don't fancy getting wet there's Bude, the south-west coast path, the Pixieland Fun Park near Kilkhampton and the Tamar Lakes Water Park.

✓ children restricted to certain areas
✓ family room
✓ garden
✓ garden toys
✓ lunchtime meals
✓ evening meals
✓ food lunchtime and evenings
✓ children's menu
✓ bottle warming
✓ no smoking area
✓ accommodation
✓ nearby camping and caravan sites
✗ nappy changing
✗ entertainment
✗ children's certificate
✓ high chairs
✗ time limit

# DEVON

## BERRYNARBOUR

# Olde Globe

Berrynarbour, Ilfracombe EX34 9SG
T 01271 882465   F 01271 889094
E karudd1@aol.com
*Licensees*: Don and Edith Ozelton
*Opening times*: 12–2.30; 7–11 (6 in summer);
12–2.30; 7–10.30 (6 in summer) Sun
*Real ales*: **Draught Bass; St Austell Dartmoor Best Bitter**; guest beers
*Directions*: off the A399

Ancient pub which has been at the hub of village life since the late 1600s; before that it was three cottages which some locals believe housed the workers building the 15th-century church opposite. Inside stone floors, an award-winning log fire plus antiques and farming implements give a picture of 'Merrie England' – there are also more up to date pictures of locals enjoying themselves.

The main draw for kids though has to be the excellent family room (which also doubles as a skittle alley) at the back of the pub (non-smoking most of the year). It houses a large ball pool where children up to seven can work off steam. There are also ride-on toys and lots of leaflets detailing local attractions. It can get very busy at weekends and during the holiday period.

Children are also allowed in the 'kitchen' bar at the front of the pub, while the no-smoking dining room is over-eights only. Over-14s are allowed into the pool room between the family room and the bar, while under-14s have to be supervised. Outside at the back there's a garden with more fun facilities, including a climbing frame, slide and 'the mouse house' (a wooden house). The pub recommends that parents keep an eye on their kids here though, but it is very relaxed. The **kids' menu** includes familiar favourites all served with chips. Some of the adult meals, such as scampi, can be served in smaller portions. Sunday lunch roasts can come in half portions – there are usually two or three choices of meat as well as Quorn sausages. Food is served all week, from 12pm–2pm, 6pm–9.30pm in summer (7pm–9pm in winter). Guest beers are Courage Best Bitter, Directors or Tribute from St Austell.

There are plenty of attractions in the area including the Big Sheep near Bideford, the Wildlife and Dinosaur Park at Combe Martin, the pristine beaches of North Devon and the Once Upon a Time theme park for children near Woolacombe.

✓ children restricted to certain areas
✓ family room
✓ garden
✓ garden toys
✓ lunchtime meals
✓ evening meals
✓ food lunchtime and evenings
✓ children's menu
✓ bottle warming
✓ no smoking area
✗ accommodation
✓ nearby camping and caravan sites
✓ nappy changing – women's toilets
✗ entertainment
✗ children's certificate
✓ high chairs
✗ time limit

## BLACKMOOR GATE

# Old Station House Inn

Blackmoor Gate, Kentisbury EX31 4NW
**T** 01598 763520
*Licensee*: Martin Shepherd
Opening Times: 11–11; 12.10.30 (Sun)
*Real ales*: **Exmoor Ale**; **Fuller's London Pride**; guest beers
*Directions*: six miles south west of Lynton at the junction of the A39, A399 and B3226

As its name suggests, there's a railway link with this very popular pub on the edge of Exmoor. Once upon a time the Barnstaple-Lynton line passed this way through what surely must have been one of the most beautiful railway routes in the south of England. Nowadays, you need a car to travel here but it's well worth the journey as landlord Martin Shepherd makes a great effort to make families welcome: 'In this day and age a pub which doesn't make parents relax is not going to succeed in this part of the world,' says this father of two under-fives.

Outside there's a substantial, well fenced timber play area with slides, rope bridges and a wood chippings surface – naturally, parents are asked not to take glasses and bottles in there. Inside, children are allowed everywhere (though under-14s have to be out by 9pm), apart from at the bar.

The bar has a pool table while the substantial dining room has raised booths along the windows, usually packed with families enjoying the food which is served 12pm–9.30pm all week. This ranges from a standard **kids' menu** with chips to small portions of the main menu (excellent home-made pizzas and pasta amongst others). There is a carvery on Saturday night and Sunday lunchtime along with the main menu – small portions are always possible. There are full nappy changing facilities, microwaves at the bar for bottle and food warming and the pub even sells baby food at reasonable prices. The staff are actively encouraged to hand out colouring books to children while they wait for their food. This enterprising attitude is something I can personally recommend. We were there with friends along with three restless and slightly grumpy under-threes waiting for their food. A staff member appeared out of nowhere and doled out lollipops and colouring pads – cue relaxed parents and happy kids.

There are usually two to three beers on tap, with guests including Courage Best Bitter, Directors and Greene King's Old Speckled Hen. Nearby attractions include the Exmoor Zoological Park, Combe Martin's Wildlife and Dinosaur Park and even a riding school which will take the youngsters. A definite must for families travelling in North Devon.

- ✗ children restricted to certain areas
- ✗ family room
- ✓ garden
- ✓ garden toys
- ✓ lunchtime meals
- ✓ evening meals
- ✓ food lunchtime and evenings
- ✓ children's menu
- ✓ bottle warming
- ✓ no smoking area
- ✗ accommodation
- ✓ nearby camping and caravan sites
- ✓ nappy changing – disabled toilets
- ✗ entertainment
- ✓ children's certificate
- ✓ high chairs
- ✓ time limit – 9pm

## EAST PRAWLE

# Pig's Nose Inn

East Prawle, Near Kingsbridge TQ7 2BY
**T** 01548 511209
www.pigsnoseinn.co.uk
*Licensees*: Peter and Lesley Webber
*Opening times*: 12–2.30, 7–11 (6.30 Sat); 12–3, 7–10.30 Sun.
*Real ales*: **Fuller's London Pride**; **Sutton Comfort**; guest beers

A sign outside this charming old pub says that dogs and children are welcome but that adults have to behave, which just about sums up the friendly and cheery atmosphere to be found here. Run by a couple who used to work in the music business (hence the regular gigs in the hall next door), this is an old smugglers' inn set on the South Devon coast

and very popular with families, especially in the summer when they make themselves at home in the three rooms plus other nooks and crannies. There's no time limit on children being in the pub, but obviously they are not allowed at the bar. Inside the pub, there are exposed beams, farm implements hanging on the wall as well as pieces of wrecked ships – after all, this is a coastline which has seen lots of wrecks. There is also a pile of toys. There's no garden but there are outdoor benches and the pub looks out onto the village green which sometimes have Shetland ponies grazing on them.

The pub is wildly popular with walkers and the menu reflects this with Lesley's legendary ploughman's (even the shallots are home-pickled) and soups (changing daily using seasonal produce) being hugely popular. The **kids' menu** includes the usual suspects (chips and all), but they will also do half portions of some of their home-made favourites including steak and kidney pie, Thai or Indian curries. They occasionally do a Sunday roast and will happily do half-portions. Food is served daily from 12pm–2.30pm; 7pm–9pm.

Attractions along the coast here include plenty of walks and bird watching but Dartmouth is also close; not far from the town you will find the Woodlands theme park with plenty of rides, slides, play areas, animals and other fun activities.

- ✗ children restricted to certain areas
- ✗ family room
- ✗ garden
- ✗ garden toys
- ✓ lunchtime meals
- ✓ evening meals
- ✓ food lunchtime and evenings
- ✓ children's menu
- ✓ bottle warming
- ✗ no smoking area
- ✗ accommodation
- ✓ nearby camping and caravan sites
- ✗ nappy changing
- ✗ entertainment
- ✗ children's certificate
- ✓ high chairs
- ✗ time limit

## Double Locks Hotel

Canal Banks, Alphington, Exeter EX2 6LT
**T** 01392 256947   **F** 01392 250247
*Licensee*: Tony Stearman
*Opening times*: 11–11; 12–10.30 Sun
*Real ales*: **Adnams Broadside; Branscombe Vale Branoc; Everards Original; Young's Bitter, Special**; guest beers
*Directions*: follow signs to Marsh Barton trading estate from Junction 31 on the M5; at second roundabout turn right and pass over a railway bridge (five ton limit) into Clapper Brook Lane East; cross canal bridge and turn right and follow alongside the canal until you reach the pub.

Even though Exeter lies to the front and the M5 to the back, the Double Locks has the feel of being in the middle of nowhere. Back in the early 18th century the Exeter canal was built and the Double Locks was originally the lock-keeper's cottage, though a bar was thoughtfully provided for thirsty seafarers.

Nowadays, the main activity on the water comes from canoeists and rowers, as the construction of the nearby M5 put paid to ships plying their trade. However, the Double Locks remains a busy and popular pub for families with a light and airy conservatory at the back which overlooks the massive outdoor play area. There is a bar area where children are not allowed, and another room, on the left of the main corridor, where they are. It's a comfortable and atmospheric place with lots of old local pictures on the walls, tiled floors and hearty helpings of good food.

There's no specific kids' menu and no chips (except during summer barbecues) but most children will find something to like (roast potatoes, sausages and beans usually go down well) and smaller portions are offered of standards such as lasagne, cottage pie and ploughman's. Hearty breakfasts are served until 12.30pm. There's a choice of roasts on Sunday (including unusual choices such as venison) and half portions are available (plus the usual weekday menu). There are always veggie options too. Food is served every day throughout the day (11am–10.30pm; Sun 12pm–10pm).

In the summer, most families decamp to the massive outside area which has a monster adventure playground (not suitable for toddlers unless closely supervised) with bridges, a fort, tyre swings and cargo netting. There's plenty of space for children to run off surplus energy and you can even pitch your own tent in the outside area if you want. Young children will need supervision as the canal is close by. Even though the pub is owned by Young's, there are usually up to a dozen beers from various breweries, some served straight from cask.

Nearby attractions include Exeter, with its magnificent cathedral and a wonderfully child-friendly museum with lots of stuffed animals from across the world, the World of Country Life at Sandy Bay, Exmouth, Powderham Castle and Crealy Adventure Park at nearby Clyst St Mary.

✓ children restricted to certain areas
✗ family room
✓ garden
✓ garden toys
✓ lunchtime meals
✓ evening meals
✓ food lunchtime and evenings
✗ children's menu
✓ bottle warming
✗ no smoking area
✗ accommodation
✓ nearby camping and caravan sites
✓ nappy changing – disabled toilets
✗ entertainment
✗ children's certificate
✗ high chairs
✗ time limit

## Elephant's Nest Inn

Horndon, Mary Tavy, Devon PL19 9NQ
**T** 01822 810273
*Licensee*: Peter Wolfes
Opening Times: 12–3, 6–11; 12–3, 6–10.30 Sun; closed Mondays from October until December 1st, then open every day until January 6, then closed Mondays until March 31st.

*Real ales*: **Palmers Copper Ale, IPA; St Austell's HSD;** guest beers
*Directions*: follow brown tourist signs from main A386

Traditional rural pub set in an idyllic remote part of Dartmoor with wonderful views. Starting off as three cottages built for local miners in the 16th century, it has been a pub for the last 100 years and has a very 'olde worlde' atmosphere inside with plenty of wood panelling, exposed beams, window seats and stone flooring. There are also a few elephant-orientated items at the bar, courtesy of a previous landlord who changed the name of the pub from the New Inn to its current one in the 1940s. However, Garry Hogg in *The English Country Inn* believed that the name first originated in the 19th century and referred to a very large landlord who, when taking up a lot of space in the bar, was described as 'being like an elephant in the nest'. The nickname stuck and the large landlord, seeing the PR value of the title, changed the pub's name. Take your pick.

As is common with most pubs, no children are allowed at the bar, but the two dining rooms double up as family rooms. However, that doesn't mean you have to have a meal if you bring the kids. Outside the secure and beautiful garden overlooks the moor and from the summer of 2003 the pub (with the aid of the Devon Wildlife Trust) will be handing out fact sheets to encourage junior naturalists to spot bugs and birds there. There are no nappy-changing facilities as such but the loos are very comfortable and clean.

Food is served 12pm–2.15pm and 6.30pm–9pm and children can have half portions of anything on the menu (or just go for the usual chicken nuggets, fish fingers, chips etc). The main bar menu includes traditional favourites such as ham, egg and chips and steak sandwiches while the à la carte menu changes daily and uses fresh local produce (examples include beef casserole with Palmers ale; pork in cider; Old English sausages with mash and gravy, fresh fish). Puddings are popular and include the traditional Devon In and Out pudding.

Although there is no accommodation, the area is well catered for with several bed and breakfasts in the area and it's an ideal base for walking on Dartmoor. Other nearby attractions include Lydford Gorge and its stunning waterfall, the Museum of Dartmoor Life at Okehampton and the National Trust property of Buckland Abbey, home of Sir Francis Drake.

- ✓ children restricted to certain areas
- ✓ family room
- ✓ garden
- ✗ garden toys
- ✓ lunchtime meals
- ✓ evening meals
- ✓ food lunchtime and evenings
- ✓ children's menu
- ✓ bottle warming
- ✗ no smoking area
- ✗ accommodation
- ✓ nearby camping and caravan sites
- ✗ nappy changing
- ✗ entertainment
- ✗ children's certificate
- ✗ high chairs
- ✗ time limit

## MOLLAND

# London Inn

Molland EX36 3NG
T 01769 550269
*Licensees*: Michael and Linda Short
*Opening times*: 12–2.30, 6–11; 12.2.30, 7–10.30 Sun
*Real ales*: **Cotleigh Tawny; Exmoor Ale**
*Directions*: From the A361, exit at B3227 and follow signs

Molland is a small isolated village on the southern edge of Exmoor with a fine old church with beautiful Georgian interiors and a Norman font. Next to it, former coaching inn the London Inn provides evidence of the cohabitation of the pub and the pulpit in the days when both were essential hubs of the small rural community. This is a very traditional and cosy country pub whose walls reflect Exmoor's long field sports tradition – a stuffed weasel, stoat and pheasant glare at you from behind their glass cases as soon as you open the front door into the vestibule; there's also a table on which to play the ancient pub game Devil Among The Tailors. Further inside, the walls have plenty of hunting prints and photos, more stuffed animals and fish, the odd set of antlers plus sewing machines and military buttons. On a winter's day there is always a roaring log fire in the main bar.

In more clement weather you can sit outside the pub or enjoy barbecues in the enclosed (but not child-proof) garden across the road. Past the bar there is a separate room, designated as the family room with boxes of toys under the seats. Unless you get too noisy, the door stays open so you still feel part of the pub.

The **kids' menu** has familiar choices, while small portions off the main menu can be served if possible. These would include soup, savoury pancakes, home-cooked ham and fish and chips (which can also be done as a take-out). There are roast lunches on Sunday with smaller roasts served if possible. In the evening the restaurant offers up more of an à la carte menu with the likes of venison in port and red wine, stuffed peppers, seafood pancakes and grilled bass with crunchy lime and coriander stuffing. Food is served all week 12pm–2pm and 7pm–9pm.

Exmoor is ideal walking and riding country, but if that doesn't appeal there is the Quince Honey Farm at South Molton, Exmoor Zoological Park (with falcony demonstrations, meet the animals and feeding time) and Moorland Wildlife Safaris, going from Dulverton and Exford.

✓ children restricted to certain areas
✓ family room
✓ garden
✗ garden toys
✓ lunchtime meals
✓ evening meals
✓ food lunchtime and evenings
✓ children's menu
✓ bottle warming
✓ no smoking area

✓ accommodation
✓ nearby camping and caravan sites
✗ nappy changing
✗ entertainment
✗ children's certificate
✗ high chairs
✓ time limit – 9pm

# Warren House Inn

Postbridge PL20 6TA
**T** 01822 880208
*Licensee*: Peter Parsons
*Opening times*: 11–11(11–3, 6–11 Mon–Thurs winter); 12–10.30 Sun
*Real ales*: **Badger Tanglefoot; Butcombe Gold; Moor's Old Freddy Walker; Sharp's Doom Bar**
*Directions*: on the B3212 between Princetown and Postbridge

This is the third highest pub in England, sitting all on its own amidst the beautiful desolate windswept spaces of Dartmoor. The nearest village is three miles away and electricity comes from a generator (but, don't worry, it's not noisy inside!). Despite its grand isolation, the Warren House Inn is popular with both locals and visitors, and families with children are more than welcome here. Built in the 1840s for the benefit of tin miners, the Warren House Inn is also famous because one of its two open fires in the bar has reputedly been burning since the inn was built. According to legend, the first fire was lit with smouldering embers taken from the mediaeval New Inn across the road, which had burnt down. Because of the possible hazards of the open fire, the bar area is banned to children, but there are two rooms designated for the use of families and there is no time limit on children.

Outside, the views are stupendous and there are a dozen picnic tables across the road on land owned by the pub. The space is down a set of steps and away from the road (but not child-proof). There is a **kids' menu** with the usual suspects, but child-sized portions can be served of the home-cooked adult choices which include soup and rabbit pie; there is also a delicious steak and ale pie which uses Moor Brewery's Old Freddy Walker as part of its filling. In the evening, the bar menu gives way to more substantial stuff, such as steaks and fresh fish. Food is served 12pm–9pm in the summer and at weekends and 12pm–2.30pm and 6pm–9pm in winter.

Nearby attractions include, of course, the moor and its many opportunities for walking and a miniature pony centre at Moretonhampstead.

✓ children restricted to certain areas
✓ family room
✓ garden
✗ garden toys
✓ lunchtime meals
✓ evening meals
✓ food lunchtime and evenings
✓ children's menu
✓ bottle warming
✓ no smoking area
✗ accommodation
✓ nearby camping and caravan sites
✗ nappy changing
✓ entertainment
✗ children's certificate
✗ high chairs
✗ time limit

## PUSEHILL

# Pig On The Hill

Pusehill, Westward Ho! EX39 5AH
**T** 01237 425889    **F** 01237 425979
**E** info@wpfcottages.co.uk
*Licensee*: John Violet
*Opening times*: 12–3, 6 (6.30 winter)–11; 12–3, 7–10.30 Sun
*Real ales*: **Country Life Old Appledore, Wallop, Golden Pig**
*Directions*: off the A39, Bideford-Abbotsham road

Just in case you forget the name of this pub, there are three tall fibreglass pigs at the entrance holding out menus. This was originally part of a farm worked by the licensee and his family before it was converted into self-catering cottages for visitors. The pub came next, in the 1980s, getting its name from a group of stone pigs on display. This is a very family friendly place, lying slap bang in an area which has a lot going on for it, including the ovine theme park The Big Sheep, the Milky Way Adventure Park at Clovelly, the old port of Bideford and the attractive old fishing village of Appledore, where there is a Maritime Museum.

There isn't a family room as such as children are allowed pretty well anywhere (except around the bar itself). There's a no-smoking restaurant and a games room adjoins the large main room with skittles, pool, video games, table football and a pile of kids books. Outside there are tables and chairs, plus a play area (swings, slides, climbing frame) which borders a pen occupied by Rodney Trotter (a pig of course), another pen with six goats and Cluckingham Palace which boasts a royal retinue of hens. The play area is not fenced in but because there is 200 yards of private driveway up to the pub, it's well off the small country road which leads to the pub.

Food is served from 12pm–2.15pm and 6.30pm–9.30pm (7pm–9pm Sundays) and includes chicken nuggets, pizza, scampi and burgers on the **kids' menu**, though they will also do small portions of choices from the main menu including lasagne, whitebait, scampi, ploughman's and broccoli bake. On Sunday lunchtimes there are usually three or four roasts (plus veggie alternative) with children's portions happily provided (there is also a reduced bar menu). Beers come from the award-winning Country Life brewery which used to brew in an area behind the bar but moved to the Big Sheep when demand meant the brewery had to expand.

✓ children restricted to certain areas
✗ family room
✓ garden
✓ garden toys
✓ lunchtime meals
✓ evening meals
✓ food lunchtime and evenings
✓ children's menu
✓ bottle warming
✓ no smoking area

✓ accommodation
✓ nearby camping and caravan sites
✓ nappy changing – disabled toilets
✗ entertainment
✗ children's certificate
✓ high chairs
✗ time limit

## WOODLAND

# Rising Sun

Woodland TQ13 7JT
**T** 01364 652544   **F** 01364 654202
www.therisingsunwoodland.co.uk
*Licensee*: Heather Humphreys
*Opening times*: 11–3, 6–11, Mon-Sat, closed
Mons in winter; 12–3, 7–10.30 Sun.
*Real ales*: **Princetown's Jail Ale**; guest beers
*Directions*: follow signs from the Plymouth-bound
A38, pub on left (1.5 miles)

There are hundreds of keys hanging from
the exposed beams in this former coaching
inn, a reminder of a former landlord who
left them there back in the 1950s. Set in
beautiful countryside south of the
Plymouth-bound A38, the Rising Sun is a
comfortable and friendly inn and
restaurant with a wide open bar area.
Landlady Heather Humphreys is keen that
families don't feel out of the action so the
family room is off to the side of the main
bar but you can still see through and feel
part of things. Children are also allowed in
the no-smoking dining room, while the
massive and secure garden comes to life in
the summer when kids converge on the
swings.

Food is served 12pm–2.15pm (until 3pm
on Sunday) and 6pm–9.15pm. The **kids'
menu** is entirely home-made with chicken
goujons, sausages and pork burgers (from
local pigs) and pasta with tomato sauce
(plus chips of course). Small portions can
also be taken off the main menu where
possible (local pork chops, chicken breast
etc). All the food is good but the pub is
particularly renowned for its fabulous
home-made pies which also can be taken
home. Sundays see roasts which can be

tailored for young appetites (the main menu
is also available). Guest beers usually come
from local micros while a local cider is also
sold. Local attractions include Dartmoor,
the River Dart Country Park outside
Ashburton (about 10 minutes drive away),
Buckfast Abbey, South Devon's beautiful
beaches, Buckfastleigh's Otter Sanctuary
and Babbacombe Model Village at Torquay.

✓ children restricted to certain areas
✓ family room
✓ garden
✓ garden toys
✓ lunchtime meals
✓ evening meals
✓ food lunchtime and evenings
✓ children's menu
✓ bottle warming
✓ no smoking area
✓ accommodation
✓ nearby camping and caravan sites
✓ nappy changing – women's toilets
✗ entertainment
✗ children's certificate
✓ high chairs
✗ time limit

# DORSET

## CHRISTCHURCH

# Olde George Inn

2a Castle Street, Christchurch PH23 1DT
**T** 01202 479383
*Licensees*: Rob Martin and Paul Goldsack
*Opening times*: 11–11; 12–10.30 Sun
*Real ales*: **Flowers Original; Hampshire's Strong
Best Bitter; Ringwood 49-er**; guest beers

At the reputed age of 600 years old, this
former coaching inn claims to be the oldest
hostelry in this picturesque and historic
town which was mentioned in the Domesday
Book. Inside it's cosy and atmospheric – low
ceilings, exposed beams, antiques – boosted
by friendly service and good food. There are

two rooms: the main bar area and one used for dining. There is also a covered courtyard which is heated in the winter months.

Children are welcome throughout the no-smoking restaurant and courtyard, but families tend to make for the courtyard, which is closed in but parents are asked to keep an eye on their charges all the same. The intriguing **kids' menu** includes mini toad-in-the-holes, cod in cola crunchies, cheese and tomato pizza and 'Jungle Pals', all of which are served with chips. Smaller portions off the main menu are not possible. Sunday lunchtime sees a roast, alongside the main menu; children sized roasts are available. Food is served all day up until 9pm (9.30pm in the summer).

As for things to do in the area, Christchurch itself is a beautiful Saxon market town with an impressive harbour and sandy beaches. Further away there's the Oceanarium at Bournemouth, while Southampton and Portsmouth with its naval history aren't too far away either.

✓ children restricted to certain areas
✗ family room
✗ garden
✗ garden toys
✓ lunchtime meals
✓ evening meals
✓ food lunchtime and evenings
✓ children's menu
✓ bottle warming
✓ no smoking area
✗ accommodation
✗ nearby camping and caravan sites
✗ nappy changing
✗ entertainment
✗ children's certificate
✓ high chairs
✗ time limit

## EAST KNIGHTON

# Countryman Inn

Blacknoll Lane, East Knighton DT2 8LL
**T** 01305 852666    **F** 01305 854125
*Licensee*: Jeremy Evans
*Opening times*: 10.30–2.30, 6–11;12–3, 6–11
*Real ales*: **Courage Best Bitter; Greene King Old Speckled Hen; Ringwood's Best, Old Thumper**

*Directions*: Off the A352 midway between Dorchester and Wareham

Thomas Hardy-country pub down a lane off the main road between Dorchester and Wareham. Converted from three cottages at the end of the 19th century, it's a busy but easy-going place with a long main bar, off which there are a couple of snugs and a family space. The decor is comfortable and rustic with settees, exposed beams and brickwork, log fires, several settles and plenty of old views of the village on the wall.

Children are allowed in the no-smoking family area and the restaurant which seats 80; the family space has books and toys, a chocolate machine and a big fish tank. There's a garden front and back, though the back is hedged in and has a selection of play equipment including tunnels, rope climbing, a slide and swing. Selections on the **kids' menu** include goujons or sausages with chips; there are also jacket potatoes and sandwiches. Smaller portions off the main menu can include pasta, curries, fish and game dishes, while there's a half-price carvery every day except for Mondays. Sunday lunch is very popular and you are advised to book. Food is served lunchtimes and evenings all week.

Kids of a martial mind will want to visit the nearby Bovington Tank Museum, where Lawrence of Arabia spent some time as a member of the Royal Tank Corps; simian minded youngsters will prefer Monkey World at Wareham. Dorchester and Weymouth, with its Skate Park, Brewers Quay shopping village and Sea Life Centre are also near.

✓ children restricted to certain areas
✓ family room
✓ garden
✓ garden toys
✓ lunchtime meals
✓ evening meals
✓ food lunchtime and evenings
✓ children's menu
✓ bottle warming
✓ no smoking area
✓ accommodation
✓ nearby camping and caravan sites

✓ nappy changing – disabled toilets
✗ entertainment
✗ children's certificate
✓ high chairs
✗ time limit

## HURN

## Avon Causeway Hotel

Hurn, Christchurch, Dorset BH23 6AF
**T** 01202 482714
www.avoncauseway.co.uk
*Licensee*: Keith Perks
*Opening times*: 11–11; 12–10.30 Sun
*Real ales*: **Red Shoot Forest Gold; Ringwood Best Bitter, Old Thumper; Wadworth Henry's Original IPA, 6X, JCB**, guest beer
*Directions*: off B3073, behind road bridge

Until 1934, this bustling and busy Wadworth-owned hotel/inn was a railway station serving a line built for the sole benefit of a local rich family who used it to get into nearby Christchurch. The public bar is to the front, with a fair selection of railway mementos and a striking solid oak floor; in the lounge area, there's a mixture of armchairs and dining tables, and then the no-smoking family area which opens out into the large garden. Children are allowed in this part. There is more railway bric-a-brac, as well as a big carved wooden duck which I'm told fascinates children.

Outside on the platform there's an old railway engine and Pullman carriage (reserved for functions and the hotel's own Murder Mystery Evenings). The garden at the rear has plenty of tables and chairs, while there's a wood-chip surfaced play area with fort, slide ropes, swings and slide; in the summer there's the occasional bouncy castle. There's also an aviary with cockatiels, budgies and canaries. The garden is fenced in and gated, there is no access to the road from it, only access to the car park or the pub itself.

There's a **kids'menu** with familiar choices, while six main dishes off the menu can be served as small portions; these include cajun chicken and scampi. There's a full carvery on Sundays (small portions available) as well as the full menu. Food is served from 12pm–2pm, 6pm–9pm Monday–Saturday, 12pm–2pm and 6pm–8pm Sundays.

The Avon Causeway is in the heritage area of the Hampshire Avon Valley between the New Forest and Ringwood Forest, but it is also only ten minutes from Bournemouth and even closer to the airport. This means it is well sited to take advantage of Bournemouth's many facilities, including the Oceanarium and the Alice in Wonderland family park, opposite the airport, as well as many country walks in the Avon valley.

✓ children restricted to certain areas
✓ family room
✓ garden
✓ garden toys
✓ lunchtime meals
✓ evening meals
✓ food lunchtime and evenings
✓ children's menu
✓ bottle warming
✓ no smoking area
✓ accommodation
✓ nearby camping and caravan sites
✓ nappy changing – disabled toilets
✗ entertainment
✗ children's certificate
✓ high chairs
✓ time limit – 9.30pm

## STOURTON CAUNDLE

## Trooper

Stourton Caundle, Sturminster Newton DT10 2JW
**T** 01963 362405
**E** rsoar@hotmail.com
*Licensee*: Richard Soar
*Opening times*: 12–2.30, 7–11; 12.2.30, 7–10.30 Sun
*Real ales*: **Adnams Bitter; Ringwood Best Bitter**; guest
*Directions*: Signed off the A357 between Sturminster Newton and Stalbridge

Blackmore Vale village in the heart of Hardy country, but Enid Blyton is the writer with a connection to this charming rural two-bar inn, which was originally called the

Catherine Wheel. It changed its name to the Trooper at the time of the Napoleonic Wars after soldiers off to fight at Waterloo gathered outside. As for Blyton she owned the Manor Farm which is opposite the Trooper and featured as Finniston Farm in one of the Famous Five mysteries. With that in mind, new licensee Richard Soar is thinking about putting a few of her books into the Trooper Bar, which is where children are allowed. The decor of the Trooper Bar is rustic through and through with over 70 horse bits displayed on the stone walls, as well as prints of troopers. There's also a countryside museum in the skittle alley, the result of the previous landlord's endeavours. It's a fascinating collection of agricultural and domestic implements including tools, milk churns, cider barrels and even a dingo trap from Australia.

Outside there's a beer garden which has an opening to the car park. There is no play equipment at time of writing but Spring should see some changes. No kids' menu either but smaller portions of the bar food menu are served. These include chips and melted cheese, scampi, sausages or ham, egg and chips. Food is only served lunchtimes, 12pm–1.45pm, Monday and Sunday lunchtimes excepted.

This is a very traditional and friendly country pub and probably better for five-year-olds onwards. It's centrally located for getting to Sherbourne (Sherbourne Castle), Yeovil (Fleet Air Arm Museum), Dorchester (the Keep Military Museum) and the sandy beaches of Weymouth.

- ✓ children restricted to certain areas
- ✓ family room
- ✓ garden
- ✗ garden toys
- ✓ lunchtime meals
- ✗ evening meals
- ✗ food lunchtime and evenings
- ✗ children's menu
- ✓ bottle warming
- ✗ no smoking area
- ✗ accommodation
- ✓ nearby camping and caravan sites
- ✗ nappy changing

- ✗ entertainment
- ✗ children's certificate
- ✗ high chairs
- ✓ time limit – 8.30pm

## TARRANT MONKTON

# Langton Arms

Tarrant Monkton, DT11 8RX
**T** 01258 830225
*Licensee*: Barbara Cossins
*Opening times*: 11.30–11; 12–10.30 Sun
*Real ales*: **Hop Back Best Bitter**; guest beers
*Directions*: signposted off the A354 NE of Blandford Forum

Tarrant Monkton is a small picturesque village which lies in rolling, green countryside between Blandford Forum and Salisbury. Unsurprisingly, the Langton Arms is appropriately charming: thatched roof, 17th century origins, opposite the church, while inside the pub, which has a public bar and lounge bar, there are bare beams, an inglenook fireplace, settles and other rustic styled furniture.

Children are allowed in the no-smoking family room which doubles up as a skittle alley (£15 deposit if you want to have a game); there is also a box of toys provided. There's also a restaurant which takes over as the family room if the lounge is booked for a function. The family room leads to a big garden where there's a wood-chipping play area with a selection of swings (including ones for the very young), a play tower, tyres and a bridge. The garden is fenced in, but as the car park is at the end parents are asked to supervise the youngsters. There is sometimes a bouncy castle in the summer.

The kids menu includes chicken goujons, lasagne, sausages, served with chips or creamed potatoes; along with a dessert it's a very reasonable £3.50. Small portions can be served off the main menu where possible; this will include vegetarian lasagne, scampi and jacket potatoes. Food is served 11.30am–2.30pm and 6pm–9.30pm in the week, and all day on Saturdays and

Sunday, with roast lunches as well as the main menu being served on Sundays (small roasts available). In addition to a selection of five real ales, there's also a real draught lager, Warsteiner. The licensee has two children of her own and the pub is very keen on being child-friendly; it also sees itself as female friendly.

Nearby attractions include Bournemouth with its beaches, the Dorset Heavy Horse and Pony Centre at Verwood, the Iron Age fort at Badbury Rings, Old Wardour Castle at Tisbury, Moors Valley Country Park and Monkey World at Wareham.

✓ children restricted to certain areas
✓ family room
✓ garden
✓ garden toys
✓ lunchtime meals
✓ evening meals
✓ food lunchtime and evenings
✓ children's menu
✓ bottle warming
✓ no smoking area
✓ accommodation
✗ nearby camping and caravan sites
✓ nappy changing – women's toilets
✗ entertainment
✗ children's certificate
✓ high chairs
✗ time limit

# GLOUCESTERSHIRE AND BRISTOL

## BRISTOL

## Annexe Inn

Seymour Road, Bishopston, Bristol BS7 9EQ
**T** 0117 9493931
www.the-annexe.co.uk
*Licensees*: Paul Bird and Roger Morgan
*Opening times*: 11–30–2.30, 6–11; 11.30–11 Sat; 12–10.30 Sun

*Real ales*: **Courage Best Bitter, Draught Bass; Marston's Pedigree; Smiles Best**; guest beer
*Directions*: close to the Gloucester County Cricket Ground

Situated next to a sports bar (the Sportsman, also owned by the same company), the Annexe is a much quieter prospect. It's a traditional single-storey pub (originally stables) with a conservatory attached to the side, which is popular with local families. The no-smoking conservatory is light and airy, fitted with blinds and heating. There are pictures of old Bristol on the wall but sadly the toys and books have now gone (as they were continually being taken away). Until 8.30pm, children are allowed here and out in the garden, a large, gated and walled space with a foliage-covered pergola shading part of the patio area.

Food is served 12pm–2pm during the week, 12pm–7pm on Saturdays and 12pm–3pm on Sundays. It's a well-priced bar-food orientated menu (sandwiches, salads, burgers, sausage and chips etc) and there is a selection of children's choices, all served with chips and beans. Smaller portions off the main menu are not served. Bristol's many activities are just a couple of miles away – these include the zoo, the newly opened British Empire museum, attractions celebrating Bristol's maritime past and for the sporting family Gloucestershire County's cricket ground.

✓ children restricted to certain areas
✗ family room
✓ garden
✗ garden toys
✓ lunchtime meals
✓ evening meals
✓ food lunchtime and evenings
✓ children's menu
✗ bottle warming
✓ no smoking area
✗ accommodation
✗ nearby camping and caravan sites
✓ nappy changing – disabled toilets
✗ entertainment
✗ children's certificate
✓ high chairs
✓ time limit – 8.30pm

## FRANCE LYNCH

## King's Head

France Lynch, Stroud GL6 8LT
**T** 01453 882225
*Licensees*: Mike and Pat Duff
*Opening times*: 12–2.30, 6–11;12–4, 7–10.30 Sun
*Real ales*: **Archers Best Bitter**; **Hook Norton Best Bitter**; guest beers
*Directions*: small hamlet northwards off the A419 between Stroud and Cirencester, two miles from Bisley; OS903035

It's a good map-reading exercise to find this friendly old pub, but well worth it. Inside you'll find a one-room bar with one end shaped like a ship's hull; children are allowed in here if they are eating. There's also a compact family room with a box of soft toys and games. Smoking is allowed throughout the pub but I'm told that there is good air conditioning.

At the front of the pub there's a big garden with a lawn, trees and shrubs plus a secure fenced in play area. This is a very popular pub for local families; a music festival is held in the garden in the summer to raise funds for the school and the local children take part. Food is hearty local produce, with a **kids' menu** including sausages or scampi and chips and jacket potatoes. Small portions off the adult menu can be provided if possible; there are also sandwiches, soups and other bar snacks. Food is served from 12pm–2pm and 6.30pm–9pm all week (except Sunday evenings). Come Sunday lunch, roasts rule the roost, along with vegetarian choices, a selection from the bar menu and the usual children's menu.

On the beer front there are two guests in the summer and one in the winter, coming from a variety of micro brewers. The excellent Czech Pilsner Budvar is also sold. This is fantastic walking country, with many walks and there's also an old fashioned playground at Charlford Botternley which is in walking distance.

✓ children restricted to certain areas
✓ family room
✓ garden
✓ garden toys
✓ lunchtime meals
✓ evening meals
✓ food lunchtime and evenings
✓ children's menu
✓ bottle warming
✗ no smoking area
✗ accommodation
✓ nearby camping and caravan sites
✗ nappy changing
✓ entertainment
✗ children's certificate
✓ high chairs
✓ time limit – 9pm

## OLD SODBURY

## Dog Inn

Badminton Road, Old Sodbury BS37 6LZ
**T** 01454 312006
*Licensees*: John and Joan Harris
*Opening times*: 11–11; 12–10.30 Sun
*Real ales*: **Draught Bass**; **Fuller's London Pride**; **Wadworth 6X**; **Wickwar BOB**
*Directions*: between Chipping Sodbury and the A46

A couple of miles north of the M4 you will find this gem of a 16th century Cotswold stone-built inn dripping in character – exposed walls and beams, settles, two big open fires and dogs everywhere (well, in pictures and plates on the wall). Children are allowed everywhere in the pub, except at the bar, but under-14s must be out before 9pm. There's a fully enclosed garden at the back with swings, slides and monkey bars for the more energetic.

This is a food-orientated pub, boasting a massive menu. The children's choice, going under the title 'puppy food', includes 'boxer' burger and chips, lasagne, pizza, fish fingers and spaghetti bolognese. Smaller portions are also available off the main menu, including pasta, curries and sweet and sour pork. Sunday sees beef, pork or nut roast, alongside the other choices (child-sized portions available, but not for nut roast). Food is served 12pm–2pm, 6pm–9.30pm and 12pm–2.30pm, 7pm–9.30pm on Sundays; the pub doesn't take bookings.

This is very close to the Cotswold Way footpath, but also handy for the Cotswold Water Park near Cirencester and the 'national' arboretum at Tetbury.

- ✗ children restricted to certain areas
- ✗ family room
- ✓ garden
- ✓ garden toys
- ✓ lunchtime meals
- ✓ evening meals
- ✓ food lunchtime and evenings
- ✓ children's menu
- ✓ bottle warming
- ✓ no smoking area
- ✓ accommodation
- ✗ nearby camping and caravan sites
- ✓ nappy changing – disabled toilets
- ✗ entertainment
- ✗ children's certificate
- ✗ high chairs
- ✓ time limit – 9pm

## PARKEND

## Rising Sun

Moseley Green, Parkend GL15 4HN
T 01594 562008
*Licensee*: Kevin Howell
Opening times: 11–3, 6.30 (6 Sat)–11 (11–11 Sat in summer); 12–3, 7–10.30 (12–10.30 summer) Sun
*Real ales*: **Freeminer Speculation Ale**; **Greene King Abbot**; guest beer
*Directions*: Parkend is north of Lydney on the B4234 and the pub is signposted

Old 17th-century inn which is situated in the middle of the Forest of Dean and surrounded by gorgeous woodland. Once upon a time the Rising Sun was reputedly a spit-and-sawdust miners' beer house, but the collieries are long shut and tourism is the area's lifeblood these days. The pub has been in the hands of the same family since the 1930s and so there's a wonderful sense of continuity about things. Inside there are three bars (one of which is no-smoking), each one continuing into the other. On the walls there is plenty of Forest of Dean mining memorabilia. Families are encouraged and children are allowed

everywhere. There is a box of toys to hand inside, while the secure garden to the side of the pub has a combination of slides and swings. Food is served lunchtimes and evenings and all day at the weekend during the summer. The **kids' menu** includes familiar choices such as chicken nuggets and scampi with chips, alongside cottage pie. At £3.25 it's well priced as this includes a 'surprise bag' for pudding, which contains doughnuts and ice cream. Smaller portions off the main menu can also be served where possible. These include sausage and chips, while child-sized roasts are served Sunday lunchtimes alongside the kids' menu. There are also penny sweets for sale behind the bar. A very friendly and popular pub which is an ideal place to repair to after a morning spent exploring the Forest, where there are plenty of walks and cycle tracks. Also close to hand is the Dean Forest Railway and Clearwell Caves.

- ✗ children restricted to certain areas
- ✗ family room
- ✓ garden
- ✓ garden toys
- ✓ lunchtime meals
- ✓ evening meals
- ✓ food lunchtime and evenings
- ✓ children's menu
- ✓ bottle warming
- ✓ no smoking area
- ✗ accommodation
- ✗ nearby camping and caravan sites
- ✗ nappy changing
- ✗ entertainment
- ✓ children's certificate
- ✓ high chairs
- ✗ time limit

## SHIREHAMPTON

## Lamplighters

Station Road, Shirehampton BS11 9XA
T 0117 982 3549
www.the-lamplighters.co.uk
*Licensee*: Leon Franklin
Opening times: 11–3, 6–11; 12–10.30 Sun
*Real ales*: **Butcombe Bitter**; **Draught Bass**; **Fuller's London Pride**; **Marston's Pedigree**

Grade II listed pub which was built in the 1760s and gets its curious name from the chap that had it built – he made his money from being contracted to light several of the Bristol parishes by means of oil-lamps. Sited opposite the village of Pill on the banks of the Avon, it has a large open planned bar area with a family room downstairs and a function room which doubles up as a restaurant on Sundays. Children are allowed in the family room, which has a few books and toys, and in the large garden which is fenced in and has plenty of swings, seesaws and a climbing frame.

The **kids' menu** has the usual choices, but the pub is reluctant to serve smaller portions off the main menu. However, Sunday lunchtime sees a roast dinner and a child's portions can be served from that; the kids' menu is also available. Food is served 12pm–2pm, 7pm–9pm during the week and 12pm–2.15pm on Sunday lunchtimes; there is no food Sunday evenings. There is a beer festival every second September weekend, when children are not encouraged to visit.

Shirehampton is on the north-western outskirts of Bristol so is well-placed for the city's attractions such as *SS Great Britain*, local museums, Bristol Zoo Gardens, Clifton Suspension Bridge and the Severn Crossing into Wales.

- ✓ children restricted to certain areas
- ✓ family room
- ✓ garden
- ✓ garden toys
- ✓ lunchtime meals
- ✓ evening meals
- ✓ food lunchtime and evenings
- ✓ children's menu
- ✓ bottle warming
- ✗ no smoking area
- ✗ accommodation
- ✗ nearby camping and caravan sites
- ✗ nappy changing
- ✗ entertainment
- ✗ children's certificate
- ✓ high chairs
- ✓ time limit – 8.30pm

## WATERLEY BOTTOM

# New Inn

Waterley Bottom, North Nibley GL11 6EF
**T** 01453 543659
*Licensees*: Jackie and Jacky Cartigny
*Opening times*: 7–11 Mon, 12–2.30, 6–11 Tuesday to Friday; 12–11 Sat; 12–10.30 Sun
*Real ales*: **Bath Gem, SPA; Cotleigh Tawny; Greene King Abbot**; guest beer
*Directions*: signed from North Nibley OS758964

Remote edge-of-Cotswolds former cider house which is hidden away at the head of a beautiful tree-filled valley – it's well worth the hunt. Inside, there's a locals' bar and a lounge bar, with children allowed in both areas – log fires in the winter make things very cosy. Outside, there's plenty of seating in the secure garden, with swings and see-saws in the small orchard at the end. Boules is also played here, which is not surprising as the landlord is French.

There's a **kids' menu** with the usual choices, while smaller portions of the main menu can be served if possible – these include lasagne, flans and pasta dishes. Roasts are served on Sundays along with specials and the main menu. Food is served 12pm–2pm and 6pm–9pm Tuesday to Friday and 12pm–2.15pm and 6pm–9pm weekends (no food served on Mondays except bank holiday lunchtimes).

This is a very friendly and relaxed place to visit with children. The location is superb and includes wonderful walking country while Berkeley Castle is only four miles away. Gloucester, with its historic docks and cathedral, is not too far either.

- ✗ children restricted to certain areas
- ✗ family room
- ✓ garden
- ✓ garden toys
- ✓ lunchtime meals
- ✓ evening meals
- ✓ food lunchtime and evenings
- ✓ children's menu
- ✓ bottle warming
- ✗ no smoking area
- ✗ accommodation
- ✓ nearby camping and caravan sites

✓ nappy changing – women's toilets
✗ entertainment
✓ children's certificate
✗ high chairs
✓ time limit – 9pm

## SOMERSET

### BRENDON HILL

## Ralegh's Cross Inn

Brendon Hill TA23 0LN
**T** 01984 640343
*Licensee*: Peter Rowan
*Opening times*: 11–2.30, 6–11 (11–11 summer);
12–2.30, 6–10.30 Sun
*Real ales*: **Cotleigh Barn Owl, Tawny; Exmoor Ale, Fox**
*Directions*: on the B3224 opposite where the B3190 descends to Watchet

Massive inn, parts of which date back to the 16th century, with stunning views over the Bristol Channel towards Wales. On a clear day, you can see the Brecon Beacons as well as Dunkery Beacon to the left, Exmoor's highest point. Located on the edge of Exmoor National Park, this was once a calling place for drovers and packhorse men and there was also an annual sheep fair held in August, sadly no more.

The inn has been added to over the years and has lots of annexes with plenty of accommodation. Inside, there's one big bar, a dining room to the right and a family space to the left which has a massive countryside mural on the wall featuring Exmoor's wildlife; also keep an eye out for the old photos detailing the history of the nearby iron mines which brought prosperity into the area in the 19th century.

Children are allowed in the no-smoking family room and dining area and there are little toys to keep toddlers amused. Outside, there's a large, grassed playing area with a massive adventure playground including a fort, swings and tyres. Even though it is a large area, it is bordered by the road and entrance to one of the car parks so supervision is essential at all times.

Food is served lunchtimes and evenings all week and the **kids' menu** has the usual choices with chips or smiley faces and beans. There's a carvery Wednesday and Sunday lunchtime and evening and Friday and Saturday evening; small portions are available.

There are plenty of walking and riding opportunities in the area, while the seaside resort of Minehead is about 20 minutes away.

✓ children restricted to certain areas
✓ family room
✓ garden
✓ garden toys
✓ lunchtime meals
✓ evening meals
✓ food lunchtime and evenings
✓ children's menu
✓ bottle warming
✓ no smoking area
✓ accommodation
✗ nearby camping and caravan sites
✗ nappy changing
✗ entertainment
✗ children's certificate
✓ high chairs
✗ time limit

### CARHAMPTON

## Butchers Arms

Carhampton TA24 6LP
**T** 01643 821333
*Licensee*: Kevin Nicholls
*Opening times*: 11.30–3 (11 Sat); 6.30–11; open all day in summer; 12–10.30 Sun
*Real ales*: **Courage Best Bitter; Young's Bitter**

On one cold January night every year the orchard adjoining to the Butchers Arms is the scene of a traditional wassailing scene where cider is drunk and a shotgun fired in the trees to ward off evil spirits. If that's not your sort of thing, do still take the family to the Butchers Arms, which is a lively community focused pub, handily based on the A39 coastal road which travels westwards to Minehead and picturesque Porlock.

Inside this ancient inn which looks as if it's been catering to travellers for centuries, it's a big open bar area with well worn stone flooring and exposed beams, plus lots of pictures of old Carhampton and horse brasses on the walls. Children are allowed at tables at the front of the pub, in the games room and the no-smoking restaurant where the tables are arranged in booths.

The food is good basic pub food with some home-cooked specials; there are also staples such as baguettes and baked potatoes. For children there's the familiar **kids' menu** which also comes with a free toy – when we visited James received a plastic dinosaur and was very much impressed. Roasts are also served on Sundays (small roasts available) alongside everything else. Service for children is quick and friendly. Food is served 12pm–2pm and 7pm–9pm, but there is none on Sunday evenings. Outside there's a securely fenced and gated play area which overlooks the busy A39.

This is an ideal spot from where to explore the coast of West Somerset and the interior of Exmoor and the licensee hopes to have accommodation up and running by spring 2003. Attractions include the West Somerset Railway (who co-host the local CAMRA branch's beer festival on Minehead platform in September), Blue Anchor Bay, Dunster Castle and very close by on the A39 there is Tropicana which has reptiles, exotic animals, a playground and a massive pirate ship, all situated in and around a stern looking 1930s building which was once a BBC transmitting station for the area. There is also a Bakerlite museum at nearby Williton.

✓ children restricted to certain areas
✗ family room
✓ garden
✓ garden toys
✓ lunchtime meals
✓ evening meals
✓ food lunchtime and evenings
✓ children's menu
✓ bottle warming
✓ no smoking area

✗ accommodation
✓ nearby camping and caravan sites
✗ nappy changing
✗ entertainment
✗ children's certificate
✓ high chairs
✗ time limit

## COMPTON MARTIN

### Ring O'Bells

Compton Martin, North Somerset BS40 6JE
**T** 01761 221284
**E** roger@ring47.freeserve.co.uk
*Licensees*: Roger and Jackie Owen
*Opening times*: 11.30–3, 6.30–11; 12–3, 7–10.30 Sun
*Real ales*: **Butcombe Bitter, Gold; Wadworth 6X**; guest beer
*Directions*: On the A368 between Bath and Weston-super-Mare, close to Blagdon and Chew Valley lakes

Mendip Hills village local which has been a pub for at least a century; before that it was a farm and cider house; more recently this Butcombe Brewery owned house has been voted local pub of the year by the CAMRA branch. Inside there's three bars boasting a variety of traditional pub interiors including an inglenook fireplace with bread oven, exposed beams, log fires and pub games.

Children are allowed in the no-smoking family room, a converted barn which has Disney characters painted on the ceiling amongst the rafters; there is also a rocking horse, toys and a big blackboard; it is linked to the main pub by a corridor. Outside there's an unfenced L-shaped garden next to the car park, so keep an eye on the little ones. There are slides, swings and a climbing frame for them to work off their energy.

The **kids' menu** features familiar choices, all served with chips; while smaller portions of the large main menu can be served. This includes, steaks, lasagne, local trout, salads and specials off the board. On Sunday lunchtimes small roasts are available, as well as the main and children's menu. Food is served from 12pm–2pm and 6.30pm–9pm throughout the week

(6.30pm–9.30pm Friday and Saturday; 7pm–9pm Sunday).

The Ring O'Bells is right in the middle of the Mendip Hills with their many walks; it is also close to Cheddar with its caves and stunning gorge and the Wookey Hole cave on the southern side of the Mendips. Weston-super-Mare, Bath and Bristol are also within easy driving distance.

✓ children restricted to certain areas
✓ family room
✓ garden
✓ garden toys
✓ lunchtime meals
✓ evening meals
✓ food lunchtime and evenings
✓ children's menu
✓ bottle warming
✓ no smoking area
✗ accommodation
✗ nearby camping and caravan sites
✓ nappy changing – unisex toilets
✗ entertainment
✗ children's certificate
✓ high chairs
✗ time limit

## PITNEY

# Halfway House

Pitney Hill, Pitney, Langport TA10 9AB
**T** 01458 252513
*Licensees*: Julian and Judy Litchfield
*Opening times*: 11.30–3, 5.30–11; 12.3.30, 7–10.30 Sun
*Real ales*: **Butcombe Bitter**; **Cotleigh Tawny**; **Hop Back Crop Circle, Summer Lightning**; **Teignworthy Reel Ale**; guest beers

Wonderful roadside pub which has won many awards, back in 1996 it was CAMRA National Pub of the Year while the most recent one came from the *Daily Telegraph* for Britain's Best Traditional Country Pub. Situated on the B3153 between Somerton and Langport, it originally started life as a couple of cottages, but has been a licensed premises for 200 years. The main part of the building is believed to be 300 years old, while the back part with its magnificent mediaeval crook beam over the fireplace is only nine years old, but it had been built to look as if it had been there for centuries. Inside the floors are well-worn stone, while the furniture is comfortable and rustic; there are log fires in the winter and the young staff are always friendly.

Families are asked to remain in the back part of the pub which is open to the main bar; it also has its own serving hatch. The loos are also here which is useful for those parents who hate having to battle with their little ones through smoky bars. There's a small garden at the front which looks onto the road, but children are best served by the side garden next to the parking space. This is away from the road, fenced and gated and has big tables, swings, a seesaw and a climbing frame.

The lunchtime menu is home-made bar food, soup and rolls, sandwiches, ploughmans and sausages from a local butcher; child's portions are served. They will also do sausage and chips for children. In the evening delicious home-cooked curries make up the menu. There are also chillis and jacket potatoes with fillings such as baked beans and cheese. Food is served Monday–Saturday 12pm–2pm and 7pm–9.30pm. There is no food on Sundays. There are usually between eight to 12 real ales served, straight from the cask, with selections (mainly from southwest micros) chalked up on a board. There is also a choice of Belgian and Czech beers and a real cider.

Nearby attractions include the Fleet Air Arm Museum at the Yeovilton air base, the Haynes Motor Museum at Sparkford, the Somerset Levels with plenty of walks and bird watching, Glastonbury with its fascinating Rural Life Museum as well as more esoteric attractions and a shopping village at Street.

✓ children restricted to certain areas
✓ family room
✓ garden
✓ garden toys
✓ lunchtime meals
✓ evening meals
✓ food lunchtime and evenings
✗ children's menu
✗ bottle warming

✗ no smoking area
✗ accommodation
✓ nearby camping and caravan sites
✗ nappy changing
✗ entertainment
✗ children's certificate
✗ high chairs
✗ time limit

## SOUTH PETHERTON

## Brewers Arms

18 St James Street, South Petherton TA13 5BW
**T** 01460 241887
*Licensee*: Duncan Webb
*Opening times*: 11.30–3, 6–11; 12–10.30 Sun
*Real ales*: **Otter Bitter**; **Worthington Bitter**; guest beers

South Petherton is a handsome hamstone village just off the A303 and the Brewers Arms is an old coaching inn with a history going back several hundred years. The original archway and cobbled yard where the coaches waited is still in evidence. Originally called the Bell Inn, it burnt down in 1924 and was rebuilt, getting its current name in the mid 1980s when a micro-brewery briefly set up shop on the property. The interior of the pub is divided into three specific areas; children are allowed in all of them, though they must keep away from the main bar area. They are also allowed in the recently opened restaurant, which can be found to the left of the bar; it's an old bakehouse complete with an old oven on display.

As for food, a **kids' menu** offers familiar choices, but smaller portions of the main menu can be served. These include pasta dishes and curries. The restaurant offers more à la carte choices, which reflect the seasons; they will include pork tenderloin with mushrooms and walnuts, seared salmon and Thai spiced chicken. Roasts are served Sunday lunchtimes (as well as the main menu), and small ones can be ordered for children. Food is served 12pm–2pm and 6pm–9pm every day, though there is a possibility that the pub might be shutting Monday nights in the winter; call to check.

The courtyard and the garden at the back are popular in the summer with families; there is only one entrance to the garden and it is reasonably narrow but it is recommended that parents keep an eye on their charges. There are usually four real ales to be found, with guests usually coming from West Country brewers. A beer festival is held in May while August bank holiday sees a festival of Somerset beers and ciders. The pub gets very crowded then but they do put on a few games such as a giant snakes and ladders.

This is very much a locals' pub, which is relaxed about children as long as they behave; being half a mile off the A303 it's very useful for a lunch break if you're travelling into Devon. Local attractions include the Fleet Air Arm Museum at Yeovilton, the Cricket St Thomas Wildlife Park and Montacute House and gardens, near where there is also a TV and Radio Memorabilia Museum.

✓ children restricted to certain areas
✗ family room
✓ garden
✗ garden toys
✓ lunchtime meals
✓ evening meals
✓ food lunchtime and evenings
✓ children's menu
✓ bottle warming
✓ no smoking area
✗ accommodation
✓ nearby camping and caravan sites
✗ nappy changing
✓ entertainment
✗ children's certificate
✓ high chairs
✗ time limit

## WIVELISCOMBE

## Bear Inn

10 North Street, Wiveliscombe TA4 2JY
**T** 01984 623537
*Licensees*: Andy and Heather Harvey
*Opening times*: 11.00–11.00; 12–10.30 Sun
*Real ales*: **Cotleigh Tawny**, seasonal beers; **Otter Bitter**; guest beers

Friendly former coaching inn run by a couple who used to manage Wetherspoon's award-winning conversion, the Commercial Rooms in Bristol. The Bear Inn can be found just off the centre of this small Somerset country town which is home to pioneering craft brewers Exmoor Ales and Cotleigh. The old Taunton-to-Barnstable road passes through the town which also makes it well-placed for Exmoor and the Brendon Hills. Inside, there's a single bar in which families are welcome though there are the usual restrictions about kids not at the bar and also not in the pool room next door. There's also a cosy family room where a few toys will keep the kids happy while you wait for your lunch. Outside, a beer garden and a gated play area with a slide, swings and a climbing frame are ideal for summer days. The **kids' menu** includes stand-bys such as chicken nuggets and sausage and chips, but small portions from the main menu will be served if possible. These include cottage pie, vegetarian options, pizzas and roasts on Sunday (the main menu is also served then). Food is served 12pm–2.20pm and 6pm–9pm all through the week.

Nearby attractions include the West Somerset Railway, Clatworthy Reservoir and Wimbleball Lake, where sailing, fishing and bird watching can be enjoyed.

✓ children restricted to certain areas
✓ family room
✓ garden
✓ garden toys
✓ lunchtime meals
✓ evening meals
✓ food lunchtime and evenings
✓ children's menu
✓ bottle warming
✗ no smoking area
✓ accommodation
✗ nearby camping and caravan sites
✗ nappy changing
✗ entertainment
✗ children's certificate
✗ high chairs
✓ time limit – 8pm

## WILTSHIRE

### BROKERSWOOD

## Kicking Donkey

Brokerswood, near Westbury, Wiltshire BA14 3EG
T 01373 823250
E kd@dotnetbiz.net
*Licensee*: Paul Taylor
*Opening times*: 11.30–3, 6–11 (11–11Fri, Sat); 12–10.30 Sun
*Real ales*: **Fuller's London Pride; Moles Tap Bitter; Wadworth 6X**; guest beers
*Directions*: between the A36 and A350

During the summer months a bouncy castle takes up permanent residence in the large garden of this 17th-century inn, which is down a quiet country lane and has a view of the Westbury White Horse. Naturally, this makes it very popular with families, especially those staying at the nearby Brokerswood (Woodland) Country Park, with its nature reserve and camping and caravan sites. Inside the pub, which used to be called the Yew Tree, it's all stone floors and walls, exposed beams, horse brasses, copper kettles and big open fireplaces.

As long as they behave, children are allowed anywhere in the pub, which has two bar areas and a separate no-smoking restaurant. There is also a compact family room called the 'Saddle Room' and full of horsey artifacts.

The **kids' menu** serves the customary choices, while smaller portions can be ordered from the main menu. These include ham, egg and chips, baguettes and curries. On Sunday lunchtimes there's a traditional roast, as well as a bar food and kids' menu. Food is served all week 12pm–2.30pm, 7pm–9.30pm (9pm on Sundays).

During the summer, people make use of the two barbecues in the fenced-off garden and the pub will also do takeaways if you are staying at the camp site. Nearby is

Longleat with its amazing safari, tour of the house and the world's longest hedge maze.

- ✗ children restricted to certain areas
- ✓ family room
- ✓ garden
- ✗ garden toys
- ✓ lunchtime meals
- ✓ evening meals
- ✓ food lunchtime and evenings
- ✓ children's menu
- ✓ bottle warming
- ✓ no smoking area
- ✗ accommodation
- ✓ nearby camping and caravan sites
- ✗ nappy changing
- ✓ entertainment
- ✗ children's certificate
- ✗ high chairs
- ✗ time limit

## COMMON PLATT

## Foresters Arms

Common Platt, Purton, Swindon SN5 5JX
T 01793 770615
*Licensees*: Laura and Phyllis Graham
*Real ales*: **Courage Best Bitter; Greene King Ruddles County; Wadworth 6X**; guest beer
*Opening times*: 11.30–3, 5.30–11 (11.30–12 Sat summer); 12–3, 7–10.30 (12–10.30 summer) Sun
*Directions*: From M4 (Junction 16) follow the signs to Purton

Solid, stone-built country-style pub which is on the edge of western Swindon. Inside, it's comfortable and cosy with old and sharp-looking forestry saws decorating the wall. Children are allowed in the family room-cum-lounge, and for the summer there's also a big garden with a fenced in play area featuring an all-wood play structure, including fort and drawbridge; a soft landing is ensured for any daring kids as wood chippings cover the floor.

The **kids' menu** includes sausages and little pizzas, all served with chips, while smaller portions can be served from the main menu where possible, including chicken tikka, baked potatoes and small steaks and gammons. There are also sandwiches and other traditional bar food.

On Sunday lunchtimes there are roasts only, with child-sized ones being available. Food is served 12pm–2pm and 7pm–9pm, 12pm–3pm on Sundays; there's no food on Sunday evenings in the winter, but during the summer food will be served all day at the weekend.

The mother and daughter licensees had just moved in when I spoke to them, and I was told that they were looking at the possibility of putting on bouncy castles and other child-friendly events during the summer. Swindon is not noted for its tourist attractions, but this pub is ideal before or after a visit to the Museum of the Great Western Railway, which is a big draw for young and old. There's also Lydiard House Park, a stately house in West Swindon with woodland walks and an adventure playground.

- ✓ children restricted to certain areas
- ✓ family room
- ✓ garden
- ✓ garden toys
- ✓ lunchtime meals
- ✓ evening meals
- ✓ food lunchtime and evenings
- ✓ children's menu
- ✓ bottle warming
- ✗ no smoking area
- ✗ accommodation
- ✗ nearby camping and caravan sites
- ✗ nappy changing
- ✗ entertainment
- ✗ children's certificate
- ✓ high chairs
- ✓ time limit – 8pm

## HAMPWORTH

## Cuckoo Inn

Hampworth, Landford SP5 2DU
T 01794 390302
*Licensee*: Tim Bacon
*Opening times*: 11.30–2.30, 6–11 (11.30–11 Sat); 12–10.30 Sun
*Real ales*: **Cheriton Pots Ale; Hop Back GFB, Summer Lightning; Ringwood Best Bitter; Wadworth 6X**; guest beers
*Directions*: four miles west on A36 from Junction 2 on M27

Hampworth is a pretty little hamlet on the edge of the New Forest and the Cuckoo Inn is appropriately rustic and picture postcard. The roof is thatched, the building is over 300 years, having been converted into a pub in the 1800s; before that it was a couple of cottages. There are four small bars inside, but children are allowed in a no-smoking family room at the back of the pub. If you're visiting the area, this is really a pub for the summertime, as there's a huge fenced-in garden with swings and a Wendy house. Even though there's a gate, the licensee does ask parents to keep an eye on their charges.

Hearteningly to parents this is a chip-free zone. Food is basic and homely with baguettes, salads, soups, quiches and risottos in the summer, all of which can be served up in small portions. In the winter the menu changes to faggots and peas, pies, soups, casseroles, baguettes and rolls. Food is served from 12pm–2pm and 6.30pm–9pm, with the exceptions of Sunday and Monday evenings. There are no roasts. Throughout the year there are between 5–12 real ales on, depending on the season. There is also a beer festival in September.

Nearby family attractions include the National Motor Museum and other attractions at Beaulieu, many walks and picnic areas in the New Forest, an Owl Sanctuary at Ringwood, Paultons family leisure park near Romsey and for older children of a more thoughtful nature Salisbury and its marvellous cathedral is just up the road.

- ✓ children restricted to certain areas
- ✓ family room
- ✓ garden
- ✓ garden toys
- ✓ lunchtime meals
- ✓ evening meals
- ✓ food lunchtime and evenings
- ✗ children's menu
- ✓ bottle warming
- ✓ no smoking area
- ✗ accommodation
- ✓ nearby camping and caravan sites

- ✗ nappy changing
- ✗ entertainment
- ✗ children's certificate
- ✗ high chairs
- ✓ time limit – 9pm

## NORTH NEWNTON

# Woodbridge Inn

North Newnton, SN9 6JZ
**T** 01980 630266    **F** 01980 630457
**E** woodbridge@btconnect.com
www.woodbridgeinn.co.uk
*Licensee*: Rebecca Croot
*Opening times*: 12–11; 12–10.30
*Real ales*: **Wadworth Henry's Original IPA; 6X;** seasonal beers
*Directions*: on A345 between Pewsey and Upavon

Grade II listed 16th-century coaching inn set in four acres of riverside paddocks on the banks of the Avon. Inside there's a big bar area with rustic furnishings, and comfortable seating by the open fire. The wall has a collection of old framed maps. There's also a small no-smoking restaurant. Children are allowed everywhere, but in the summer they will want to be outside in the extensive and secure beer garden, where there is a play area with rattle bridge, towers, slide and boules piste, including kids boules. Families are also encouraged to bring footballs to have a kickabout in the paddocks. There are also horses and chickens to see. The riverside paddocks are fenced and secure so there is no worries about the little ones near the river.

On the food side, there are the usual **kids' menu** choices, though there are also chip free alternatives such as sausages, new potatoes and gravy as well as salads. Smaller portions are also available off the main menu, such as chicken dishes, scampi, open sandwiches and nachos. On Sundays there are kid-sized roasts plus everything else. Food is served from 12pm–10pm every day. As well as bottle- and food-warming facilities, this friendly and welcoming inn will puree up food for the very young.

This is rich country for fans of ancient

remains with Stonehenge, Silbury Hill, Avebury Stone Circle and Wiltshire White Horses all within easy striking range. For the more familiar attractions, Wilton House has an excellent play area and Andover has a Jungle Jungle play area.

✗ children restricted to certain areas
✗ family room
✓ garden
✓ garden toys
✓ lunchtime meals

✓ evening meals
✓ food lunchtime and evenings
✓ children's menu
✓ bottle warming
✓ no smoking area
✓ accommodation
✓ nearby camping and caravan sites
✗ nappy changing
✗ entertainment
✗ children's certificate
✓ high chairs
✗ time limit

# Yorkshire

*Alice Hawthorn*
NUN MONKTON, YORKSHIRE

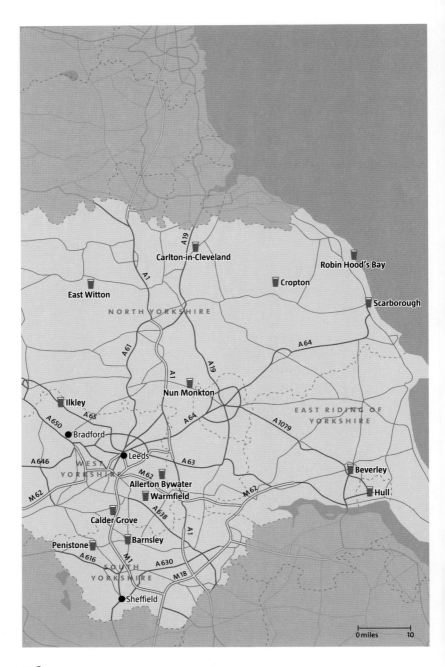

Carlton-in-Cleveland

Robin Hood's Bay

Cropton

East Witton

Scarborough

NORTH YORKSHIRE

Nun Monkton

Ilkley

EAST RIDING OF
YORKSHIRE

Bradford

Leeds

Beverley

Allerton Bywater

Hull

WEST
YORKSHIRE

Warmfield

Calder Grove

Penistone

Barnsley

SOUTH
YORKSHIRE

Sheffield

0 miles    10

Every Sunday throughout the year, the Victoria Hotel in Robin Hood's Bay fires its cannon at midday. Yorkshire folk have always liked to make a big noise about themselves – and why not? The spirit of Freddie Truman has never faded away.

England's most vociferous county is a stunning blend of dales and moorland, rugged coastlines and popular seaside resorts, as well as bustling, modern cities such as fashion-conscious Leeds and Sheffield, where there's plenty for the family to do. Things are changing everywhere. Take Hull, for instance. Long seen as a North Sea port and home to the lugubrious poet Philip Larkin, it's now a vibrant and energetic city, symbolised by the Deep, a world ocean discovery centre.

York, of course, is known throughout the world for its long tradition and history which has included the Romans, Normans and Vikings. The latter are celebrated by Jorvik, a dramatic reconstruction of Viking York – smells and all. TV fans in the area might like to take a visit to Castle Howard, a breathtaking 18th-century house which starred in the 1980s TV classic *Brideshead Revisited*.

Out in the countryside, there are cosy pubs with good real ale from the likes of Black Sheep and Timothy Taylor. Check out the brewpub Cropton which offers a friendly welcome and plenty to keep the kids happy while you enjoy a pint and a pie. It's not the only good choice: one pub boasts a play area which is more assault course than swings and slides. Another produces home-made chips (getting rarer and rarer to find) to go with its renowned ham and eggs, which have become a favourite of TV celebrity Richard Whiteley.

The coast is also a great draw, from Scarborough and its miles of sandy beaches to brooding Whitby Abbey which provided an atmospheric setting for Bram Stoker's Dracula. Incidentally, Robin Hood's Bay isn't far away which is where we came in.

## EAST YORKSHIRE

# Hodgson's

Fleming House, Flemingate, Beverley, HU17 0NU
**T** 01482 880484
www.hodgsonspub.com
*Licensee*: Janet Morris
*Opening times*: 12–11; 12–10.30 Sun
*Real ales*: **Tetley Bitter, Mild**; guest beers

Impressive looking early 19th-century building which only became a pub in 1996 and was until recently home to the now defunct Wawne Brewery. It's a big friendly pub with a public bar at the front and a large lounge at the rear which also has live entertainment and discos throughout the week; there's also a skittle alley at the back.

Children are allowed in the front room where there is a toybox; if eating they are also welcome in lounge where there is a no-smoking area. There's also a big field at the back of the pub where they can let off steam but it's not always available as it doesn't belong to the pub.

Food is served lunchtimes and evenings through the week, with the **kids' menu** featuring familiar choices. Smaller portions off the main menu can also be served including haddock and chips, lamb chops, gammon and steak and ale pie. Sunday lunchtime sees a carvery (small portions available) as well as the main menus.

Very handy to go to after visiting the Army Transport Museum which is directly across the road.

✓ children restricted to certain areas
✗ family room
✗ garden
✗ garden toys
✓ lunchtime meals
✓ evening meals
✓ food lunchtime and evening
✓ children's menu

✓ bottle warming
✓ no smoking area
✗ accommodation
✗ nearby camping and caravan sites
✗ nappy changing
✗ entertainment
✗ children's certificate
✓ high chairs
✓ time limit – 8pm

# Mission

11–13 Posterngate, Hull HU1 2JN
**T** 01482 221187
*Licensees*: Ronald and Carol Aston
*Opening times*: 11–11; 12–3, 7–10.30 Sun
*Real ales*: **Old Mill Bitter, Old Curiosity**

City centre pub which was originally a seamen's mission but was converted into its present use in 1995. Owned by Old Mill Brewery, it has a large spacious interior with pews, a pulpit and stained glass windows.

Children are allowed in the designated family area which is called the chapel – that's because it used to be one even though these days you don't feel as if you're sitting in rows waiting for a sermon. This is the sort of city pub which is more suitable for children at lunchtimes as it can get loud and busy in the evening, especially on Monday and Tuesday nights when it's student night and loud music is common.

Food is served lunchtimes only and the limited but good value **kids' menu** has pizzas, sausage and chicken nuggets all with chips. There is also ice cream for 50p. On Friday and Saturday lunchtimes kids can get smaller portions off the main menu, including home-made pies and sweet and sour pork. There's a carvery on Sunday with small portions available as well as the kids' menu.

An impressive-looking pub which is useful for the city centre whose attractions include local museums as well as the Deep, which tells the story of the world's oceans; it also has the world's deepest underwater tunnel through which you can travel in an acrylic lift and see all manner of sealife.

✓ children restricted to certain areas
✓ family room
✗ garden
✗ garden toys
✓ lunchtime meals
✗ evening meals
✗ food lunchtime and evening
✓ children's menu
✓ bottle warming
✓ no smoking area
✗ accommodation
✗ nearby camping and caravan sites
✓ nappy changing – disabled toilets
✗ entertainment
✗ children's certificate
✓ high chairs
✓ time limit – 7pm

## HULL

## Old Grey Mare

193 Cottingham Road, Hull HU5 2EG
**T** 01482 448193   **F** 01482 449316
*Licensee*: Mark Walton-Cole
*Opening times*: 11–11; 12–10.30 Sun
*Real ales*: **Courage Directors**; **Marston's Pedigree**;
**Theakston Cool Cask**

If you've got an older child at Hull University
and want to embarrass them by taking the
rest of the family down for a visit then this
is the place to go as it is opposite the
university and has accommodation. The Old
Grey Mare is a smartly decorated pub/hotel
with a central bar in the middle of a large
L-shaped room and attracts a mix of locals,
university staff and students. It might be
open-planned but there are several different
areas, including a large no-smoking one.

Children are allowed everywhere and
they've even got their own separate toilets.
There's a beer garden and patio for summer
eating and drinking but take care as it leads
into the car park. One stress-reducing and
canny initiative is the sale of 'crazy
playcones', which are filled with toys, sweets
and games and retail at £2.50. Food is served
all day throughout the week with a well-
priced **kids' menu** featuring familiar choices
until 7pm. Smaller portions off the main
menu can also be served where possible;

these include battered cod and gammon.
Sunday lunchtimes sees a choice of roast or
a vegetarian option with child's portions
available; the kids' menu is available too.

A useful stop if you're travelling into
Hull from the north, while in the town
maritime-minded youngsters will love the
Deep (see Mission entry for details).

✗ children restricted to certain areas
✗ family room
✓ garden
✗ garden toys
✓ lunchtime meals
✓ evening meals
✓ food lunchtime and evening
✓ children's menu
✗ bottle warming
✓ no smoking area
✓ accommodation
✗ nearby camping and caravan sites
✗ nappy changing
✗ entertainment
✓ children's certificate
✓ high chairs
✓ time limit – 7.30pm

## NORTH YORKSHIRE

## CARLTON-IN-CLEVELAND

## Blackwell Ox Inn

Carlton-in-Cleveland TS9 7DJ
**T** 01642 712287
www.theblackwellox.co.uk
*Licensee*: Jeff Burton
*Opening times*: 11.30–3, 5.30–11; 11.30–11 Sat;
12–10.30 Sun
*Real ales*: **Black Sheep Best Bitter**; **Worthington
Bitter**; guest beers
*Directions*: off A172, three miles south of Stokesley

Situated in a pretty village on the northern
edge of the Cleveland Hills, this is very
much a traditional pub. However if you and
your family enjoy Thai food, this is the
place to come as three internationally

trained Thai chefs work in the kitchens. British food is not ignored either though. Open fires are the norm during the winter and there's a central bar area with two no-smoking areas where children are allowed (designated as family areas). Outside there are two beer gardens, one with an adventure playground which is described as more assault course than gentle swings and slides! There are also picnic benches out in the garden.

Food is served lunchtimes and evenings throughout the week with a more interesting **kids' menu** than normal which includes chicken goujons, egg noodles, sausage and lasagne, served with chips and beans. Smaller portions off the menu are served where possible and include pasta, small fish and items off the aforementioned Thai menu.

The pub also has its own caravan site, with space for both tourers and residential ones, some of which are especially for families. As for things to do, this is very much 'pack-your-walking-boots' territory with plenty of rambles in the area.

- ✓ children restricted to certain areas
- ✓ family room
- ✓ garden
- ✓ garden toys
- ✓ lunchtime meals
- ✓ evening meals
- ✓ food lunchtime and evening
- ✓ children's menu
- ✓ bottle warming
- ✓ no smoking area
- ✗ accommodation
- ✓ nearby camping and caravan sites
- ✗ nappy changing
- ✗ entertainment
- ✗ children's certificate
- ✓ high chairs
- ✓ time limit – 9pm

## CROPTON

# New Inn

Cropton, near Pickering YO18 8HH
**T** 01751 417330   **F** 01751 417582;
www.croptonbrewery.co.uk
*Licensee*: Philip Lee

*Opening times*: 11–11; 12–10.30 Sun
*Real ales*: **Cropton King Billy, Two Pints, Honey Gold, Scoresby Stout, Balmy Mild, Monkmans Slaughter**; guest beers
*Directions*: turn off A170 between Pickering and Kirkbymoorside

Friendly family-run country inn on the southern edge of the North Yorkshire Moors National Park which started brewing its own beers in 1984, reviving a Cropton tradition that went back to 1613. Like most New Inns, this one is hundreds of years old and has a traditional interior, though a modern note is struck by a display of paintings on the walls by local artists; if you fancy one, they are for sale.

Children are allowed in the no-smoking restaurant, games room and the conservatory which acts as the family room. This opens out onto a beer garden with picnic tables, while beyond are the landscaped gardens which open up into the car park so keep an eye on children. There is also a fish pond which is gated off from the main area.

Food is served all week, both lunchtime and in the evening. The **kids' menu** offers up familiar choices but also includes small steak pies. On Sundays, there are small roasts available alongside the normal kids' menu. This is a very traditional and welcoming country inn which has a fair selection of its home-brewed ales, as well as a real cider.

There's an abundance of country walks in the area, while other attractions include the Flamingo Theme Park and Zoo at Kirby Misperton and the World War II museum Eden Camp near Malton, both of which are a short drive away.

- ✓ children restricted to certain areas
- ✓ family room
- ✓ garden
- ✗ garden toys
- ✓ lunchtime meals
- ✓ evening meals
- ✓ food lunchtime and evening
- ✓ children's menu
- ✓ bottle warming
- ✓ no smoking area

✓ accommodation
✓ nearby camping and caravan sites
✗ nappy changing
✗ entertainment
✗ children's certificate
✓ high chairs
✗ time limit

## EAST WITTON

# Cover Bridge Inn

East Witton DL8 4SQ
T 01969 623250
E enquiries@thecoverbridgeinn.co.uk
www.thecoverbridgeinn.co.uk
*Licensee*: Nick Harrington
*Opening times*: 11–11; 12–10.30 Sun
*Real ales*: **Black Sheep Bitter**; **Taylor Landlord**;
**Theakston Old Peculier**; guest beers
*Directions*: on A6108, ¾ mile north of village

Charming old coaching inn which dates
back to the 1670s and can be found in a
beautiful location on the banks of the River
Cover in Wensleydale. Inside the
atmosphere is traditional and cosy with
open fires in the winter, bench seating and
old beams. There are usually no less than
eight real ales available.

Children are allowed throughout the
multi-roomed pub which includes a no-
smoking dining room, while there's a large
beer garden with a Wendy house, swings
and climbing frame.

Food is served lunchtimes and evenings.
The **kids' menu** has familiar choices though
with home-made chips, while small
portions off the main menu are available
where possible. These include home-made
pies, steaks, scampi and the pub's
renowned ham and eggs. The latter gained
celebrity status when served on TV to
*Countdown*'s Richard Whiteley who lives
nearby and occasionally pops in the pub.
Sunday lunchtime sees a choice of two
roasts (children's portions served) as well as
a slimmed-down selection from the main
bar menu.

As this is gorgeous Dales country there
are many local walks, while also worth a

visit is the Forbidden Corner in nearby
Coverdale, 'a unique labyrinth of tunnels,
chambers, follies and surprises created in a
four acre garden'.

✗ children restricted to certain areas
✗ family room
✓ garden
✓ garden toys
✓ lunchtime meals
✓ evening meals
✓ food lunchtime and evening
✓ children's menu
✓ bottle warming
✓ no smoking area
✓ accommodation
✓ nearby camping and caravan sites
✓ nappy changing – women's toilets
✗ entertainment
✗ children's certificate
✓ high chairs
✗ time limit

## NUN MONKTON

# Alice Hawthorn

The Green, Nun Monkton YO26 8EW
T 01423 330303
E alicehawthorn@hotmail.com
www.alicehawthorn.co.uk
*Licensee*: Shane Winship
*Opening times*: 12–2, 6–11; 12–10.30 Sun
*Real ales*: **Camerons Strongarm**; **John Smith
Bitter**; **Taylor Landlord**; guest beer
*Directions*: off the A59, York–Harrogate road

Rural village local which was named after a
famous racehorse of the 19th century and is
situated in a village which has a maypole
and duck pond on its village green. In World
War II, it was a favourite watering hole with
Canadian airmen who were stationed
nearby and the dwindling survivors from
those tumultuous days still turn up from
time to time to remember their precarious
youth. These days it's also popular with
those using the nearby rivers Ouse and Nidd
as well as walkers. The pub will happily
suggest local walks of interest if you ask.

Inside there's a heavily beamed lounge
with plenty of brass and a brick fireplace, a
public bar and no-smoking dining room

with children allowed everywhere. Outside there's a secure garden with a play area which includes swings and a slide.

Food is served lunchtimes and evenings throughout the week with the **kids' menu** featuring familiar choices, but smaller portions off the main menu can also be served where possible; examples include scampi and curry. Sunday lunchtime sees a choice of roast (small portions available) alongside the main menus.

There's also a paddock attached to the pub where you can pitch your tent – but do call first. As well as the local walks, York with all its historical attractions (including the National Railway Museum) is a short drive away.

✗ children restricted to certain areas
✗ family room
✓ garden
✓ garden toys
✓ lunchtime meals
✓ evening meals
✓ food lunchtime and evening
✓ children's menu
✓ bottle warming
✓ no smoking area
✗ accommodation
✓ nearby camping and caravan sites
✗ nappy changing
✗ entertainment
✓ children's certificate
✓ high chairs
✗ time limit

## ROBIN HOOD'S BAY

# Victoria Hotel

Station Road, Robin Hood's Bay YO22 4RL
**T** 01947 880205
*Licensee*: Lydia Gibson
*Opening times*: 12–2.30 (12–11 summer); 12–11 Fri, Sat; 12–10.30 Sun
*Real ales*: **Camerons Bitter, Strongarm**; guest beer

As the name might suggest, the Victoria was constructed in the time of said queen and is an imposing building which sits on the cliff overlooking the old fishing village which was named after everyone's favourite outlaw. No one knows quite what

he was doing so far from Nottingham though one legend suggests that Robin came to the bay to try and find ships for an expedition to the continent.

There are marvellous views of the bay and village from the hotel which has a welcoming bar, restaurant and a no-smoking family room where children are allowed. Colouring books and pencils are supplied to keep them entertained while parents enjoy a drink and study the menu. There's a garden outside which is safe and fenced off but parents should be aware that it is also on the edge of a cliff: so keep a beady eye out. Every Sunday at midday a cannon is fired from the clifftop.

Food is served lunchtimes and evenings throughout the week with the **kids' menu** featuring familiar choices as well as beef stew. More interesting is the main menu with its highly regarded homecooked dishes; smaller portions are available where possible and these include sausage and mash and salads.

A beautiful spot for a drink and something to eat with the old rambling village of Robin Hood's Bay well worth investigating, while Whitby with its ghoulish associations with Dracula (perfect teenage fodder) is a short drive to the north.

✓ children restricted to certain areas
✓ family room
✓ garden
✗ garden toys
✓ lunchtime meals
✓ evening meals
✓ food lunchtime and evening
✓ children's menu
✓ bottle warming
✓ no smoking area
✓ accommodation
✗ nearby camping and caravan sites
✓ nappy changing – women's toilets
✗ entertainment
✗ children's certificate
✓ high chairs
✗ time limit

## SCARBOROUGH

# Cricketers

119 Marine Road, Scarborough YO12 7HU
**T** 01723 365864
**E** cricketerspublichouse@supanet.com
*Licensee*: Stuart Neilson
*Opening times*: 12–11; 12–10.30 Sun
*Real ales*: **Taylor Landlord**; **Tetley Bitter**; guest beers

If you and your family are cricket fans, this is the place for you – it's situated right next door to the second home of Yorkshire CC and gets wildly busy whenever there's a match on. Situated on a clifftop with splendid views over North Bay, it's a traditional pub with children allowed everywhere. However in the summer there is an upstairs function room which is used as a family room – not a tough call as it hosts children's entertainment in summer including karaoke. There is also a pool table for the older kids. There is a garden but children must be supervised.

Food is served all day throughout the week with the **kids' menu** featuring familiar choices as well as a free drink. There is also a roast choice served daily and small portions are available. Scarborough has plenty to occupy the family, including three miles of golden beaches, 12th-century Scarborough Castle and the Sealife Centre in North Bay which is home to over 70 species of marine creatures.

✗ children restricted to certain areas
✓ family room
✓ garden
✗ garden toys
✓ lunchtime meals
✓ evening meals
✓ food lunchtime and evening
✓ children's menu
✓ bottle warming
✗ no smoking area
✗ accommodation
✗ nearby camping and caravan sites
✓ nappy changing – women's toilets
✓ entertainment
✗ children's certificate
✓ high chairs
✗ time limit

## *SOUTH YORKSHIRE*

## BARNSLEY

# Keresforth Hall

Keresforth Hall Road, Kingstone, Barnsley S70 6NH
**T** 01226 284226
www.keresforth.co.uk
*Licensee*: John Fulton
*Opening times*: 11–2, 7–11; 12–10.30 Sun
*Real ales*: **Clark's Classic Blonde**; guest beers

Family owned and run establishment which can be found on the edge of Barnsley where the town starts to give way to the countryside. Originally the seat of the local Lancaster family, it has extensive rural views from its large gardens, while the interior is comfortable and friendly.

Children are allowed in the light and modern Peacock Conservatory which is a casual drinking and dining area with peacocks on the wallpaper, and a big stuffed one keeping watch over everyone. The conservatory is also no-smoking and recently won a clean air award, while there are board games available for children. Outside to the front there's a walled garden which leads out into the car park, so keep an eye on small children. Swings, a slide and a climbing frame are available while summer bank holidays sees occasional barbecues and bouncy castles.

Food is served lunchtimes and evenings Monday-Saturday and all day up to 6pm on Sunday. The **kids' menu** features familiar choices as well as a healthy option of jacket potatoes, pasta or salad. Smaller portions off the main menu can also be served for most dishes, including a selection off the carvery which is available evenings and weekend lunchtimes. As well as the carvery on Sunday lunchtime choices from the main menus are also served.

This is a pleasant part of Barnsley and close to Locke Park where there are activity walks. Further afield the Elsecar Heritage Centre is a short drive away and here you will find various craft units and a steam engine area which gets visits from Thomas the Tank Engine.

✓ children restricted to certain areas
✓ family room
✓ garden
✓ garden toys
✓ lunchtime meals
✓ evening meals
✓ food lunchtime and evening
✓ children's menu
✓ bottle warming
✓ no smoking area
✗ accommodation
✗ nearby camping and caravan sites
✓ nappy changing – cloakroom
✓ entertainment
✗ children's certificate
✓ high chairs
✗ time limit

## PENISTONE

# Cubley Hall

Mortimer Road, Penistone S36 9DF
T 01226 766086   F 01226 767335
E cubley@ukonline.co.uk
*Licensee*: John Wigfield
*Opening times*: 11–11; 12–10.30 Sun
*Real ales*: **Tetley Bitter**, **Burton Ale**, **Imperial**; guest beers
*Directions*: off the A629

Cubley Hall started life as a moorland farm back in the 1700s when it was on the main pack-horse route over the Pennines. Other incarnations have been a private house and an orphanage, which is when it was supposed to have been haunted by the ghost of Flora who appeared at the bedsides of sick children. It became a free house in 1983 and has also since developed into a popular hotel and restaurant, with the conversion of an oak-beamed and slate-floored barn.

Inside the sympathetically refurbished interior there's plenty of room and children are allowed in the designated family room which is spacious and overlooks the hostelry's pleasant gardens; they are also allowed in the no-smoking restaurant for meals on Sundays. Outside there is a secure play area with climbing frame and slides.

Excellent food is served all day throughout the whole week and while the **kids' menu** features familiar choices it also has home-made lasagne and sautéed chicken pieces with garden peas and pasta. A free vanilla ice cream cornet comes with the meal. Sunday lunchtime sees a carvery with child-sized portions available; selections from the kids' menu are also served.

Penistone is located on the edge of the Peak District National Park and there are many local walks. Further afield in Rotherham there's Magna, a science adventure centre with sound and light shows, giant water cannons and rockets amongst its attractions.

✓ children restricted to certain areas
✓ family room
✓ garden
✓ garden toys
✓ lunchtime meals
✓ evening meals
✓ food lunchtime and evening
✓ children's menu
✓ bottle warming
✓ no smoking area
✓ accommodation
✗ nearby camping and caravan sites
✓ nappy changing – women's toilets
✗ entertainment
✗ children's certificate
✓ high chairs
✗ time limit

*WEST YORKSHIRE*

## ALLERTON BYWATER

# Boat Inn

Boat Lane, Allerton Bywater WF10 2BX
T 01977 552216
www.boatpub.co.uk
*Licensee*: Kieron Lockwood
*Opening times*: 12–3, 6–11; 12–11 Sat; 12–10.30 Sun

*Real ales*: Boat Man In The Boat, Tetley Bitter; guest beers

Old 17th-century inn which is situated in a lovely position by the River Aire. If you're a rugby league fan then this is the place to go as it is run by the son of former Great Britain rugby league captain Brian Lockwood and full of his sporting mementos around the bar. The Boat Brewery can also be found at the back of the pub.

Children are allowed in the no-smoking family/dining room which opens out to the beer garden and the newly built play area; here there is a plastic tree house, climbing frame and other play facilities. If you're on a camping holiday, then the pub is only too happy to let you and the family pitch the tent in the large two-acre garden, providing you call first.

Food is served 12pm–2pm, 6pm–9pm Monday–Friday, 12pm–2.30pm, 6pm–9.30pm Saturday and 12pm–3.30pm, 6pm–9pm Sunday. The **kids' menu** has familiar choices though smaller portions off most of the main menu can also be served; these include chillis, pasta, salads and steaks; there are also sandwiches. It is advised to book for food. Sunday lunchtimes sees a roast (kids' portions available) as well as specials and the children's menu.

Located in good walking country, while for more materialistic pleasures there's a designer outlet village just a short drive away in Castleford.

✓ children restricted to certain areas
✓ family room
✓ garden
✓ garden toys
✓ lunchtime meals
✓ evening meals
✓ food lunchtime and evening
✓ children's menu
✓ bottle warming
✓ no smoking area
✗ accommodation
✗ nearby camping and caravan sites
✓ nappy changing – disabled toilets
✗ entertainment
✗ children's certificate
✓ high chairs
✗ time limit

# Navigation

Broad Cut Road, Calder Grove WF4 3DS
**T** 01924 274361
*Licensee*: Samantha Hall
*Opening times*: 12–11; 12–10.30 Sun
*Real ales*: **Taylor Landlord**; **Tetley Bitter**; guest beers summer
*Directions*: 400 yards off Denby Dale Road over canal bridge

Historical two-roomed pub now owned by Punch Taverns situated in an unique position on an island. The river Calder is on one side and the Aire & Calder Navigation canal on the other. Unsurprisingly, this makes it a popular stop for narrow-boaters in the summer. No children allowed in the lounge, with families directed to the no-smoking family room which has its own soft play area; there's further fun to be had outside with a large play area which includes wooden climbing frames, slides and a large plastic playhouse; be aware that the garden, even though it is large, is next to the towpath of the canal. A bouncy castle is also available through the summer.

Food is served 12pm–9pm every day in summer, lunchtimes and evenings and all day at weekends in the winter. There is a **kids' menu** with familiar choices, which come with a free toy. Smaller portions off the main menu are available as well; these include scampi, curry, chilli and gammon. There's a roast on Sunday lunchtime with children's portions available; the kids' menu is also served then.

You can enjoy a canalside walk after lunch, while further afield towards Wakefield there's Pugneys Country Park, Kirklees Light Railway and Sandal Castle. Note: even though it will remain open, a large refurbishment of the pub is planned in the autumn of 2003.

✓ children restricted to certain areas
✓ family room
✓ garden
✓ garden toys
✓ lunchtime meals
✓ evening meals

✓food lunchtime and evening
✓children's menu
✓bottle warming
✓no smoking area
✗ accommodation
✗ nearby camping and caravan sites
✓nappy changing – ladies
✗ entertainment
✗ children's certificate
✓high chairs
✗ time limit

## ILKLEY

# Riverside Hotel

Riverside Gardens, Bridge Lane, Ilkley LS29 9EU
**T** 1943 607338　**F** 01943 607338
*Licensees*: Christine and Kelvin Dobson
*Opening times*: 11–11; 12–10.30 Sun
*Real ales*: **Samuel Smith OBB; Taylor Best Bitter; Tetley Bitter**

Smart hotel built at the end of the Victorian era and located in a charming spot alongside the River Wharfe. Nearby is also the old Pack Horse Bridge which is where the Dalesway officially starts. Inside there's a tastefully decorated two-roomed bar with children allowed anywhere apart from at the main bar area; the dining room is no-smoking.

There's a beer garden outside but no swings or slides, but after finishing your drink and meal the play area in the Riverside Gardens Park is a 200-yard stroll away; it is separate from the hotel so you can't take your drink over. Here children can find swings, slides and other play activities; in the summer there is usually a bouncy castle.

The hotel serves food from midday–6pm every day throughout the whole week. The **kids' menu** has familiar choices as well as a small shepherd's pie, which makes a change from chicken nuggets. Sunday lunchtimes sees a choice of roasts (small portions available) as well as the kids' menu: please note even though food is served until 6pm on Sunday, the roast choice is only available between 12–2pm.

A very friendly establishment which has a good local feel, even though it also caters

for the many visitors to this popular Yorkshire town. There are plenty of things to do in Ilkley itself including walks in the Riverside Park Gardens, the Manor House Museum and a local swimming pool. There is also the world-famous Ilkley Moor where nature-loving youngsters can follow a nature trail.

✗ children restricted to certain areas
✗ family room
✗ garden
✗ garden toys
✓lunchtime meals
✓evening meals
✓food lunchtime and evening
✓children's menu
✓bottle warming – milk only
✓no smoking area
✓accommodation
✓nearby camping and caravan sites
✗ nappy changing
✗ entertainment
✗ children's certificate
✓high chairs
✓time limit – 9pm

## WARMFIELD

# Plough

45 Warmfield Lane, Warmfield WF1 5TL
**T** 01924 892007
*Licensee*: Brian Stringer
*Opening times*: 12–11; 12–10.30 Sun
*Real ales*: **John Smith's Bitter; Theakston Best Bitter, Mild, Old Peculier**
*Directions*: 400 yards from A655

Traditional 18th-century inn situated in the Lower Calder Valley which has been added to over the centuries but still manages to retain a rustic charm with solid wooden beams, open log fires and old pictures of the village on the wall. One reason to visit is that children's meals are free providing the adults with them are also eating. Can't be bad!

Children are allowed in the dining area and a separate family room which can be found to the side of the pub. Here there are a couple of rides, a driving machine and for the older kids a pool table. There's a walled beer garden to the front of the pub with a play area; there's also an occasional bouncy castle during the summer.

Food is served lunchtimes and evenings throughout the week with familiar choices on the free **kids' menu** (see above); smaller portions off the main menu can also be served where possible. These include corned beef hash and scampi; there are also sandwiches. Sunday lunchtime sees roast dishes only with small portions available for children.

Family attractions in the area include Pugneys Country Park which is a short drive away to the south of nearby Wakefield. Here there are lakeside walks, picnic spots and opportunities for birdwatching.

✓ children restricted to certain areas
✓ family room
✓ garden
✓ garden toys
✓ lunchtime meals
✓ evening meals
✓ food lunchtime and evening
✓ children's menu
✓ bottle warming
✗ no smoking area
✓ accommodation
✗ nearby camping and caravan sites
✗ nappy changing
✗ entertainment
✗ children's certificate
✓ high chairs
✓ time limit – 9pm

# Is Pub Food making our children sick?

Sausage and chips, burger and chips, fish fingers and chips, chicken nuggets and chips. Standard kids' fare in the majority of our pubs. There's no doubt that children almost universally adore this kind of food, so much so that in this book we've gone to great pains to point out when chips AREN'T available – to forestall any tantrums. But is this kind of 'chips with everything' menu really good for our children? Should we be concerned that this is the accepted diet for kids in British pubs?

Children's food expert Amanda Cross, author of *Food Boosters for Kids* (Hamlyn), says a little of this kind of food, as an occasional treat, is fine. But if children eat this sort of food on a regular basis then, yes, we should be worried. 'Junk foods are laden with saturated fats, salt and additives,' she says, 'all of which are detrimental to your child's health.' She explains that a diet based on these foods can lead to 'attention deficit disorder, compromised immune system functioning and habits that will lead children to a lifetime of obesity, disease and disability.'

Strong words indeed. Surely the odd chip can't do that much harm? 'No food is a problem if you only consume it once a week,' says nutritional health expert and author Linda Lazarides,

'but I am worried that chips, nuggets etc. are now known as "children's foods" as if somehow they ought to be standard fare. Chips may contain a minute amount of vitamin C but they would never come high on the list of vitamin C-containing foods. What's really going on is that proper nutritional standards are now being sacrificed to convenience.'

Unfortunately chips (along with processed foods such as burgers, sausages and chicken nuggets) are all very high in salt. Many studies have shown that a high sodium (salt) intake is associated with high blood pressure. A salt-rich diet can also increase the amount of calcium excreted in the urine, reducing the levels of this essential mineral available for healthy growth. In addition they are usually deep-fried making them high in hydrogenated fat, responsible for increasing the risk of coronary heart disease. To add insult to injury, Linda Lazarides points out that foods loaded with fat, sugar, salt and flavour enhancers actually get kids addicted to them.

'Parents see no harm in what they're doing,' she says, 'because the lack of nutrition education in schools means that most people grow up unconsciously relying on TV advertising for their nutrition information. Children are shown so often on TV eating chips and convenience food that it's easy to imagine this is what children are supposed to eat.'

All pretty depressing. Yet it needn't be so. While the odd chip won't do any damage, it's worth trying to wean your children onto a wider variety of foods. Pubs, of course, will say that they're merely giving people what they want. But it's a bit disingenuous and pubs could, frankly, do better. Children are far more open to trying new foods while out and a pub which offers a wider choice of child-friendly options could be a parent's godsend. We found that, while the vast majority of pubs think no further than the chip, there are a small but growing number of publicans who are more imaginative.

The Cambridge Blue in Cambridge is a chip and chicken nugget free zone. 'We don't have a fryer because we try and encourage healthy eating,' says the pub's chef Catherine Durance. 'In our experience kids are always happy to have something which is especially prepared for them but which is still considered to be an adult choice, hence half portions of the main menu. They mainly go for sausage and mash but half portions of the Sunday roast are also popular.'

Heather Humphreys is the landlady of the Rising Sun in Woodland in Devon and even though the pub serves chicken goujons and chips on its kids' menu, they are home-made as is everything else on the menu. 'We don't do chicken nuggets because we don't know what's in them,' she says. 'We've always done our own chicken goujons (which we call nuggets) and what we do is buy chicken breasts and make them from that. We also do our own chips. It all goes down well with children. We also offer potatoes and vegetables and they can have things off the main menu in small portions. I think the reason a lot of them like chicken nuggets is that they are conditioned to like them what with McDonald's etc. It does take a bit more time to prepare but our priority is doing local food and cooking it ourselves.'

'Other pub lunches might be baked potatoes with home-made baked beans and a crunchy raw salad with peanuts and fruit pieces,' suggests Linda Lazarides, 'Or sweet and sour fish and vegetables on a bed of rice. Or pasta with a sauce made from fresh tomatoes and olive oil, topped with cheese.'

If you're laughing hollowly at the very idea of your local coming up with anything like this, you may be better off trying the advice of Mary Whiting, author of *Dump the Junk!* (Moonscape). She suggests that when eating in pubs you avoid the children's menu altogether and either order small portions off the main menu (most pubs in the book offer this option) or simply ask for another plate and share your food with them. This actually works quite well, especially on Sunday lunchtimes when many pubs offer a heaped plate of roast meat, potatoes and veg. When I go for Sunday lunch at my local we always ask for a small plate for James.

How wonderful it would be if pubs could lead the way in encouraging children (and the rest of us) into healthier eating. Publicans are happy to serve real ale (or at least the ones in this book do) so why won't they serve real food too?

## Tips for Landlords

Keen to offer more kid-friendly choices but don't know how? Try these:

- Real pizzas with smiley faces (tomatoes and strips of carrot for the features).
- Humus with chunky crudités for dipping.
- Home-made fish cakes – or fingers (grilled, not deep fried).
- Soups: most children will eat soup if it's pureed – no bits!
- Real burgers with crunchy salad.
- Pasta (interesting shapes such as spirals work well) with Bolognese or tomato sauce.
- Home-made potato wedges or chips.
- Salad bars: kids love making their own choices.
- Fresh fruit salad.

# Scotland

*Craw Inn*
AUCHENCROW, BORDERS

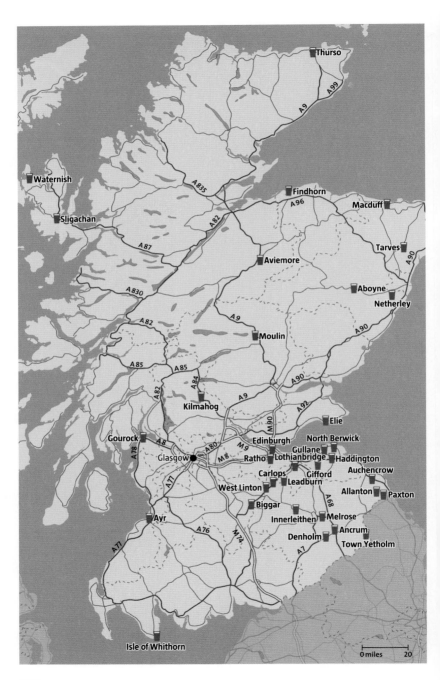

0 miles 20

SCOTTISH pubs have the luck of being located in some of the most spectacular scenery in the British isles – overshadowed by brooding mountains, still and tranquil by the side of moody lochs or neighbours to ruined castles where dark deeds were the order of the day. They can be found in atmospheric market towns, quiet isolated villages and within the boundaries of bustling cities. There also seems to be more acceptance of children in pubs than south of the border, with a lot of pubs having children's certificates. Furthermore, the Scottish brewing scene is growing with more small breweries thriving and the likes of Caledonian and Belhaven going from strength to strength.

The country has many faces. There are the rolling mountains and hillsides of the border country with its bloody history of battles, cattle raids and long-lasting feuds. In stark contrast, further north you will find the massive peaks of the Highlands where dedicated souls battle the crags and peaks of some of the cruellest mountains in Britain. You could stop off for a spot of skiing in the Cairngorms or, if you fancy swapping a ski-lift for a cosy railway carriage, there's the Strathspey Steam Railway which runs into Aviemore. You can also take in the Highland Games in the summer.

Those families who like mucking about in boats are more likely to make for the cool, clear waters around the islands, or maybe spend time casting flies on rushing rivers; and what about taking the kids on a monster hunt around the shores of Loch Ness?

This outdoor life is the number one family activity and there are all sorts of countryside walks ranging from gentle ambles with a buggy along a long sandy beach where Mel Gibson once held Horatio's fate in his hands to more strenuous treks in the rugged landscapes further north where red deer, grouse and osprey are often seen. These are also great areas for cycling with the facilities and touring options for cyclists improving all the time. Many pubs will let you know about local walks and rides – ask your landlord.

For more urbane and weatherproof pleasures there's the splendour of Edinburgh where the sights include Arthur's Seat, Princes Street, the Scott Monument, Greyfriars Bobby and the National Museum of Scotland. Even though the city centre bars and pubs are not too conducive to children, there are ones on the outskirts which are: how does a pint of Deuchars IPA with a plate of haggis, neeps and tatties while keeping an eye on the Firth of Forth grab you?

The east coast has the islands and the city of Glasgow and its environs. There are also seaside resorts such as Ayr and Gourock, which overlooks the Firth of Clyde. The pubs in this area are a resourceful bunch: if it's a rainy summer's day and you're on Skye there's an award-winning pub with its own indoor play area; there are also usually eight real ales on in this establishment during the summer. Book the holiday now!

# BORDERS

## ALLANTON

## Allanton Inn

Allanton TD11 3JZ
**T** 01890 818260
*Licensee*: John Philt
*Opening times*: 12–2.30, 6–11 (1am Fri); 12–1am Sat; 12–11 Sun
*Real ales*: beer range varies
*Directions*: off B6437

Former coaching inn in a conservation village surrounding by rolling Borders countryside; keep an eye out for the original hitching rings for horses which can still be seen on the outside of the inn. The bar is at the front and has stone flagstones, while the rear has a pool table and variety of other pub games; there's a log fire in the winter. There's also a safe garden where kids can run off steam.

Children are allowed in the games room and there are toys for them to play with; they are also welcome in the no-smoking dining room if eating.

Food is served lunchtimes and evenings through the week. The **kids' menu** has familiar choices while smaller portions off the main menu can be served where possible; examples include steak pie, scampi and sandwiches. Roast dishes are served Sunday lunchtime (small portions available), plus the main menus. There is usually an interesting selection of three real ales.

A traditional and friendly pub which can serve as a base for touring the Borders, while further afield it's a short drive to the historic towns of Berwick-upon-Tweed or Coldstream.

✓ children restricted to certain areas
✗ family room
✓ garden
✗ garden toys
✓ lunchtime meals
✓ evening meals
✓ food lunchtime and evening
✓ children's menu
✓ bottle warming
✓ no smoking area
✓ accommodation
✓ nearby camping and caravan sites
✗ nappy changing
✗ entertainment
✓ children's certificate
✓ high chairs
✗ time limit

## ANCRUM

## Cross Keys Inn

The Green, Ancrum TD8 6XH
**T** 01835 830344
**E** crosskeys@ukgateway.net
*Licensee*: David Arnold
*Opening times*: 12–11 (midnight Thurs, Sat, 1am Fri); 12.30–11 Sun
*Real ales*: **Caledonian Deuchars IPA**; guest beers summer
*Directions*: on B6400, off A68

There was a battle in this part of the world back in 1545, when the Scottish army trounced an English one 5000 strong. Local legend has it that one of the casualties on the Scottish side was a young woman called Lilliard who, according to a totally implausible rhyme, went down fighting while standing on the stumps of her amputated legs! Things are quieter now and the Cross Keys is a haven of calm where you can mull over the area's bloody history. Unchanged since the start of the last century, when the local brewery did a spot of modernisation, this is a gem of a country pub with half-pine panelling and tables made from old sewing stands in the main bar, while in the roomy back lounge (which was once the cellar) you can still see the overhead tramlines used to move the barrels.

Children are allowed in the lounge which stretches back into several areas including a no-smoking dining space. There's also a pleasant garden at the back.

Food is served lunchtimes and evenings throughout the week. The **kids' menu** changes quite regularly and features familiar dishes, including home-made chicken nuggets; however, the kitchen will also do the sort of unusual things that kids like such as jam or bacon sandwiches. Do ask is what I was told. Smaller portions can also be served off the main menu, including scampi or steak and ale in a Yorkshire pudding.

Apart from doing a battlefield tour on Ancrum Moor, try a visit to Harestanes Countryside Visitor's Centre which is very close to Ancrum. Here converted farm buildings are home to a selection of indoor and outdoor activities with guided walks, activities and events taking place.

✓ children restricted to certain areas
✗ family room
✓ garden
✗ garden toys
✓ lunchtime meals
✓ evening meals
✓ food lunchtime and evening
✓ children's menu
✗ bottle warming
✓ no smoking area
✓ accommodation
✗ nearby camping and caravan sites
✗ nappy changing
✗ entertainment
✓ children's certificate
✓ high chairs
✗ time limit

## AUCHENCROW

# Craw Inn

Auchencrow TD14 5LS
T 01890 761253
*Licensee*: Trevor Wilson
*Opening times*: 12–2.30, 6–11 (midnight Fri); 12–12 Sat; 12.30–11 Sun
*Real ales*: beer range varies
*Directions*: on B6438, follow signs from A1

Peaceful rural inn dating from the early 18th century which retains its character even though it has been refurbished down the years; at about the time of the inn's construction the village had a reputation for being home to many witches and some were reputedly hanged in the pub's garden. Inside there's a wooden-beamed bar with bench seating, a lounge and restaurant where local produce is used in many dishes.

Children are allowed in the no-smoking restaurant and designated parts of the bar. There's also a beer garden at the back of the pub where families can sit out in the summer.

Food is served lunchtimes and evenings throughout the week, with a **kids' menu** featuring familiar choices. Smaller portions off the main menu can also be served; these will include pate, home-made soups, sandwiches and baguettes, though the restaurant has more elaborate dishes many of which cannot be cut in half. There are usually two real ales available, mainly coming from smaller breweries.

This unspoilt village is a few minutes drive from the A1 and on the edge of the Lammermuir Hills where there are plenty of walking opportunities. Other attractions within a short drive include Eyemouth Museum and Duns Castle Nature Reserve.

✓ children restricted to certain areas
✗ family room
✓ garden
✗ garden toys
✓ lunchtime meals
✓ evening meals
✓ food lunchtime and evening
✓ children's menu
✗ bottle warming

✓ no smoking area
✓ accommodation
✗ nearby camping and caravan sites
✓ nappy changing – disabled toilets
✗ entertainment
✓ children's certificate
✓ high chairs
✓ time limit – 8pm

## CARLOPS

### Allan Ramsay Hotel

Main Street, Carlops EH26 9NF
**T** 01968 660258
www.allanramsayhotel.co.uk
*Licensee*: David Kinnear
*Opening times*: 12 (12.30 Sun)–midnight
*Real ales*: **Caledonian Deuchars IPA**; guest beer

The name of this small village nestling beside the Pentland Hills reputedly comes from the Gaelic for witch's leap. Legend has that local witches would get their jollies by jumping off a couple of stones near the pub. As for the Allan Ramsey, the origins of this family-run hotel are more prosaic, having been converted from a flax mill which was built in the 1790s. Inside, there's an open-planned bar area with plenty of character and tartan upholstery, while budding numismatists (coin-collectors to the rest of us) will want to look at the collection of pre-decimal pennies which are embedded in the bar (the 'penny bar').

Children are allowed everywhere but after 8pm they have to leave or decamp to the restaurant if they're eating; there's a garden for summer eating and drinking.

Food is available all day throughout the whole week, with a **kids' menu** serving familiar choices. Smaller portions off the main menu are also served including home-made burgers, risottos, half a haddock and vegetarian options. A busy Sunday lunchtime sees a roast (small portions available) alongside the main menus as well as several specials such as Irish stew to warm up the walkers who stop by.

Located in beautiful countryside there are plenty of opportunities for country walks and pony-trekking, while Edinburgh is a short drive away.

✗ children restricted to certain areas
✗ family room
✓ garden
✗ garden toys
✓ lunchtime meals
✓ evening meals
✓ food lunchtime and evening
✓ children's menu
✓ bottle warming
✗ no smoking area
✓ accommodation
✓ nearby camping and caravan sites
✗ nappy changing
✗ entertainment
✓ high chairs
✗ children's certificate
✗ time limit

## DENHOLM

### Fox & Hounds Inn

Main Street, Denholm TD9 8NU
**T** 01450 870247
*Licensee*: Stewart Mabon
*Opening times*: 11–3, 5–midnight (1am Fri);
11–1am Sat; 12.30–midnight Sun
*Real ales*: **Wylam Gold Tankard**, guest beer

Traditional local dating from the 1750s and situated opposite the village green. Inside there's a cosy main bar area with original beams and stuffed animal heads hanging on the walls.

Children are allowed in the separate dining area. They can also go outside to the sheltered courtyard and there's a play area with swings and climbing frame.

Food is served at lunchtimes throughout the week all year round, and evenings March-November. The **kids' menu** offers familiar choices with chips as well as jacket potatoes. Smaller portions off the main menu can be served including lasagne, scampi and small fish dishes. Most Sunday lunchtimes see a choice of roasts (small portions available) alongside the main menu.

There are a few country walks in the area and the pub has several books detailing them, while Jedburgh, which is associated with Mary Queen of Scots, is five miles away.

✓ children restricted to certain areas
✗ family room
✓ garden
✓ garden toys
✓ lunchtime meals
✓ evening meals
✓ food lunchtime and evening
✓ children's menu
✓ bottle warming
✗ no smoking area
✓ accommodation
✓ nearby camping and caravan sites
✓ nappy changing – women's toilets
✗ entertainment
✓ children's certificate
✓ high chairs
✓ time limit – 8pm

## INNERLEITHEN

# Traquair Arms Hotel

Traquair Road, Innerleithen EH44 6PD
**T** 01896 830229   **T** 01896 830260
**E** traquair.arms@scottishborders.com
www.traquair-arms-hotel.co.uk
*Licensee*: Dianne Johnston
*Opening times*: 12–11 (midnight Fri, Sat);
11.30–11.30 Sun
*Real ales*: beer range varies
*Directions*: B709, off A72

Family-run hotel which dates from the 18th century and isn't too far from the famous Traquair House Brewery which usually supplies one of the real ales on tap here (the hotel is the only establishment outside Edinburgh which sells Traquair House's splendid beers on draft). The other two are selected from a wide range produced by the other Borders brewery Broughton and may include the likes of Greenmantle and Merlin's Ale. Inside there's a comfortable lounge with log fires in the winter, local pictures on the wall and a tank of goldfish. There is also a comfortable no-smoking dining room. Children are welcome throughout.

Food is served all day from midday until 9pm all week. The **kids' menu** has familiar choices with chips, though smaller portions off the main menu are available

where possible; these include home-made pies as well as sandwiches. There are also daily specials.

The hotel is set in a beautiful part of the Borders area, and there are many riverside and forest walks including the Southern Upland Way. Close by and well worth a visit is Traquair House which is the oldest inhabited house in Scotland; note that it is closed during the winter.

✗ children restricted to certain areas
✗ family room
✓ garden
✗ garden toys
✓ lunchtime meals
✓ evening meals
✓ food lunchtime and evening
✓ children's menu
✓ bottle warming
✓ no smoking area
✓ accommodation
✓ nearby camping and caravan sites
✓ nappy changing – women's toilets
✗ entertainment
✗ children's certificate
✓ high chairs
✗ time limit

## MELROSE

# King's Arms Hotel

High Street, Melrose TD6 9PB
**T** 01896 822143
www.kingsarmsmelrose.co.uk
*Licensees*: Mike and Helen Dalgetty
*Opening times*: 11 (12 Sun)–midnight
*Real ales*: **Tetley Bitter**, **Burton Ale**; guest beer

Rugby fans will feel at home in this old coaching inn which goes back to the 1790s. Famous Scottish side Melrose used the establishment as a meeting place in their early days, while the main bar has a rugby theme plus a largescreen TV for sports events. Tradition also gets a nod in with a wooden floor, church pews and old pictures of the area on the wall. There's also a comfortable lounge, with an old decoratively carved door set into the ceiling, and a no-smoking restaurant. Children are allowed in the lounge and restaurant.

Food is served lunchtimes and evenings all week, with the large **kids' menu** offering familiar choices as well as pasta and curries. Smaller portions can be ordered off the main menu including pizza, pasta, lasagne, haddock and chips and sandwiches at lunch. Sunday lunchtime sees a roast with small ones for the children; the main menus are also available.

The historic town of Melrose is set in the midst of beautiful Borders countryside and has several opportunities for walks and cycle rides.

- ✓ children restricted to certain areas
- ✗ family room
- ✗ garden
- ✗ garden toys
- ✓ lunchtime meals
- ✓ evening meals
- ✓ food lunchtime and evening
- ✓ children's menu
- ✓ bottle warming
- ✓ no smoking area
- ✓ accommodation
- ✓ nearby camping and caravan sites
- ✗ nappy changing
- ✗ entertainment
- ✓ children's certificate
- ✓ high chairs
- ✓ time limit – 8pm

## PAXTON

## Cross Inn

Paxton TD15 1TE
**T** 01289 386267
*Licensee*: Matthew Caulfield
*Opening times*: 11–2.30 (closed all day Mon), 6.30–midnight; 12.30–2.30, 6.30–midnight Sun
*Real ales*: beer range varies
*Directions*: off B6460

Victorian-era village local which started off as the Cross Inn but until recently was known as the Hoolits Nest, on account of the amount of owls in the bar collected by the licensees and brought in by customers. Even though the owls remain and there's no hiding place from them, the pub went back to its old name during the Millennium celebrations to coincide with the restoration of an old cross outside the pub.

Children are allowed everywhere, though families usually eat in the cosy no-smoking dining room. There's a beer garden outside, but no swings (the local park and playground is just across the road from the pub).

Food is available lunchtimes and evenings all week (apart from Monday), with the **kids' menu** serving familiar choices, while smaller portions off the blackboard menu are also available where possible. These will include scampi, small fish dishes and pasta. There are occasional roasts at Sunday lunchtimes (small portions available), but if not it will be the main menus. One of the two real ales available is usually from Broughton.

Attractions in the area include Paxton House where the garden has an adventure playground and children are invited to spot different animals, including red squirrels, in the grounds.

- ✓ children restricted to certain areas
- ✗ family room
- ✓ garden
- ✗ garden toys
- ✓ lunchtime meals
- ✓ evening meals
- ✓ food lunchtime and evening
- ✓ children's menu
- ✓ bottle warming
- ✓ no smoking area
- ✗ accommodation
- ✗ nearby camping and caravan sites
- ✗ nappy changing
- ✗ entertainment
- ✓ children's certificate
- ✓ high chairs
- ✗ time limit

## TOWN YETHOLM

## Plough Hotel

High Street, Town Yetholm TD5 8RF
**T** 01573 420215
*Licensee*: Andrew Wilson
*Opening times*: 11–2.30, 5–11 (midnight Thurs, 1am Fri); 11–1 Sat; 12.30–midnight Sun
*Real ales*: beer range varies

Town Yetholm is a picturesque little village very close to the English border and within sight of the foothills of the Cheviots; the Pennine Way actually comes to an end close by in Kirk Yetholm. The Plough is an 18th-century former coaching inn which has been tastefully modernised but still retains its traditional character. There's a public bar, games room and dining room which is no smoking; children are allowed in the latter two, but they have to be eating in the dining room. Inside the bar areas there is plenty of memorabilia of the famous Yetholm gypsy king and queen, as well as a board which lists all the winners of the local leek-growing competition going back to the 1960s. Outside kids can run off some of their energy in the secure garden.

Food is served lunchtimes and evenings through the week but not on Monday or Tuesday in the winter. The **kids' menu** offers familiar choices while smaller portions can be served off the main menu including scampi and lasagne. Sunday lunchtime sees a choice of roast (small ones available), alongside the main menus. There is usually one real ale on, including the likes of Taylor's Landlord.

A very rural pub which is close to many walks, including the St Cuthbert's Way, while the town of Kelso is only seven miles away and has the Floors Castle plus a cinema and swimming pool.

✓ children restricted to certain areas
✗ family room
✓ garden
✗ garden toys
✓ lunchtime meals
✓ evening meals
✓ food lunchtime and evening
✓ children's menu
✓ bottle warming
✓ no smoking area
✓ accommodation
✓ nearby camping and caravan sites
✗ nappy changing
✗ entertainment
✓ children's certificate
✓ high chairs
✓ time limit – 8.30pm

## WEST LINTON

# Gordon Arms Hotel

Dolphington Road, West Linton EH46 7DR
T 01968 660208
Licensee: Tony McDonald
Opening times: 11-midnight (1am Fri, Sat);
11–midnight Sun
Real ales: **Caledonian Deuchars IPA**; guest beer
Directions: on A702

Busy hotel in a commuter village lying on the southern side of the impressive Pentland Hills, where peaks rise up to 1500 feet and desolate valleys cut through the range. Inside there's an L-shaped bar with stone walls, a real fire in winter and a collection of sofas and chairs plus a comfortable lounge which is where children are allowed at the time of writing (however, as from June 2003 they will be allowed anywhere in the pub due to a change in local licensing laws; I was also told that there were plans for the hotel to be totally no-smoking sometime in 2003). Elsewhere there's also a neat restaurant which is renowned for its hefty helpings of good food, while outside there is a small beer garden connected to the car park.

Food is available all day throughout the week. This is a chicken nugget-free zone for children who can be served smaller portions off the main menu, including pasta, pizzas and chicken. Sunday lunchtime sees a roast sirloin with small portions available; the main menu is also served.

If you're staying here, leave some room from the night before as the delicious breakfasts are reputedly huge! An ideal base for exploring the Pentland Hills, while Edinburgh is 17 miles to the north along the A702.

✓ children restricted to certain areas
✗ family room
✓ garden
✗ garden toys
✓ lunchtime meals
✓ evening meals
✓ food lunchtime and evening
✓ children's menu
✓ bottle warming
✓ no smoking area

# SCOTLAND

✓ accommodation
✓ nearby camping and caravan sites
✗ nappy changing
✗ entertainment
✓ children's certificate
✓ high chairs
✓ time limit – 9pm

## CENTRAL

### KILMAHOG

## Lade Inn

Kilmahog FK17 8HD
**T** 01877 330152
**E** steve@theladeinntrossachs.freeserve.co.uk
www.theladeinn.com
*Licensee*: Stephen Nixon
Opening hours: 12.30–2.30, 5.30–11; 12–11
Sat; 12.30–10.30 Sun
*Real ales*: **Broughton Greenmantle**; guest beers
*Directions*: at A84/A821 Junction, one mile west of
Callander

The first Ben of the Highlands, Ben Ledi,
overlooks the small village of Kilmahog and
this former coaching inn is a perfect
jumping-off point for exploring the
spectacular scenery of the area. Inside
there's a lounge bar which also acts as a
dining area (parts of which are no-
smoking), while there's also a comfortable
bar which always has a log fire lit during the
cold months. The decor is rustic and
traditional, while there are regular ceilidhs
held on Saturday evenings.

Children are allowed everywhere as long
as they are eating with their family, while
there are books and toys to keep them
entertained. In the summer, families can go
outside to the secure garden which is split
into two halves, one with tables and the
other, which is open grass, for children to
play in. Also in the summer the Lade often
has family events such as face painting

while there are magicians for special
occasions such as Mothering Sunday.

Food is served lunchtimes and evenings
Monday–Friday and midday–9pm at the
weekend. There is a **kids' menu** with familiar
choices, though smaller portions can be
served off the main menu if possible.
Examples include scampi or haddock and
chips. Guest ales come from various
Scottish breweries.

As well as great walks and cycling, there
is plenty to do in the area including the
Hamilton Toy Museum and the Rob Roy
Tourist and Visitor Information Centre in
nearby Callander.

✗ children restricted to certain areas
✗ family room
✓ garden
✗ garden toys
✓ lunchtime meals
✓ evening meals
✓ food lunchtime and evening
✓ children's menu
✓ bottle warming
✓ no smoking area
✓ accommodation
✓ nearby camping and caravan sites
✓ nappy changing – women's toilets
✗ entertainment
✓ children's certificate
✓ high chairs
✓ time limit – 9pm

## DUMFRIES AND GALLOWAY

### ISLE OF WHITHORN

## Steam Packet Inn

Harbour Row, Isle of Whithorn DG8 8LL
**T** 01988 500334    **F** 01988 500627
**E** steampacketinn@btconnect.com
www.steampacketinn.com
*Licensee*: Alasdair J G Scoular
*Opening times*: 11–11 (11–2.30, 6–11 winter);
12–11 Sun
*Real ales*: **Theakston XB**; guest beer

The Isle of Whitehorn is not actually a real island, but a delightful village situated on the southern tip of the Machars peninsula, in an area where getting about by boat is as common as using a taxi in central London. The Steam Packet can be found by the harbour and it has been run by the same family for over 20 years. Inside there is a public bar (stone-clad walls, flagstone floors and a big log fire), lounge and two dining areas, including a no-smoking conservatory; there are views over the sea from two of the bars.

Children are allowed everywhere apart from the public bar. Outside there is a garden which is very pleasant in the summer.

Food is served lunchtimes and evenings throughout the week, with the **kids' menu** serving familiar choices with potato waffles and beans, though chips and salad are available if required. However, smaller portions are available where possible off the main menu which has an emphasis on serving fresh Scottish produce, especially seafood. Examples include small steaks and a serving of mussels which is apparently a perennial favourite with youngsters. Sunday lunchtime sees a choice of roast (kids' portions available) plus the main menus.

A friendly quayside inn which has a good mix of locals, fishermen and visitors, while there are plenty of walks and several beaches close by. The Isle of Man is only 18 miles away and can be seen quite clearly most days.

✓ children restricted to certain areas
✗ family room
✓ garden
✗ garden toys
✓ lunchtime meals
✓ evening meals
✓ food lunchtime and evening
✓ children's menu
✓ bottle warming
✓ no smoking area
✓ accommodation
✗ nearby camping and caravan sites
✗ nappy changing
✗ entertainment
✓ children's certificate
✓ high chairs
✗ time limit

## FIFE

**ELIE**

# Braid's Bar at the Victoria Hotel

High Street, Elie KY9 1DB
**T** 01333 330305
**E** gordon@the-vic.com
www.the-vic.com
*Licensee*: Gordon Davidson
*Opening times*: 11–midnight (1am Fri, Sat); 11–midnight Sun
*Real ales*: **Caledonian 80/-, Deuchars IPA**; guest beers

Elie is an unspoilt seaside community on the southern tip of what writer Ian Rankin calls 'the former kingdom of Fife'. The village overlooks the Firth of Forth while the Fife coastal path runs nearby. Braid's is a wood-panelled bar to be found in a 300-year-old former coaching inn where the traditional interior contrasts with the very modern touch of a largescreen TV.

Children are allowed in the main bar and the no-smoking dining room, and there are books and colouring pens to keep them entertained. Outside there's a large beer garden with chairs and tables which becomes very popular during the summer.

Food is served lunchtimes and evenings all week and, although there isn't a kids' menu, smaller portions off the main menu are always possible. These include fish, chicken, burgers, mince and fish fingers, served with chips (so they won't really notice the difference).

As for family activities in the area there's the Elie Water Sports Centre plus plenty of walks, while the historic town of St Andrews is a 20-minute drive away.

✗ children restricted to certain areas
✗ family room
✓ garden
✗ garden toys
✓ lunchtime meals

✓ evening meals
✓ food lunchtime and evening
✗ children's menu
✓ bottle warming
✓ no smoking area
✓ accommodation
✗ nearby camping and caravan sites
✗ nappy changing
✗ entertainment
✓ children's certificate
✓ high chairs
✓ time limit – 9.30pm

# GRAMPIAN

## Boat Inn

Charlestown Road, Aboyne AB34 5EL
**T** 013398 86137
**E** boatinnltd@aol.com
*Licensee*: Wilson Forbes
*Opening times*: 11–2.30, 5–11 (midnight Fri);
11–midnight Sat; 11–11 Sun
*Real ales*: **Draught Bass**; guest beers
*Directions*: north bank of River Dee, near bridge

Back in the early 19th-century a flood washed away the old bridge. If you wanted to cross you had to take the boat – hence the name of this charming riverside inn which dates back to the days of Bonnie Prince Charlie and is a very popular establishment.

Despite changes over the years, the open-planned interior remains very traditional and comfortable with a wood-burning stove adding welcome cosiness in the winter months; there are also further seating areas (some of which are no-smoking) above the main bar which are reached via a staircase. Young train fanatics (and in fact most children – and a fair few fathers too) will be entranced by the model train that travels round the whole pub at picture rail height. Children are allowed

everywhere, but families normally tend to make for the dining area.

Food is served lunchtimes and evenings throughout the week, with the **kids' menu** featuring familiar choices. If the thought of turkey dinosaurs and chips makes the heart sink, there are smaller portions off the main menu also available where possible. These include beefsteak pie, fish, mince and potatoes and lasagne. There is a choice of roast on Sunday (small portions available), served alongside the main menus. The guest beers are usually from Scottish breweries as the landlord has a policy of promoting Scottish real ales.

Accommodation is provided by one self-catering flat (sleeps four) in the pub. A good place to refresh the family before or after one of the many walks in the area. Also worth visiting is the Muir of Dinnet nature reserve and Aboyne's castle.

✗ children restricted to certain areas
✗ family room
✗ garden
✗ garden toys
✓ lunchtime meals
✓ evening meals
✓ food lunchtime and evening
✓ children's menu
✓ bottle warming
✓ no smoking area
✓ accommodation
✓ nearby camping and caravan sites
✗ nappy changing
✗ entertainment
✗ children's certificate
✓ high chairs
✗ time limit

## Kimberley Inn

Findhorn IV36 3Y
**T** 01309 690492
www.thekimberleyinn.com
*Licensee*: John Hessle
*Opening times*: 11–12:30 (1.30am Fri, Sat);
11–12.30 Sun
*Real ales*: beer range varies
*Directions*: on the shore of Findhorn Bay

Back in the 1970s the small village of Findhorn became famous due to the Findhorn Foundation. This new-age community managed (apparently with the help of nature spirits) to grow immense vegetables (despite the inhospitable conditions). The Foundation is still active and open to visitors all year round (the vegetable furore seems to have died down though). Less esoteric pleasures can be had at the Kimberley Inn, a popular and friendly pub which obtained its current name in the late 19th-century, after the famed diamond mines in South Africa.

Beautifully located, overlooking Findhorn Bay, the Kimberley has a main bar area where there's a roaring log fire in the winter, plus a couple of no-smoking areas. Children are allowed everywhere but families are recommended to take them to the no-smoking areas. There's also a patio at the front of the pub from where you can observe the wildlife in the bay. Food is served lunchtimes and evenings Monday–Thursday and all day the rest of the week. There's a **kids' menu** which offers up familiar choices with chips, as well as chicken tikka. Sadly there are no smaller portions off the main menu which features local produce (including bread from Findhorn Foundation) and fresh seafood, but if you've got a couple of kids with you they might like to share; the kitchen occasionally gets breaded haddock and will divide if there are two children sharing. Real ales come from the likes of Fuller's, Tetley, Orkney and Caledonian.

There is plenty to do in the area including walking, cycling, swimming, birdwatching and planespotting at nearby RAF Kinloss.

✗ children restricted to certain areas
✗ family room
✓ garden
✗ garden toys
✓ lunchtime meals
✓ evening meals
✓ food lunchtime and evening
✓ children's menu
✓ bottle warming
✓ no smoking area
✗ accommodation

✓ nearby camping and caravan sites
✗ nappy changing
✗ entertainment
✓ children's certificate
✓ high chairs
✓ time limit – 8pm for under 14s; 10pm for under 16s

## MACDUFF

# Knowes Hotel

78 Market Street, Macduff AB44 1LL
T 01261 832229
www.knowes.co.uk
*Licensee*: John Lovie
*Opening times*: 12–midnight (12–2, 5-midnight winter Mon-Fri); 12.30–11 Sun
*Real ales*: beer range varies

Friendly family-run hotel which dates from the 1880s and enjoys wonderful views over Banff Bay and across the Moray Firth to the Caithness coastline. Inside there's a very traditional feel to things and children are allowed everywhere apart from the bar area, while the no-smoking conservatory is designated as the family room. Here children will find books to amuse them. No garden but the hotel is next to the local playing fields.

Food is served lunchtimes and evenings through the week with the **kids' menu** featuring familiar choices with chips. However, smaller portions are always available off the excellent main menu which makes use of fresh local produce; these include pasta, scampi or haddock. There's a Sunday roast (small portions available) which is served alongside the main menus.

There's plenty to do in this beautiful part of north-east Scotland including the Macduff Marine Aquarium which is a stone's throw away. Other attractions within close striking distance include Fraserburgh Lighthouse Museum and Aden Country Park.

✓ children restricted to certain areas
✓ family room
✗ garden
✗ garden toys
✓ lunchtime meals
✓ evening meals
✓ food lunchtime and evening

✓ children's menu
✓ bottle warming
✓ no smoking area
✓ accommodation
✗ nearby camping and caravan sites
✓ nappy changing – women's toilets
✗ entertainment
✓ children's certificate
✓ high chairs
✗ time limit

## NETHERLEY

# Lairhillock Inn

Netherley AB39 3QS
**T** 01569 730001
**E** lairhillock@breathemail.net
www.lairhillock.co.uk
*Licensee*: Roger Thorne
*Opening times*: 11–2.30, 5–11 (midnight Fri);
11–12 Sat; 11–11 Sun
*Real ales*: **Courage Directors; Taylor Landlord;**
guest beers
*Directions*: off B979, three miles south of B9077

Former coaching inn which can be found amidst beautiful countryside just a 15-minute drive from Aberdeen. Inside there's a lounge, no-smoking conservatory, award-winning 'Crynoch' restaurant and snug bar.

Children are allowed everywhere but families tend to opt for the conservatory which is designated as the family room. Keep children amused with board games such as chess, dominoes and Jenga which are available behind the bar. There's a beer garden outside with a rockery, flower beds and paths, so keep an eye on straying children.

Food is served lunchtimes and evenings through the week, while there are snacks also available on Saturday and Sunday evenings. There's a **kids' menu** and refreshingly it's not the normal stuff but rather soup, penne pasta, bangers and mash, lasagne and baked potatoes all available; no chips! The house real ale comes from the Isle of Skye brewery.

A popular establishment for families and ideal as a base for exploring the local countryside. The town of Stonehaven is a short drive away where there is an open-air

swimming pool and the traditional Fireball Festival which takes place on December 31. Film fans might like to search out Dunnottar Castle on the coast which was used as a location in the movie *Hamlet* starring Mel Gibson.

✗ children restricted to certain areas
✓ family room
✓ garden
✗ garden toys
✓ lunchtime meals
✓ evening meals
✓ food lunchtime and evening
✓ children's menu
✓ bottle warming
✓ no smoking area
✗ accommodation
✗ nearby camping and caravan sites
✓ nappy changing – women's toilets
✗ entertainment
✗ children's certificate
✓ high chairs
✗ time limit

## TARVES

# Aberdeen Arms Hotel

The Square, Tarves AB41 7GX
**T** 01651 851214
www.aberdeenarmstarves.com
*Licensee*: Lucy Lee
*Opening times*: 12–2 (not Mon), 5–11; 12–11 Sun
*Real ales*: **Courage Directors; Wells Bombardier**

Family-run country pub/hotel which was built as a farm in 1810 and became a hotel in the 1860s, when it was also a stopping place for coaches on their way to Aberdeen. The farming connection is continued inside the hotel's bistro with various agricultural bric-a-brac on the stone walls; there's also a massive wooden plaque which commemorates a battle scene with Cavaliers and Roundheads having a go at each other.

Children are allowed everywhere apart from the public bar, which still leaves the lounge (no-smoking until 8pm) and the totally no-smoking bistro. No nappy changing area as such, but the hotel say that the ladies' loo is large enough to carry out such an activity with comfort (lone fathers will have to do the familiar car seat shuffle instead).

Food is served lunchtimes (except Monday) and evenings throughout the week, with the **kids' menu** featuring the usual choices with chips. However, smaller portions of most selections off the main menu can be served; these include haddock, scampi, chicken and curries. There's a Sunday carvery most weekends during the tourist season with small portions available, as well as the main menus.

The Aberdeen Arms is popular with walkers and travellers but is also close to National Trust owned Haddo House, which has a country park with lots of chances to spot the local wildlife. Also nearby is the Prop of Ythsie (pronounced icy), just outside Tarves. This is a folly which was built back in the 19th century and offers a wonderful view of the surrounding countryside if you have the energy to go up the steps.

✘ children restricted to certain areas
✘ family room
✘ garden
✘ garden toys
✔ lunchtime meals
✔ evening meals
✔ food lunchtime and evening
✔ children's menu
✔ bottle warming
✔ no smoking area
✔ accommodation
✘ nearby camping and caravan sites
✔ nappy changing – women's toilets
✘ entertainment
✔ children's certificate
✔ high chairs
✔ time limit – 8pm

## HIGHLANDS & ISLANDS

### AVIEMORE

# Old Bridge Inn

23 Dalfaber Road, Aviemore PH22 1PU
**T** 01479 811137
**E** sales@aviemore-bunkhouse.com
www.oldbridgeinn.co.uk
*Licensee*: Nigel Reid
*Opening times*: 11–11 (midnight Thurs, Fri, Sat); 12.30–11 Sun
*Real ales*: beer range varies
*Directions*: 100 yards from Cairngorm ski road junction

Popular pub with walkers, skiers and locals all enjoying the atmosphere, good food, Highland real ales and musical nights. Children are allowed everywhere apart from the main bar area until 8pm, though they must be having a meal with their parents. There's a no-smoking dining area.

Food is served lunchtimes and evenings throughout the whole week and parents hoping to give their children a break from the ubiquitous chip will breathe a sigh of relief as the **kids' menu** has spaghetti bolognese, bangers and mash and jacket potatoes – but no chips. Smaller portions off the main menu and specials board can also be served; examples have included lamb casserole and baked ham in creamy white wine sauce. Sunday roasts are served (smaller portions available) as well as the main menus.

The Old Bridge Inn can be found alongside the River Spey and is ideally placed for the Speyside Way and for getting into the Cairngorms where there are plenty of opportunities for wildlife spotting. If you fancy going off the rails, the Strathspey Steam Railway also runs from Aviemore to Boat of Garten, a thrilling ride through beautiful countryside.

- ✗ children restricted to certain areas
- ✗ family room
- ✗ garden
- ✗ garden toys
- ✓ lunchtime meals
- ✓ evening meals
- ✓ food lunchtime and evening
- ✓ children's menu
- ✓ bottle warming
- ✓ no smoking area
- ✗ accommodation
- ✓ nearby camping and caravan sites
- ✗ nappy changing
- ✗ entertainment
- ✓ children's certificate
- ✓ high chairs
- ✓ time limit – 8pm

## SLIGACHAN

## Sligachan Hotel

Sligachan, Isle Of Skye IV47 8SW
**T** 01478 650204
**E** reservations@sligachan.co.uk
www.sligachan.co.uk
*Licensee*: Ian Campbell
*Opening times*: 11–9.30 (1am summer); 11–11 Sun
*Real ales*: beer range varies
*Directions*: A850/A863 junction

Family-run white-painted hotel which lies in the shadow of the Cullin Mountains, one of the most magnificent mountain ranges in the British Isles. Built in the early years of the 19th century, the Sligachan is a Mecca for climbers, walkers and those who just like to inhale the surrounding scenery. During the summer if the weather is wet there's an inside kids' play area with a ball pool, while the outside assault course style playground comes into its own when the sun is shining. No wonder the hotel recently won an award for being the most child-friendly establishment on the island. Inside there are two bars, one of which has a dining area, while the other is a smaller more cosy one. Families usually make for the larger bar off which lies the ball-pool area; there is also a no-smoking area here.

Food is served from midday–9pm, though during the quiet winter months this might vary, so call to check. The **kids' menu** has familiar choices but smaller portions off the main one are also available. Examples include lasagne, fish and chips, haggis and tatties plus curries. There are also roast lunches on Sundays (small portions available) alongside the main kids' menu.

A wonderfully child-friendly place to visit or even stay (there are three family rooms) with plenty of rambles and awe-inspiring landscape right at the front door. The hotel also has a real ale and music festival in the autumn and usually stocks up to eight real ales on handpump during the summer.

- ✗ children restricted to certain areas
- ✗ family room
- ✓ garden
- ✓ garden toys
- ✓ lunchtime meals
- ✓ evening meals
- ✓ food lunchtime and evening
- ✓ children's menu
- ✓ bottle warming
- ✓ no smoking area
- ✓ accommodation
- ✗ nearby camping and caravan sites
- ✓ nappy changing – disabled toilets
- ✗ entertainment
- ✗ children's certificate
- ✓ high chairs
- ✓ time limit – 8pm

## THURSO

## Central Hotel

Traill Street, Thurso KW14 8EJ
**T** 01847 893129
**E** central.hotel@btinternet.com
*Licensee*: Brian Cardosi
*Opening times*: 11–midnight (1am Fri, Sat); 12.30–11.45 Sun
*Real ales*: beer range varies

There's no garden at this town centre pub, but who cares when there's an interior bouncy castle and soft play area which is open daily 11am–7pm (12.30pm–7pm Sundays). There are also colouring books and pens, so there's plenty to keep children from the dreaded "I'm bored" syndrome. Children are allowed in the large upstairs bar/restaurant, part of which is no-smoking, but they must be eating with their parents.

A word of advice: let them have a spell on the bouncy castle before food!

Meals are served 11am–8.30pm Monday–Saturday and 11.30am–8.00pm on Sundays. The pub will also do takeaways. The **kids' menu** includes familiar choices, while smaller portions off the main menu are also available including macaroni, cauliflower cheese and chicken fillets. There are also roasts on Sundays (kids' portions available), plus the main menus. A handy place for exploring Thurso which can trace its origins back to Viking times. Places to visit include the Thurso Heritage Museum which includes a reconstruction of a crofter's kitchen. The beach is only five minutes away. Thurso is also the main ferrying point for crossing over to the Orkney Isles. Other family attractions include the Halkirk Highland Games held in the summer at the town of the same name.

✓ children restricted to certain areas
✗ family room
✗ garden
✗ garden toys
✓ lunchtime meals
✓ evening meals
✓ food lunchtime and evening
✓ children's menu
✓ bottle warming
✓ no smoking area
✓ accommodation
✓ nearby camping and caravan sites
✓ nappy changing – women's toilets
✓ entertainment
✓ children's certificate
✓ high chairs
✓ time limit – 8pm

## WATERNISH

## Stein Inn

Waternish, Isle of Skye IV55 8GA
**T** 01470 592362
www.steininn.co.uk
*Licensee*: Angus McGhie
*Opening times*: 4–11 (midnight Fri); 12–midnight Sat, summer; 12.30–11 Sun
*Real ales*: **Isle Of Skye Red Cullin**; guest beers
*Directions*: north of Dunvegan on B886, four and a half miles from Fairy Bridge

Spectacular sunsets and imposing scenery are the stuff of Skye and the views from outside this 18th-century inn nestling in a small fishing village are no exception to the rule. It's no wonder that the Stein is equally popular with walkers and those who turn up by boat (if you are sailing round the Highlands, there are mooring facilities here). Children are allowed in the dining room and family lounge where there's an open fire (both rooms are no-smoking). There's also a small indoor play area off the lounge with building bricks and a chalk board. There are no restrictions during the day but children have to be eating with their parents between 6pm–8pm (8pm is when children have to be out). On a sunny day, take the kids outside to a picnic area at the front where you can luxuriate in the scenery that makes Skye so magnificent.

Food is available 12pm–4pm and 6pm–9.30pm every day throughout the week in summer, but it is cut back to mainly evenings-only apart from Sunday lunch during the rest of the year (there is no food Monday night in the winter apart from bank holidays). Home-cooked local produce is favoured by the kitchen, though the **kids' menu** features the familiar choices. However, some of the dishes on the menu can be served in smaller portions; these include scampi, macaroni cheese and soups. During the winter there is only soup on offer Sunday lunchtimes, while the rest of the time sees a roast choice (small portions available), plus a few bar snacks such as sandwiches, toasties or a plate of chips.

A very friendly and accommodating place where you can hear the Gaelic language spoken. Skye is an astounding place to visit with lots of natural beauty and wildlife so if you and the family are walkers then the prospect must be mouth-watering. Sea dogs on the other hand can be piped aboard the boat trips that go round Loch Bay.

✓ children restricted to certain areas
✓ family room
✓ garden
✗ garden toys

✓ lunchtime meals
✓ evening meals
✓ food lunchtime and evening
✓ children's menu
✓ bottle warming
✓ no smoking area
✓ accommodation
✗ nearby camping and caravan sites
✓ nappy changing – disabled toilet
✗ entertainment
✓ children's certificate
✓ high chairs
✓ time limit – 8pm

## LOTHIANS

## Old Chain Pier

Old Trinity Crescent, Edinburgh EH5 3ED
**T** 0131 552 1233
www.oldchainpier.co.uk
*Licensee*: Drew Nicol
*Opening times*: 12–11 (midnight Thu–Sat);
12.30–11 Sun
*Real ales*: **Caledonian Deuchars IPA; Taylor
Landlord; Tetley Burton Ale**; guest beers
*Directions*: on foreshore between Granton and
Newhaven

The original Old Chain Pier was built in the
1820s and destroyed during a storm in 1898
and this popular pub is sited in the former
booking office (check out the ancient
pictures of the pier on the wall). One of its
most curious past licensees was Betty Moss
who ran the pub after the Second World War
and reputedly called time by firing a starting
pistol; she also filled the pub with all sorts
of strange objects including a German
helmet and a shrunken head, a lot of things
being brought in by the sailors who flocked
there when they docked nearby.

The Old Chain Pier has a good reputation
for its real ales and food and children are
allowed in the balcony area of the main bar
from where there are excellent views over
the Firth of Forth; colouring books are
supplied. They are also welcome in the light
and airy no-smoking conservatory. During
the summer a few tables and chairs are put
outside, children must be supervised there.

Food is served midday–9pm (12.30pm–
8pm Sundays) all year round and there is no
kids' menu, so no chicken nuggets; but
there are chips. However, smaller portions
off the main menu can be served including
vegetable lasagne, stews, soups, filled
baguettes or just a plate of chips. There is a
choice of a roast on Sunday (kids' portions
available) alongside the main menu. There
are nappy changing facilities in the ladies,
but dads are also welcome to use them.

A friendly pub which is close to the historic
Newhaven harbour area, where some of the
earliest photographs in the world were taken.

✓ children restricted to certain areas
✓ family room
✗ garden
✗ garden toys
✓ lunchtime meals
✓ evening meals
✓ food lunchtime and evening
✓ children's menu
✓ bottle warming
✓ no smoking area
✗ accommodation
✗ nearby camping and caravan sites
✓ nappy changing – women's toilets
✗ entertainment
✓ children's certificate
✓ high chairs
✓ time limit – 7pm

## Stable Bar

30 Frogston Road East, Edinburgh EH16 6TJ
**T** 0131 664 0773
www.stablebar.co.uk
*Licensee*: Forbes Crawford
*Opening times*: 11–midnight; 12.30–11 Sun
*Real ales*: **Caledonian Deuchars IPA, 80/-;
Inveralmond Ossian's Ale**
*Directions*: on the southern edge of city by camp site

Friendly converted stable block on the south
side of Edinburgh and close to the nearby
Mortonhall camp site which attracts tourists

from all over the world in the summer, giving the Stable Bar a cosmopolitan air. The entrance is through a cobbled courtyard where you can drink in the summer, while the main bar has stone walls and a log fire in the winter. There is also a cosy no-smoking restaurant at the rear of the pub.

Children are allowed everywhere and colouring books, draughts and chess are available.

Food is served all day throughout the whole week with the **kids' menu** having familiar choices with chips and baked beans. According to the friendly barman I spoke to, smaller portions off the main menu can also be served 'depending on the mood of the chef'. I think he was joking. Choices for children include scampi, hot baguettes, soup, and macaroni. No roasts on Sunday, but the main menus and specials are available.

Mortonhall camp site has several woodland walks which are signposted, but the Hillend ski slope is about a mile away – go before you eat!

- ✗ children restricted to certain areas
- ✗ family room
- ✗ garden
- ✗ garden toys
- ✓ lunchtime meals
- ✓ evening meals
- ✓ food lunchtime and evening
- ✓ children's menu
- ✓ bottle warming
- ✓ no smoking area restaurant
- ✗ accommodation
- ✗ nearby camping and caravan sites
- ✗ nappy changing
- ✗ entertainment
- ✗ children's certificate
- ✓ high chairs
- ✗ time limit

## Starbank Inn

64 Laverockbank Road, Edinburgh EH5 3BZ
**T** 0131 552 4141
www.starbankinn.co.uk
*Licensee*: Valerie West
*Opening times*: 11–11 (midnight Thu–Sat); 12.30–11 Sun
*Real ales*: **Belhaven Sandy Hunter's Ale, 80/-, St Andrew's Ale; Caledonian Deuchars IPA; Taylor**

**Landlord**; guest beers
*Directions*: on foreshore near Newhaven

You can keep an eye on the Firth of Forth from the front bar of this light and comfortable stone-built pub whose main bar area is U-shaped (there used to be a telescope but sadly it was stolen); there's also a no-smoking conservatory-style restaurant. The decor is brewery memorabilia, along with a large mirror which is apparently traditional for pubs in this part of the world. Eight real ales are normally available, from all over the British Isles.

Children are allowed everywhere while there is a single set of dominoes available if you want to start them on pub games early!

Food is served lunchtimes and evenings through the week and all day at the weekends. Be warned: no chips. However, smaller portions off the excellent main bar menu will introduce them to the delights of Scottish favourites such as mince and tatties and haggis, neeps and tatties; there's also haddock mornay, chicken and vegetarian dishes, filled rolls, soup, home-made pate and toast and a pint of prawns which might be good to share.

Well situated for having a look at the Newhaven Harbour area where there's a heritage museum in the old fish market, detailing the history of the long-gone fishing industry.

- ✗ children restricted to certain areas
- ✗ family room
- ✗ garden
- ✗ garden toys
- ✓ lunchtime meals
- ✓ evening meals
- ✓ food lunchtime and evening
- ✗ children's menu
- ✓ bottle warming
- ✓ no smoking area
- ✗ accommodation
- ✗ nearby camping and caravan sites
- ✗ nappy changing
- ✗ entertainment
- ✗ children's certificate
- ✓ high chairs
- ✓ time limit – 8.30pm

## GIFFORD

# Goblin Ha' Hotel

Main Street, Gifford EH41 4QH
T 01620 810244
www.goblin-ha-hotel.co.uk
*Licensee*: Douglas Muir
*Opening times*: 11–2.30, 4.30–11; 11-midnight
Fri, Sat; 11–11 Sun
*Real ales*: **Caledonian Deuchars IPA, Hop Back
Summer Lightning, Taylor Landlord**; guest beer

Family-owned hotel located in a charming village which dates from the 1700s, when the local aristocrat airily decided to build himself a new house in the village of Bothans and so shunted the locals into nearby Gifford. Apparently, the term Goblin Ha' (or Hall) refers to a long filled-in underground basement in the ruins of a local castle, attached to the hotel, which is a relic of the warlike days of the Middle Ages. Nowadays all is much more peaceful and the hotel offers a friendly welcome.

Inside, the public bar has a low ceiling with church pews serving as seating; there's also a games room. Elsewhere there's a newly refurbished cosy lounge/dining area. Children are allowed everywhere. Outside there's a large beer garden with a play area planned for the summer of 2003; the local park is also opposite the hotel and has its own play area.

Food is served lunchtimes and evenings throughout the week with a **kids' menu** offering familiar choices. Smaller portions off the main menu are also available including battered fish and mushy peas, lasagne, mince pie and baps. Sunday lunchtime sees a roast (small portions possible) alongside the main menu.

A delightful countryside retreat which is also within easy striking distance of Edinburgh and the sandy beaches at Gullane and North Berwick.

- ✘ children restricted to certain areas
- ✘ family room
- ✔ garden
- ✘ garden toys
- ✔ lunchtime meals
- ✔ evening meals

- ✔ food lunchtime and evening
- ✔ children's menu
- ✔ bottle warming
- ✘ no smoking area
- ✔ accommodation
- ✔ nearby camping and caravan sites
- ✔ nappy changing – disabled toilets
- ✘ entertainment
- ✔ children's certificate
- ✔ high chairs
- ✘ time limit

## GULLANE

# Old Clubhouse

East Links Road, Gullane EH31 2AF
T 01620 842008
www.oldclubhouse.com
*Licensees*: Guy and Brenda Campanile
*Opening times*: 11–11 (midnight Thu, Fri, Sat);
12.30–11 Sun
*Real ales*: **Caledonian Deuchars IPA, 80/-**; guest
beer (summer)

Half-timbered former golf clubhouse originally set up by local players of the game in 1890 when there was only one course in the area. Now there are seven including the world-famous Muirfield. Inside there's a spacious bar area with a wide view towards the Lammermuir Hills and there's also a no-smoking brasserie to the side of the building. Stuffed birds and animals line the walls, while caricatured statuettes of the likes of the Marx Brothers and Laurel and Hardy hang around the bar. There's also a patio to the front for outside drinking and eating in the summer.

Children are allowed everywhere. Food is served from midday–10pm throughout the week and there is no specific kids' menu: smaller portions off the extensive main menu are served instead. These include burgers, fish, seafood and even (real) chicken nuggets.

Gullane is set on the shores of the Firth of Forth in rugged East Lothian and it's a magnet for golfers, so not surprisingly the Old Clubhouse is popular with them but it also attracts locals and tourists drawn by the surrounding landscape and coastal position where there are plenty of opportunities for birdwatching. Of course you and the family could go with the flow and play some golf – there's a free children's golf course opposite the Old Clubhouse.

- x children restricted to certain areas
- x family room
- x garden
- x garden toys
- ✓ lunchtime meals
- ✓ evening meals
- ✓ food lunchtime and evening
- x children's menu
- ✓ bottle warming
- ✓ no smoking area
- x accommodation
- x nearby camping and caravan sites
- ✓ nappy changing – women's toilets
- x entertainment
- ✓ children's certificate
- ✓ high chairs
- ✓ time limit – 8pm

## HADDINGTON

# Tyneside Tavern

10 Poldrate, Haddington EH41 4DA
**T** 01620 822221
www.tynesidetavern.co.uk
*Licensee*: Paul Kinnock
*Opening times*: 11–11 (midnight Thu, 12.45am Fri, Sat); 12.30–midnight Sun
*Real ales*: **Courage Directors**; guest beers
*Directions*: A6137, south of centre

Traditional stone-built inn which opened as an alehouse in 1819 and has been slaking thirsts and appetites ever since. Keep an eye out for the list of past landlords which can be seen near the entrance (why should churches have a monopoly on this fascinating tradition eh?). Inside it's cosy and rustic with a long bar warmed by a large stone fireplace; there's also a lounge which is where children are allowed. There are several large Sky TV screens dotted throughout the pub, while there's a patio garden for summer drinking and eating and, at the time of writing, the licensees were planning a play area.

Food is served lunchtimes and evenings throughout the week. The **kids' menu** has familiar choices with chips, while smaller portions off the large main menu are also possible. Examples include scampi, steak pie, chicken fillets and veggie burgers. A friendly place and very handy for getting to the Museum of Flight at East Fortune Airfield, which is just a short drive away.

- ✓ children restricted to certain areas
- x family room
- ✓ garden
- x garden toys
- ✓ lunchtime meals
- ✓ evening meals
- ✓ food lunchtime and evening
- ✓ children's menu
- ✓ bottle warming
- x no smoking area
- x accommodation
- x nearby camping and caravan sites
- x nappy changing
- x entertainment
- ✓ children's certificate
- ✓ high chairs
- ✓ time limit – 8pm

## LEADBURN

# Leadburn Inn

Leadburn EH46 7BE
**T** 01968 672952
*Licensee*: Adrian Dempsey
*Opening times*: 11–11 (11.45 Fri, Sat, midnight summer); 12–11 (midnight summer) Sun
*Real ales*: beer range varies
*Directions*: A701/A703/A6094 Junction

The Leadburn was built in the 1770s and is reckoned to be one of the oldest hostelries in Scotland. Inside there's a straightforward public bar with slate floor, pot-bellied stoves and wonderful views of the Pentland Hills.

Children are welcome everywhere but families usually wend their way to the comfortable lounge (part of which is no-smoking) and the light and airy totally no-smoking conservatory, where there is a massive grapevine. Outside there is a patio garden with seats looking across the hills; there is also a converted railway coach which can be booked for private functions. There are usually four real ales available.

Food is served lunchtimes Monday–Friday and all day at the weekend.

The **kids' menu** includes familiar choices with chips or baked potatoes, while smaller portions off the main menu are always possible, the philosophy being that whatever the customer asks for the pub will endeavour to provide. So examples include steak pie, fish, scampi and salads.

The Leadburn Inn is only a short drive from Edinburgh and its many attractions, but as it is on the edge of the Scottish Borders it is also well-placed for walking.

- ✗ children restricted to certain areas
- ✗ family room
- ✓ garden
- ✗ garden toys
- ✓ lunchtime meals
- ✓ evening meals
- ✓ food lunchtime and evening
- ✓ children's menu
- ✓ bottle warming
- ✓ no smoking area
- ✓ accommodation
- ✗ nearby camping and caravan sites
- ✓ nappy changing – women's and men's toilets
- ✗ entertainment
- ✓ children's certificate
- ✓ high chairs
- ✗ time limit

## LOTHIANBRIDGE

## Sun Inn

Lothianbridge, near Dalkeith EH22 4TR
**T** 0131 663 2456
*Licensee*: Shirley Tyldesley
*Opening times*: 11–12; 12–midday
*Real ales*: **Caledonian Deuchars IPA**; guest beer (summer)

Built back in 1870s but only a pub for the last 60 years or so, the Sun Inn can be found in the shadow of the impressive and now disused 23-span Waverley Line viaduct. The line closed in the late 1960s but there are plans to bring it back to life before the end of the decade. Maintaining the trackside theme, there's a suspended model railway system within the pub as well as a few paintings by local artists (if they're to your taste and you're feeling flush, they're up for sale). The main bar is comfortable and

caters to both drinkers and diners, while there is also a no-smoking dining area. Children are allowed everywhere. There's a garden at the back with a play area which includes a swing and Wendy House; the pub hopes to add more in summer.

Food is served lunchtimes and evenings Monday–Thursday and all day Friday–Sunday. There is a well-priced menu for children up to age 10 which includes familiar choices with a juice and ice cream thrown in. Smaller portions off the main menu can also be served including macaroni cheese, steak pies, and lasagne. Sunday lunchtime sees a roast of the day with half portions for children; the main menus are also available.

A friendly establishment which is on the outskirts of Dalkeith and only a short drive from the centre of Edinburgh, while older children with an eye to impressing their teachers with an unusual school project might be interested in the mining museum at Newtongrange.

- ✗ children restricted to certain areas
- ✗ family room
- ✓ garden
- ✓ garden toys
- ✓ lunchtime meals
- ✓ evening meals
- ✓ food lunchtime and evening
- ✓ children's menu
- ✓ bottle warming
- ✓ no smoking area
- ✓ accommodation
- ✓ nearby camping and caravan sites
- ✗ nappy changing
- ✗ entertainment
- ✗ children's certificate
- ✓ high chairs
- ✗ time limit

## NORTH BERWICK

## Nether Abbey Hotel

20 Dirleton Avenue, North Berwick EH39 4BQ
**T** 01620 892802
www.netherabbey.co.uk
*Licensee*: Stirling Stewart
*Opening times*: 11.30–11.30 (midnight Thu, 1am Fri, Sat); 12–11.30 Sun
*Real ales*: **Caledonian Deuchars IPA**; guest beers

Family-run hotel located in a pretty Victorian seaside town with sandy beaches and a picturesque harbour. You wouldn't think that, several centuries ago, North Berwick was alleged to have been the meeting place for scores of witches attempting to do harm to James VI of Scotland (later on also James I of England). Things have settled down since and the Nether Abbey Hotel is an ideal place to contemplate the nefarious doings of the past.

Inside there's a restaurant, patio dining area and the 'Fly Half' bar, while decent weather sees the bar stretching outside thanks to a movable canvas roof. Also outside there's a secure garden with a play area which includes a Wendy House, swings and a slide. Children are allowed everywhere while food is served lunchtimes and evenings throughout the week. The **kids' menu** features familiar choices with chips as well as spaghetti bolognese, while smaller portions off the main menu can be served including fish and chips, scampi and steak pie. Sunday lunchtimes sees a choice of roast (small portions available) alongside the main menus.

There are plenty of beach walks in the area, while bird-watchers are directed to the recently opened Scottish Seabird Centre in the town which is an ideal location for birdspotting. Further afield, Edinburgh is only 30 minutes away by car or train.

✗ children restricted to certain areas
✗ family room
✓ garden
✓ garden toys
✓ lunchtime meals
✓ evening meals
✓ food lunchtime and evening
✓ children's menu
✓ bottle warming
✗ no smoking area
✓ accommodation
✓ nearby camping and caravan sites
✓ nappy changing – women's toilets
✗ entertainment
✓ children's certificate
✓ high chairs
✓ time limit – 9.30pm

## RATHO

# Bridge Inn

27 Baird Road, Ratho EH28 8RA
**T** 0131 333 1320
www.bridgeinn.com
*Licensee*: Ronnie Rusack
*Opening times*: 11–11 (midnight Fri, Sat); 11–11 Sun
*Real ales*: **Belhaven 80/-**; **Deuchars IPA**; guest beer

The Bridge Inn is only minutes from junction 2 on the M8 and also just a short distance from Edinburgh Airport yet it sits in rolling countryside alongside the Union Canal. Landlord Ronnie Rusack has tirelessly campaigned for the restoration of said canal over the years and received an MBE for his efforts. Thankfully, his hard work has paid off and with the completion of the British Waterways Millennium Link Project it will soon be possible to travel by canal from east to west coast.

The landlord also pioneered the idea of Children's Licenses in Scotland so it's not surprising that this old inn, which was originally built as a farmhouse in the 1750s, is a deeply family-friendly place. Children are allowed in the comfortable no-smoking family room in the 'Pop Inn' lounge where there are excellent views over the canal; toys and books are also available. Outside there's a well-stocked play area which includes a carousel. It is described as 'parent-powered', so make sure you've got enough energy before you promise your children a turn on it!

Food is served all day throughout the week with children under age 12 choosing from the 'Bridge Inn Bill' menu which offers soup, corn on the cob, fresh haddock bits, pizza, home-made burgers and sliced chicken. If you are desperate for chicken nuggets the kitchen will produce home-made ones. There are also smaller portions available off the main menu and these include fish, pasta and vegetarian dishes. Roasts are available on Sunday with small ones for the kids; choices from the main menus are also served.

A popular canalside inn which has its own restaurant canal boats which offer a variety of cruises on the Union Canal, including ones for children parties and the Santa cruise at Christmas. Inspired.

✓ children restricted to certain areas
✓ family room
✓ garden
✓ garden toys
✓ lunchtime meals
✓ evening meals
✓ food lunchtime and evening
✓ children's menu
✓ bottle warming
✓ no smoking area
✗ accommodation
✗ nearby camping and caravan sites
✓ nappy changing – disabled toilets
✗ entertainment
✓ children's certificate
✓ high chairs
✓ time limit – 9.30pm

## STRATHCLYDE

### AYR

## Chestnuts Hotel

52 Racecourse Road, Ayr, KA7 2UZ
T 01292 264393
E info@chestnutshotel.com
www.chestnutshotel.com
*Licensee*: Grant Steel
*Opening times*: 11–midnight; 12.30–midnight Sun
*Real ales*: beer range varies

Solidly-built family-run hotel which makes an ideal base for touring Robert Burns' country – the cottage in which the poet was born sits just a mile away and is kept as a museum. Children are allowed in the wood-panelled lounge bar known as the '19th hole' which reflects the hotel's nearness to over a dozen golf courses. This room has a cosy log fire and features a high pitched ceiling with several hundred whisky water jugs hanging down. Children are also welcomed in the non-smoking restaurant

and the secure beer garden which is home to swings, a climbing frame and slide. Colouring books are provided indoors.

Food is served from lunchtimes and evenings while there are also high teas from 3pm–5pm Fri–Sun. The **kids' menu** has familiar choices including burgers, sausages and pasta. Some items off the main menu can be served in smaller portions including haddock and chips, steak pie and lasagne. Sunday roast lunches are served alongside the general menus; sadly no small portions. There are three real ales usually available, coming from the likes of Fuller's, Taylor and Caledonian plus smaller local micros such as Arran and Kelburn. As well as being handy for tracing the life of Rabbie Burns, the Chestnuts is on the south side of the popular holiday resort of Ayr which has numerous parks and walks (the beach is only two minutes away); while part of southeast Ayrshire is in the Glen Troon National Forest Park which is home to a variety of wildlife.

✓ children restricted to certain areas
✓ family room
✓ garden
✓ garden toys
✓ lunchtime meals
✓ evening meals
✓ food lunchtime and evening
✓ children's menu
✓ bottle warming
✓ no smoking area
✓ accommodation
✓ nearby camping and caravan sites
✗ nappy changing
✗ entertainment
✓ children's certificate
✓ high chairs
✓ time limit – 8pm

### BIGGAR

## Crown Inn

109 High Street, Biggar MC12 6DL
T 01899 220116
*Licensee*: Stewart Barry
*Opening times*: 11–11; 12.30–11 Sun
*Real ales*: Greene King Abbot; Shepherd Neame Spitfire; guest beers

Children are allowed everywhere in this traditional 200-year-old town pub which has an unusual, generous and enormously welcome policy of free meals for kids (off the **kids' menu**) providing the parents are eating. There are several rooms to choose from including a separate no-smoking area (the snug). Expect a song or two as the Crown attracts musicians and there are plenty of instruments around the place for them to pick up and play. If you're musically inclined, this is the place to impress (or embarrass) the family. The walls are also covered with historical pictures of Biggar. There's a very secure garden outside.

Food is served midday–9pm every day and the kids' menu includes burgers, chicken nuggets etc with chips. Half portions can also be served off the main menu where possible; these include macaroni cheese and scampi. Sunday lunchtime sees a roast (small portions available) alongside the main menus.

Biggar is an attractive little town on the northern edge of the Borders area and there are plenty of walks to be had. In the town itself there are two historic museums and a puppet theatre.

✘ children restricted to certain areas
✘ family room
✓ garden
✘ garden toys
✓ lunchtime meals
✓ evening meals
✓ food lunchtime and evening
✓ children's menu
✓ bottle warming
✓ no smoking area
✘ accommodation
✓ nearby camping and caravan sites
✘ nappy changing
✘ entertainment
✓ children's certificate
✓ high chairs
✓ time limit – 9pm

## GOUROCK

# Spinnaker Hotel

121 Albert Road, Gourock PA19 1BU
**T** 01475 633107    www.spinnakerhotel.co.uk
*Licensee*: Stewart McCartney
*Opening times*: 11–midnight; 12.30–midnight Sun
*Real ales*: **Belhaven 80/-**; guest beers
*Directions*: on the main coastal road in Gourock

Gourock is a popular seaside resort at the entrance to the Firth of Clyde. Great views of the Firth and the hills of Argyll can be had from this small family-run hotel. Inside there's a bar, dining room and no-smoking lounge area.

Children are allowed everywhere. Outside at the front there's a small beer terrace but children must be supervised as it overlooks the road.

Food is served midday–8pm (12.30pm–8pm Sunday), with the **kids' menu** offering familiar choices, though smaller portions can be served off the main menu. These include pasta, baked potatoes, steak pie, soup and sandwiches. Children are also given a party bag with their meal (remember to ask for this).

There's plenty to do in the area including the Cornalees Bridge Centre which is just outside Greenock and has woodland, moorland and hill walks along the historic Greenock Cut; or you might just want to watch the maritime activity on the Clyde which can include everything from trawlers to yachts to the odd submarine.

✘ children restricted to certain areas
✘ family room
✓ garden
✘ garden toys
✓ lunchtime meals
✓ evening meals
✓ food lunchtime and evening
✓ children's menu
✓ bottle warming
✓ no smoking area
✓ accommodation
✘ nearby camping and caravan sites
✓ nappy changing – at rear of dining room
✘ entertainment
✘ children's certificate
✓ high chairs
✓ time limit – 8pm

## TAYSIDE

### MOULIN

# Moulin Inn

11–13 Kirkmichael Road, Moulin PH16 5EW
T 01796 472196
E sales@moulinhotel.co.uk
www.moulinhotel.co.uk
*Licensee*: Chris Tomlinson
*Opening times*: 12–11; Sun 12–11
*Real ales*: **Moulin Light, Braveheart, Ale of Atholl, Old Remedial**
*Directions*: 3/4 mile NE of Pitlochry

Friendly and busy edge-of-Highlands hotel which has a history going back to the late 17th-century when it was initially built as an inn. The centuries have seen it grow into a hotel, but there's still plenty of charm and tradition within: ancient wooden beams, stone fireplaces with roaring log fires in the winter, plenty of cosy nooks and crannies and real ale from the brewery at the back of the establishment.

Children are allowed in a large area which is separate from the main 'locals' bar and also used for dining. Outside there's a courtyard for summer eating and drinking but look out for small children as it is open to the road.

Food is served all day throughout the whole week and while the **kids' menu** has familiar choices, smaller portions off the extensive home-cooked menu which uses local produce is available where possible. Examples include small steak pies, casseroles and salads. Sunday lunchtime usually sees the main menus and a selection of specials. Brewery trips are possible from Thursday–Monday between midday and 3pm.

A friendly and comfortable place which can be found in a small village less than a mile from Pitlochry, which has always been seen as the 'gateway to the Highlands', so there are plenty of country activities to be undertaken locally, while historically-minded buffs might want to visit the battlefield of Killecrankie, where in 1689 a body of Highlanders loyal to the deposed James II gave a good walloping to government troops.

✓ children restricted to certain areas
✗ family room
✓ garden
✗ garden toys
✓ lunchtime meals
✓ evening meals
✓ food lunchtime and evening
✓ children's menu
✓ bottle warming
✗ no smoking area
✓ accommodation
✓ nearby camping and caravan sites
✓ nappy changing – main toilets
✗ entertainment
✗ children's certificate
✓ high chairs
✗ time limit

# How the Children's Certificate was meant to make Pubs more Family-friendly, but failed

Some pubs are a veritable gold mine for certificates, all neatly framed and proudly displayed. CAMRA branch commendations jostle for space with thanks from local charities about the money raised by the pub's patrons, while some landlords proudly show off their British Institute of Innkeeping (BII) qualifications. Who knows, there might be a pub out there with the owner's O-Level certificates on the wall. However, there's one credential which is rarely seen: the Children's Certificate.

Frankly I'm not that surprised as the CC seems to be a mystery not just to pubgoers but to those behind the pumps as well; a further sign of the deep confusion that has surrounded the issue of children in pubs for years. During the writing of this book, when I asked whether pubs had a CC more than a few licensees or their bar staff looked blank and frankly expressed total ignorance of what it meant.

Simply explained, the Children's Certificate was introduced in 1995 with the aim of making British pubs more family-friendly. Before then, pubs could only allow children under-14 inside their doors if they had a dedicated family room – and the children had to stay firmly within its bounds. As the family room was often the dingiest room, furthest from the main hubbub of the pub, it often signalled a bit of a sentence. There was also some confusion about children in licensed premises as some pubs allowed children in as long as they stayed away from the bar, while other landlords used the excuse of a lack of a family room to completely ban them.

However if a pub had a certificate this meant that under-14s could be allowed freely into the establishment providing they were away from the bar, accompanied by an adult and left by 9pm. It seemed an

eminently sensible idea and, according to figures from the BII, it was reckoned that well over half the pubs in England and Wales had shown interest in the certificates prior to their introduction. However, up until now a meagre 4% have applied for them. In Scotland the take-up has been higher with nearly 20% of pubs applying, but that's still a small minority. And the price of the CC's failure is that it looks as if it will vanish sometime in 2003. So why has it been such a problem?

Detractors say that the Certificate (which is issued by Licensing Magistrates) places unreasonable restrictions on pubs. True, it seems plain daft to ban children from a pub where dominoes is played. On the other hand, some of the restrictions are eminently sensible – for example, pubs having to include no-smoking areas and stopping children from using gaming machines.

The problem seems to be that the certificate is just too dogmatic: it simply doesn't make an allowance for all the different types of pub.

Large establishments like those of the Wetherspoons chain (which all have CCs) are all relatively new and find it simple to adapt their premises to fit the criteria of the CC. However, it's not always that easy for landlords of smaller, older pubs which may have unusual layouts. One licensee who didn't want his name or the name of his pub mentioned, told me why he didn't apply for a children's certificate. 'My pub was built back in 1865 and we are a one-bar country pub so it wouldn't be practical for the purposes of the Children's Certificate – a child wouldn't be able to get through the door if we had one. We encourage families in an area away from the bar and it's always worked well so I'm very much of the theory that if it ain't broke don't fix it.'

David Woolman, who runs the Wheel & Compass at Market Harborough where children are very welcome in the lounge and dining room, which are away from the bar, also agrees.

'I reckon a lot of people do not take up Children's Certificates because of the rules over things such as nappy changing facilities,' he says. 'To do that sort of thing I would have to extend the size of my loos and that would cost a lot. All these things I would love to do but I can't pay for it.'

On the other hand the Bridge Inn at Ratho near Edinburgh does have a certificate and the licensee Ronnie Ratho was a leading light in pushing the idea of Children's Certificates.

'Children's Certificates have helped to give a better atmosphere to pubs as they start to involve the whole family,' says the Bridge Inn's general manager Jim Slavin. 'Whereas before the kids were excluded into an annex, now they have their own part of the pub which helps to change the ambience.

'The take-up in Scotland is sadly quite small, maybe it's because of some of the restrictions such as no-smoking areas or the provision of facilities. Some licensing boards in different parts of Scotland insist on different changing areas while some boards are stricter than others.'

However, the Children's Certificate is soon likely to be a thing of the past if the government's planned Licensing Bill becomes law. Even though the prospect of 24-hour drinking is what makes the headlines, there are a couple of issues regarding children and pubs which should make for a more family-friendly atmosphere without turning them into alcoholic branches of McDonald's.

'When the Licensing Bill goes through the idea is that Children's Certificates won't exist anymore,' says Karen Kelshaw of the British Beer and Pub Association. 'It will be up to individual licensees to decide when children can come in. The government wants to encourage more friendly-family pubs. The publican will be free to choose his or her own policy with the idea that red tape will be removed.'

Now that sounds more like it. But will the government really bring itself to dispense with red tape, instead of festooning more of it around? Sounds about as likely as a two-year old sitting quietly through Wagner's *Ring Cycle* to me.

# Wales

*Crown Inn*
LLANFIHANGEL GLYN MYFYR, CONWY

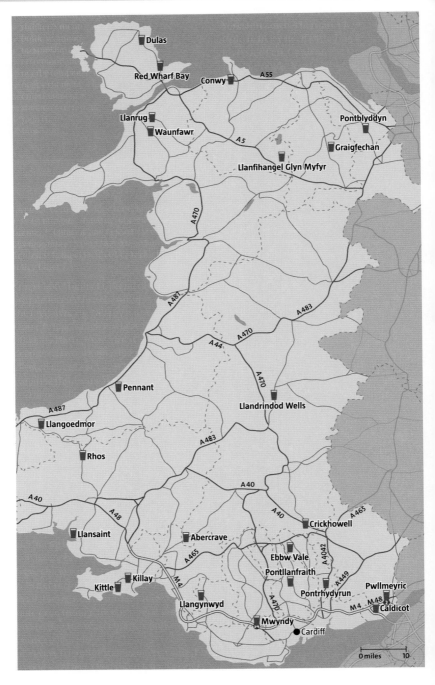

Dulas
Red Wharf Bay
Conwy
A55
Pontblyddyn
Llanrug
Waunfawr
A5
Graigfechan
Llanfihangel Glyn Myfyr
A470
A487
A483
A470
A44
A470
Pennant
A487
Llandrindod Wells
Llangoedmor
Rhos
A483
A40
A40
A48
Crickhowell
A465
Llansaint
Abercrave
A40
Ebbw Vale
A4042
Kittle
Killay
A465
Pontllanfraith
A449
Pwllmeyric
M4
Pontrhydyrun
M48
Llangynwyd
A470
Caldicot
M4
Mwyndy
Cardiff

0 miles    10

WALES is a country of contrasts: stunning craggy mountain scenery, tranquil green vales and valleys, beautiful sandy beaches and rugged coastlines. Oh, there are a few towns and cities in between as well. Writing as a Welshman, I'm pleased to note a new sense of confidence abroad – some believe brought about by devolution. In the past Wales' licensing trade was blighted by the scourge of temperance and the ridiculousness of Sunday closing. But now the country offers an excellent selection of pubs for the family, providing good real ales, some fine food and plenty of amusement for children of all ages.

In the north of the country, where the clean golden beaches of Anglesey and Llandudno make for a wonderful family day out, there are pubs which have been around for centuries but are bang up to date with their family-friendly facilities. Fed up of the beach? No problem. Head in the opposite direction and get walking, riding or canoeing in the wild mountains and foothills of Snowdonia. Or explore the surprisingly bloody history of Wales in historic towns such as Conwy and Caernarfon. Into wildlife? Get out the binoculars on the Great Orme above Llandudno or in Clocaenog Forest. The Bronze Age mines at Llandudno are ideal for older children while all ages (and their parents) approve of the (very green) Greenwood Centre which educates while it entertains. There are also country parks, the bright and breezy seaside resort at Rhyl and just over the border, the massive shopping outlet complex at Cheshire Oaks.

As for beer, there are not many breweries in North Wales, with regionals from the north-west being heavily represented, but a visit to Waunfawr where the Snowdonia Parc Hotel has its own brewery is a must. Not only is there the chance of sampling the excellent beer, but the hotel goes all out to entertain children with loads of toys inside and out, as well as the chance to watch steam trains go by.

Further south, the countryside is different but also stunning in its own way. The Gower Peninsula, the Brecon Beacons and the unspoilt beaches of Cardiganshire are all beautiful and well worth exploring. Then there's the Wye Valley and the southern valleys where coal was once king. Wales is well set-up for tourists and you'll find plenty of farm parks, wildlife centres and other attractions – something for all ages and tastes. You can even play Wild West gunslingers at the cowboy town Gunsmoke at Seven Sisters. If you're lucky you might catch a glimpse of the rare red kite in its mid-Wales heartland. Then there's the capital city of Cardiff with its museums, cinemas and shops. Just outside the city sits the fascinating Museum of Welsh Life at St Fagans.

Pubs range from sparkling new modern ones, where a pint of real ale goes hand in hand with an indoor play area, to an ancient inn which sees the 'Mari Llwyd' festival take place every New Year. The major breweries of Wales are situated in the south but there is also a goodly selection of micros producing award-winning beers. You can expect a warm welcome or, as they say in Wales, 'Croeso'.

## GLAMORGAN

### MWYNDY

## Barn at Mwyndy

Cardiff Road, Mwyndy, near Miskin CF72 8PJ
**T** 01443 222333   **F** 01443 227766
*Licensees*: Mark and Christine Wilby
*Opening times*: 11–3, 5–11 (11–11 Sat); 12–10.30 Sun
*Real ales*: beer range varies
*Directions*: M4 Junction 34, up A4119, through two sets of lights, 100 yards on right filter lane; down lane, pub on right-hand side.

Award-winning converted 16th-century barn apparently haunted by the ghost of a teenage milkmaid who had an affair with the lord of the manor several hundred years ago. Inside, there's a selection of farming and fishing bric-a-brac hanging among the rafters, including a traditional Welsh coracle; a minstrel-style gallery provides a comfortable space for diners.

Children are allowed anywhere in the split-level bar pub, though parents are requested not to let them run about. The upstairs and downstairs restaurants are both no-smoking. Outside there's a large, secure beer garden which has a play area on soft bark. A clown performs occasionally during the summer, and there are also a brace of beer festivals held through the year when the place can get very busy; at the winter one held in January this year a magician was booked to entertain the children.

The **kids' menu** features familiar choices, served with a choice of mash or chips and peas or beans. At £2.25 it's a bargain, especially as ice cream is thrown into the price. Young diners are also given colouring pencils and paper. Small portions are available off the main menu if possible; these include curries and scampi; there are also filled baps. Sundays sees a roast lunch (small portions available) as well as the full main menu; there are also barbecues in the summer, weather permitting. Food is served 12pm–2pm, 6pm–8.30pm during the week, with all day servings at the weekend (food finishes at 7pm on Sunday).

There are usually six real ales available, from local breweries and further afield. In the immediate area there is a farm park and many walks, while attractions a short drive away include the Museum of Welsh Life at St Fagans and the confident capital city of Cardiff with its museums, shops, cinemas and waterfront development.

x children restricted to certain areas
x family room
✓ garden – outdoor drinking area
✓ garden toys
✓ lunchtime meals
✓ evening meals
✓ food lunchtime and evenings
✓ children's menu
✓ bottle warming
✓ no smoking area
x accommodation
✓ nearby camping and caravan sites
✓ nappy changing – women's toilets
✓ entertainment
✓ children's certificate
✓ high chairs
x time limit

## KILLAY

# Railway Inn

553 Gower Road, Upper Killay SA2 7DS
**T** 01792 203946
*Licensees*: William Carter and Christine Hatton
*Opening times*: 11–11; 12–10.30 Sun
*Real ales*: **Swansea Deep Slade Dark**; **Bishopwood Bitter**; Original Wood; guest beers

The Gower peninsula is one of the most beautiful parts of Wales. Stretching out westwards from Swansea, it has long been designated an Area of Outstanding Beauty with its sheltered sandy bays and charming seaside resorts.

The village of Killay stands on the very western edge of Swansea and this compact family-owned pub is an ideal place to stop before or after exploring the Gower. It was built back in 1864 at the same time as the local railway line was laid down, but the rolling stock and sleepers vanished in the 1960s and the old disused railway line is now a bicycle track which can be ridden all the way to Cardiff. Naturally, it's a magnet for cyclists, families and walkers. From the outside, the Railway looks like an ordinary, solidly-built house, while inside the decor is unspoilt and traditional with plenty of railway memorabilia to remind customers of the pub's origins and past.

Children are allowed in a small family room which is equipped with a few books, while outside there are a couple of patios.

Food is limited to rolls in the summer, and there are no chips.

This is probably best for over-8s, a place to recuperate after a long walk in the nearby Clyne Valley Country Park.

✓ children restricted to certain areas
✓ family room
✓ garden – outdoor drinking area
✘ garden toys
✘ lunchtime meals
✘ evening meals
✘ food lunchtime and evenings
✘ children's menu
✓ bottle warming
✘ no smoking area
✘ accommodation

✓ nearby camping and caravan sites
✘ nappy changing
✘ entertainment
✘ children's certificate
✘ high chairs
✓ time limit – 7pm

## KITTLE

# Beaufort Arms

18 Pennard Road, Kittle SA3 3JS
**T** 01792 234521
*Licensee*: Bertha Lebrocq
*Opening times*: 11.30–11; 12–10.30 Sun
*Real ales*: **Brains Buckley's Best Bitter**, **Rev James**, seasonal beers

One of the oldest pubs on the Gower peninsula and once the home of monks in the Middle Ages. Surprisingly there are no reports of any ghosts. Owned by Brains of Cardiff, it has a beamed ceiling and lots of exposed stone in the oldest part of the building.

Children are allowed in part of the lounge bar, which is non-smoking, and a family dining room. Outside there's a play area with slides, swings and a Wendy House; parents are advised to supervise their children. In the summer there is a bouncy castle and regular fundays with barbecues and DJs for the family.

Food is served all day until 9.30pm in the summer, while in the winter it's lunchtimes and evenings Monday–Thursday and all day Friday–Sunday. The **kids' menu** features familiar choices, while some selections off the main menu are available in smaller portions. These include chicken dishes as well as traditional bar food choices such as ham or sausage and chips. There are also sandwiches. On Sundays there's a roast alongside the main menu, with small portions available.

The beaches of south Gower are close by and there are also many walks in the area.

✓ children restricted to certain areas
✓ family room
✓ garden
✓ garden toys

✓ lunchtime meals
✓ evening meals
✓ food lunchtime and evenings
✓ children's menu
✓ bottle warming
✓ no smoking area
✗ accommodation
✓ nearby camping and caravan sites
✗ nappy changing
✓ entertainment
✓ children's certificate
✓ high chairs
✓ time limit – 9.30pm

## Old House/Yr Hen Dŷ

Llangynwyd CF34 9SB
**T** 01656 733310
www.oldhouse-llan.co.uk
*Licensee*: Richard David
*Opening times*: 11–11; 12–10.30 Sun
*Real ales*: **Flowers IPA**, **Original**; **Worthington Bitter**;
guest beer
*Directions*: on top of the hill, west of A4063

Nearly 850 summers have passed since this ancient thatched inn was built back in 1147 and not surprisingly it's full of character, history and atmosphere. For instance it was the local of noted Welsh poet Wil Hopcyn, who plied his trade in the early 1700s. Another intriguing survival from the past is the Mari Llwyd festival which happens every New Year and involves groups of locals led by someone wearing a horse's head drinking and dancing through the village before arriving at the pub and engaging in a battle of verse.

Given the age of the establishment, it's not surprising to find a generous amount of thick ancient beams inside plus a big inglenook fireplace; brass ornaments and jugs hang from every available space. Church pews provide atmospheric seating. There's also a no-smoking conservatory with a decking area outside leading to a fenced garden which backs onto a field. The garden has an adventure playground which is joined by a bouncy castle for the duration of the summer.

Children are allowed everywhere apart from the bar area, but a lot of families make a beeline for the conservatory which has beautiful hilly views.

Food is served lunchtimes and evenings all through the week. The **kids' menu** (which is strictly for the under-11s) has familiar choices, while smaller portions off the main menu can be ordered if possible; this will include gammon and chips, a child's curry and bangers and mash. Sunday lunchtime sees a selection of roasts (small portions available) alongside the kids' menu. This is a wonderful walking area while the Garw Fechan Woodland Park is also close. Cowboy fans however might want to make the short journey by car to Gunsmoke cowboy town at Seven Sisters, nine miles north of Neath, where 10-gallon hats are essential headgear.

✗ children restricted to certain areas
✗ family room
✓ garden
✓ garden toys
✓ lunchtime meals
✓ evening meals
✓ food lunchtime and evenings
✓ children's menu
✓ bottle warming
✓ no smoking area
✗ accommodation
✗ nearby camping and caravan sites
✗ nappy changing
✓ entertainment
✗ children's certificate
✓ high chairs
✗ time limit

# GWENT

## Measure Inn

63–65 Newport Road, Caldicot NP26 4BR
**T** 01291 424808
*Licensee*: Malcolm Godbold

*Opening times*: 12–11; 12–10.30 Sun
*Real ales*: **Greene King IPA, Old Speckled Hen**;
guest beer

Large pub situated a short stroll from the local shopping precinct. The extensive interior comprises a public bar and a split-level lounge decorated in dark, subdued colours. This gives access to the contrasting and much lighter decor of the family room. No children are allowed in the main bar, but over-14s can go into the lounge with adults, while children have the family room. This is open from 12pm–9pm and it's a roomy space, split into two levels.

There is a small indoor play area, 'Mouseketeers Funland', which is a ball-pit with a miniature staircase above. There are also a variety of electronic games for older children. The lower level in the family room is no-smoking and leads out into the garden and enclosed play area with seating to enable adult supervision. Children up to 10 are allowed to use the play area, which has wood chippings on the floor and two climbing frames.

Children's menu meals range from £1.99 (for the younger ones) to £2.85, and have familiar options all served with fries, beans or peas; a fizzy drink is also thrown in. Older children can choose from a menu that includes gammon, small steaks, barbecued chicken and burgers. There are also vegetarian options. On Sundays there is a special roast lunch offer of £5 for an adult and child meal; the main menu is also available. Food is served 12pm–3pm, 4pm (5pm Sunday)-8pm.

Nearby family attractions include Caldicot Castle and country park, with a costume and furniture museum and children's activity station, Caerwent Roman Town (Venta Silurum) and Chepstow Castle and Museum with life-sized figures of mediaeval Marcher lords and Civil War battle scenes. The Wye Valley is also nearby with Tintern Abbey and a countryside centre at the restored former Tintern railway station.

✓ children restricted to certain areas
✓ family room
✓ garden
✓ garden toys
✓ lunchtime meals
✓ evening meals
✓ food lunchtime and evenings
✓ children's menu
✓ bottle warming
✓ no smoking area
✗ accommodation
✗ nearby camping and caravan sites
✓ nappy changing – unisex nursing/nappy changing room
✗ entertainment
✓ children's certificate
✓ high chairs
✓ time limit – 9.30pm

## EBBW VALE

# Brewsters

Victoria Business Park, Waun Lwyd,
Ebbw Vale NP23 8AM
**T** 01495 307185   **F** 01495 301114
www.brewsterthebear.co.uk
*Licensee*: Andrew Garforth
*Opening times*: 11–11; 12–10.30 Sun
*Real ales*: **Greene King Old Speckled Hen**
*Directions*: Situated on the A4046, 1 mile south of Ebbw Vale town centre adjacent to the entrance of the Festival Shopping Park

Recently built family pub/restaurant to the south of the town centre and the steel works site; part of the Whitbread-owned Brewsters chain. Sited in part of a former National Garden Festival Park and surrounded by wooded hills, it has a spacious interior with a brightly coloured no-smoking family dining area; children are allowed everywhere apart from the adults-only drinking space. A couple of nice touches is that some loos have been specially adapted to cater for children, while staff are trained to make children of all ages feel welcome. There is also a 'Fun Factory' play area, which is common to all pubs in the Brewsters chain; this has an hour limit and is divided into different sections for different age groups. There is a mix of play equipment, with a ball swamp, climbing frame and play stations. Children wear tagged aprons which sound an alarm if they wander too near an exit; the main dining room also gives views of the Fun Factory. There is a play area in the garden, which is safely enclosed within a fence; children are very fond of the large enclosed climbing frame with safety rails to help prevent accidents.

Food is served from 11.30am–10pm (12pm–10pm Sunday), with special menus for the under- and over-7s, with prices ranging from £2.99–£5.99; the **kids' menu** has familiar choices with chips; while over-7s can have hot dogs, burgers, chicken korma or pasta. On Sunday there is also a children's roast or vegetarian option available; the regular kids' menu is also served.

Local attractions include Festival Park country walks and an owl sanctuary, while the Brecon Beacons National Park is within easy reach by car.

✓ children restricted to certain areas
✓ family room
✓ garden
✓ garden toys
✓ lunchtime meals
✓ evening meals
✓ food lunchtime and evening
✓ children's menu
✓ bottle warming
✓ no smoking area
✗ accommodation
✗ nearby camping and caravan sites
✓ nappy changing – unisex nursing/nappy changing room
✓ entertainment
✓ children's certificate
✓ high chairs
✗ time limit

## PONTLLANFRAITH

# Crown

Bryn View, Pontllanfraith NP12 2HE
**T** 01495 223404
*Licensee:* Nancy Jones
*Opening times:* 12–3, 5–11; 12–11 Fri & Sat; 12–10.30 Sun
*Real ales:* **Courage Best Bitter; John Smith Bitter;** guest beers

Twin-roomed pub which can be found on the corner of two roads in a village which has steadily become incorporated into the former mining community of Blackwood. A hostelry on this site has been traced back to the 1660s, but the interior is very modern and tidy, with the work of local photographers on the wall.

Children are allowed in the lounge where there is a dedicated no-smoking area. Outside there's a play area with swings, Wendy House and slide which is popular with families in the summer, though keep an eye out for small children as the area leads onto the car park.

Food is served lunchtimes and evenings all week, apart from Sunday evenings. The **kids' menu** has the usual chicken nuggets, sausages and fish fingers, all served with chips, while older children might want to try choices from the bar food menu. These include curries, pasta and scampi. On Sundays there is a roast alongside the main menu; small roasts are also available.

Pontllanfraith is right in the middle of the old mining area of South Wales with the likes of Merthyr Tydfil, Rhymney and Tredegar just up the valley, while the award-winning manor house of Llancaiach Fawr is a short drive westwards along the A472 at the village of Nelson. Here visitors can try out old furniture, dress in period costume and sample the stocks!

✓ children restricted to certain areas
✗ family room
✓ garden
✓ garden toys
✓ lunchtime meals
✓ evening meals
✓ food lunchtime and evenings
✓ children's menu
✓ bottle warming
✓ no smoking area
✗ accommodation
✗ nearby camping and caravan sites
✗ nappy changing
✗ entertainment
✗ children's certificate
✓ high chairs
✓ time limit – 9.30pm

## PONTRHYDYRUN

# Ashbridge Inn

Avondale Road, Pontrhydyrun NP44 1DE
**T** 01633 876678
www.brewsterthebear.co.uk
*Licensee*: Beryl Jones
*Opening times*: 11–11, 12–10.30 Sun
*Real ales*: **Boddingtons Bitter; Flowers Original**
*Directions*: From Jn26, M4 follow the A4042 to
Pontypool. After eight miles turn left at
roundabout (A4051 Cwmbran). Turn left at next
roundabout (1/2 mile). Pub on left

Attractive family pub/restaurant north of
Cwmbran and part of the Brewsters chain.
Converted from an old barn – there are
pictures of it in its former days – entry is
through a great wooden door. Inside, the
decor is in keeping with the building's rural
origins.

There are extensive dining areas with
children allowed everywhere apart from
the adults only (16+) area. The no-smoking
family dining area is very popular and
includes ice cream and fruit juice
machines. There is also a children's room,
the 'Fun Factory' (see Brewsters entry at
Ebbw Vale for details). The outside garden is
securely fenced in with plenty of tables and
chairs and it hoped that play equipment
including a bouncy castle will be set up by
the summer of 2003.

Food is served from 11.30am–10pm
(12pm–10pm Sunday). There are three
different **kids' menus** all with familiar
dishes: 'Tiny Tots'; under-7s (create your
own ice cream) and a 'Big Deal' menu which
caters up to 12-year olds and is a bit more
sophisticated. Sunday sees regular menus,
roast lunches and a child's portion of a roast
meal. There is also a specials board and
Heinz baby food is sold.

Local attractions include Cwmbran
Community Farm, Pontypool Park and
Leisure Centre with a shell grotto and ski
slope and for the historically minded the
Cordell Trail starts and ends in Pontypool.

✓ children restricted to certain areas
✓ family room
✓ garden
✓ garden toys
✓ lunchtime meals
✓ evening meals
✓ food lunchtime and evenings
✓ children's menu
✓ bottle warming
✓ no smoking area
✗ accommodation
✗ nearby camping and caravan sites
✓ nappy changing – unisex nursing/nappy
    changing room
✓ entertainment
✓ children's certificate
✓ high chairs
✗ time limit

## PWLLMEYRIC

# New Inn

Pwllmeyric NP16 6LF
**T** 01291 622670    **F** 01291 630103
*Licensee*: Lisa Clarke
*Opening times*: 11–11; 12–10.30 Sun
*Real ales*: **Boddingtons Bitter; Draught Bass;
Wadworth 6X**
*Directions*: Off M48 Junction 2 via A466 to
roundabout then A48 westbound to Newport,
the pub is on the left at the bottom of the hill.

Three-storey roadside inn which was built
in 1745. The adults-only public bar is very
traditional and has a pool table, while the
lounge (children are allowed here) is
decorated with dark wood panelling which
was salvaged from a former luxury liner,
the *Duchess of Bedford*, after it was broken
up in Newport. There is also an attractive
fireplace, pictures of old Chepstow and
breweriana from the now closed Usher's
brewery.

The no-smoking lower lounge area
doubles as a family dining room and also
gives access to the outdoor play area. There
is also a 'Clumsy Clown' children's room
with a colourful split-level play area and a
small counter to purchase sweets and soft
drinks. Time limits and entry charges are
specified on a notice board outside the
room. Even though the nappy changing

facilities are situated in the ladies, staff assistance is available for fathers. There is a secure play area out in the garden with a climbing apparatus and a noughts and crosses game for younger children. The **kids' menu**, which includes vegetarian and coeliac options, offers familiar choices, all served either with French fries, potato waffles, spiral fries, potato heads plus beans or peas. Sunday sees the same options. Food is served 12pm–3pm, 5pm–9pm (12pm–9pm Saturday and Sunday). The pub is very family-friendly but more suitable for younger children than teenagers.

Local attractions include Caldicot Castle and country park with a costume and furniture museum, and children's activity station, Caerwent Roman Town (Venta Silurum) and Chepstow Castle and Museum with life-sized figures of mediaeval Marcher lords and Civil War battle scenes. The Wye Valley is also nearby with Tintern Abbey and a countryside centre at the restored former Tintern railway station.

✓ children restricted to certain areas
✗ family room
✓ garden
✓ garden toys
✓ lunchtime meals
✓ evening meals
✓ food lunchtime and evenings
✓ children's menu
✓ bottle warming
✓ no smoking area
✗ accommodation
✓ nearby camping and caravan sites
✓ nappy changing -ladies
✓ entertainment
✗ children's certificate
✓ high chairs
✗ time limit

# MID WALES

## ABERCRAVE

# Copper Beech Inn

133 Hoel Tawe, Abercrave SA9 1XS
**T** 01639 730269
*Licensee*: Linda Messer
*Opening times*: 11–11; 12–10.30 Sun
*Real ales*: Beer range varies
*Directions*: off A4067

Originally built as a mine-owner's house in the 19th-century, this friendly single-bar inn can be found on the southern side of the Brecon Beacons National Park. It's popular with visitors to the area, especially cavers, but also functions as an important meeting place for the local community. Inside, the heavily beamed interior has plenty of copper items hanging around as the inn's name suggests. There's a large bar area plus dining and games room. A beer garden lies to the front and side with stunning views from the front towards the Brecon Beacons. Be advised, the gardens are not secure so keep an eye on young children. At present there is no play equipment but the landlady tells me that she is thinking about it for next summer.

Children are allowed everywhere and food is served both lunchtime and evening all week. The **kids' menu** has the usual small-person pleasers with chips, while half portions off the main menu can be served where possible – examples include a steak for two children or pasta. Sunday lunchtime sees roasts, plus the main menus; kids' roasts available.

Five real ales are usually on tap, including at least one from Wye Valley.

There's plenty to do in the area including a multitude of walks in the Beacons, pony trekking and the National Showcaves Centre for Wales at Dan-yr-Ogof which has a dinosaur park, Iron Age village and a spectacular 'cathedral' cave.

x children restricted to certain areas
x family room
✓ garden
x garden toys
✓ lunchtime meals
✓ evening meals
✓ food lunchtime and evenings
✓ children's menu
✓ bottle warming
x no smoking area
✓ accommodation
✓ nearby camping and caravan sites
x nappy changing
x entertainment
✓ children's certificate
✓ high chairs
✓ time limit – 9.30pm

## CRICKHOWELL

# Bear Hotel

High Street, Crickhowell, Powys NP8 1BW
**T** 01873 810408   **F** 01873 811696
**E** bearhotel@aol.com
www.bearhotel.co.uk
*Licensees*: Judy and Stephen Hindmarsh
*Opening times*: 11–3, 6–11; 12–3, 7–10.30 Sun
*Real ales*: **Brains Reverend James; Draught Bass;
Greene King Old Speckled Hen; Hancock's HB**

Historic award-winning coaching inn set
right in the middle of this small town which
lies between Brecon and Abergavenny.
Inside the rambling, multi-roomed interior
there are plenty of wooden beams, stone
floors, wrought iron chandeliers, elaborate
drapes and rich red rugs, all adding to a
cosy and welcoming atmosphere.

Children are allowed in the top bar
which doubles up as the family room, as
well as two adjoining dining rooms which
can be reached through the top bar. There is
also a small garden at the back of the inn
which opens onto the car park.

The Bear is noted for its food, which is
served 12pm–2pm and 6pm–10pm
(7pm–9pm Sunday) throughout the week.
For children there is the 'Cubs' Menu which
has familiar choices such as scampi or pizza
alongside Welsh Rarebit and pasta; small
portions off the regular bar menu are also
served, including fresh salmon fishcakes

with a lemon cream sauce, home-made
faggots and grilled bacon with bubble and
squeak, plus sandwiches and baguettes.
Kid-sized ice creams and sorbets are also on
the menu. Roasts (small portions available)
are served on Sundays alongside the main
bar menu. There is an à la carte restaurant
open evenings Monday–Saturday and for
Sunday luncheon; children under seven are
not allowed in here and booking is
recommended. The Bear Hotel is a delightful
place to visit or stay at, which manages to
keep the balance between locals enjoying a
pint or special meal and visitors exploring
the beautiful scenery of the nearby Brecon
Beacons. Other attractions in the area
include the Brecknock Museum in Brecon,
Langorse Lake, the secondhand book mecca
of Hay-on-Wye and the Brecon Beacons
Mountain Centre at Libanus near Brecon.

✓ children restricted to certain areas
✓ family room
✓ garden
x garden toys
✓ lunchtime meals
✓ evening meals
✓ food lunchtime and evenings
✓ children's menu
x bottle warming
✓ no smoking area
✓ accommodation
✓ nearby camping and caravan sites
x nappy changing
x entertainment
x children's certificate
✓ high chairs
x time limit

## LLANDRINDOD WELLS

# Llanerch 16th Century Inn

Llanerch Lane, Llandrindod Wells LD1 6BQ
**T** 01597 822086
**E** llanerchinn@lc24.net
*Licensee*: Simon Buckley
*Opening times*: 11.30–3 (11 summer), 5–11;
11–11.30 Thu, Fri, Sat; 12–10.30 Sun
*Real ales*: **Hancock's HB**; guest beers
*Directions*: town centre, near police station

Atmospheric 16th century inn originally
built as a staging post, and which still has

some intriguing original features such as a Jacobean staircase. Inside, children are allowed in most places apart from the main bar area, but that still leaves several rooms including a lounge which is non smoking until 8pm. Outside there's a beer terrace and a secure leafy orchard in which children can discover a play area containing swings, climbing frame and seesaw. There's also an extensive outside seating area and a boules pitch.

The 'table toppers' menu has the usual chicken nuggets and cod bites, as well as chicken curry with chips, while smaller portions of the main menu will be served if possible; examples include scampi or cod and chips and lasagne. There is also a good selection of snacks. Sunday lunchtimes sees a roast alongside the main menu (small roasts available) and food is served both lunchtime and evening all through the year.

During August Llandridnod Wells has a week-long Victorian festival with street entertainers and open air shows. The town is also only a short drive from the Brecon Beacons National Park, and lots of walks in the Elan Valley where you might catch a glimpse of the reintroduced Red Kite.

✓ children restricted to certain areas
✗ family room
✓ garden
✓ garden toys
✓ lunchtime meals
✓ evening meals
✓ food lunchtime and evenings
✓ children's menu
✓ bottle warming
✓ no smoking area
✓ accommodation
✗ nearby camping and caravan sites
✗ nappy changing
✗ entertainment
✗ children's certificate
✓ high chairs
✓ time limit – 10pm in Winter

## NORTH-EAST WALES DENBIGHSHIRE

### GRAIGFECHAN

## Three Pigeons Inn

Graigfechan LL15 2EU
**T** 01824 703178    **F** 01824 703812
*Licensees*: Morton and Heather Roberts
*Opening times*: 12–3, 5.30–11; 12–11 Sat; 12–10.30 Sun
*Real ales*: **Draught Bass; Hancock's HB; Enville Ale; Plassey's Fusilier**
*Directions*: on B5429 three miles south of Ruthin

Welsh drovers were hardy souls who took cattle and sheep from the wilds of Wales to the markets of England. They had their regular calling places and the Three Pigeons was one of them – it was originally a drovers' inn before being rebuilt in 1777. Even though work has been carried out in the last ten years and produced a balcony dining area with wonderful views of the Vale of Clwyd, the solid-looking stone-built pub still retains its old traditional atmosphere with exposed oak beams and lots of polished brass.

Children are allowed in the dining room, lounge bar and games room (which doubles up as the family room and games, toys and books are available) but must be out by 8.30pm, though the licensees say that they try to be flexible. Outside there's a safe large grassed area with a playshed and big Lego; there's also a Wendy House with soft cushions. As this area is popular with tourists there's also an adjacent camping/caravan site complete with loos and showers.

The **kids' menu** includes chicken dippers, fish fingers, sausages, all with chips. Smaller portions of the main menu can be served, including mild curries. Sunday lunchtime is devoted to roasts (small roasts available), with the usual children's menu also available. Food is served lunchtimes and evenings all week, apart from Sunday evenings.

This is a beautiful part of the world with the seaside resorts of Rhyl and Llandudno within easy reach; nearer is the Ruthin Gaol Visitor Centre, Ruthin Craft Centre, a section of Offa's Dyke and the Plassey Country Park near Wrexham.

✓ children restricted to certain areas
✓ family room
✓ garden
✓ garden toys
✓ lunchtime meals
✓ evening meals
✓ food lunchtime and evenings
✓ children's menu
✓ bottle warming
✓ no smoking area
✗ accommodation
✓ nearby camping and caravan sites
✗ nappy changing
✗ entertainment
✗ children's certificate
✓ high chairs
✓ time limit – 8.30pm

## FLINTSHIRE

### PONTBLYDDYN

## New Inn

Corwen Road, Pontblyddyn CH7 4HR
**T** 01352 771459
**E** DaveAndSandra@NewInnPontblyddyn.fsnet.co.uk
www.newinnpontblyddyn.fsnet.co.uk
*Licensees*: Dave and Sandra Hunt
*Opening times*: 12–11; 12–10.30 Sun
*Real ales*: **Brains' Rev James**; guest beers
*Directions*: three miles from Mold on the A5104 Corwen road

Eighteenth-century pub which originally started off as three terraced houses; it has also done time as a general stores-cum-pub. Now it's a family-run business where

children are welcome in the downstairs lounge and the upstairs dining room. The lounge also doubles up as a family room, and has table football, crayons and colouring books and other games. The dining room is more formal but is no-smoking. Outside in the safe garden, there's a play area which has a slide, tyre swings, a rope climb and springers.

The **kids' menu** features familiar choices which are very reasonable at £2.50 (ice cream included in the price). There are also the usual bar snacks, baguettes and sandwiches. Sugar-free drinks and sweets are also on sale. For £3.50 the pub can do child-sized portions off the main menu; these include a small gammon or a chicken dish, as well as a free ice cream. Sunday sees a beef roast, with the child's portion also including the free ice cream; both main and kids' menus are available as well. Food is served from 12pm–8.30pm (9.30pm Friday and Saturday) all week except for Mondays (bank holidays excepted).

Family attractions include the historical city of Chester with its Roman walls, Cheshire Oaks shopping outlet, Mold Market on Wednesdays and Saturday, country walks, farm parks and the nearby seaside town of Rhyl. No dogs.

✓ children restricted to certain areas
✓ family room
✓ garden
✓ garden toys
✓ lunchtime meals
✓ evening meals
✓ food lunchtime and evenings
✓ children's menu
✓ bottle warming
✓ no smoking area
✗ accommodation
✓ nearby camping and caravan sites
✗ nappy changing
✗ entertainment
✓ children's certificate
✓ high chairs
✓ time limit – 9pm

## NORTH WEST WALES
## ANGLESEY

### DULAS

## Pilot Boat Inn

Dulas LL70 9EX
**T** 01248 410205
*Licensee*: Mark Williams
*Opening times*: 11.30–11; 12–10.30 sun
*Real ales*: **Robinson's Best Bitter**; seasonal beers
*Directions*: on A5025 between Amlwch and Benllech

The lack of public transport might be an issue in some rural areas, but the Pilot Boat Inn is one country place where you'll always see a bus. That's because the beer garden in this friendly inn has a converted double-decker fun bus over which children are encouraged to clamber. There's also an assault course for the more energetic. Clearly, the licensees believe in making children feel at home.

Inside, children are allowed in most places though the lounge, with an unusual boat-shaped bar, and the pool room double up as a family room. The decor is flagstones, a stone fireplace and wooden beams; there is a collection of banknotes from all over the world pinned up and the walls have pictures of boats and anything nautical.

The **kids' menu** features familiar choices and at £2.99 is good value, as there is an ice lolly thrown in with the price. Some of the adults meals can be served in kids' portions, including gammon, egg and chips and chicken curry. Food is served from midday–9pm every day.

The Pilot Boat Inn is in an area of outstanding beauty, and there are lots of lovely beaches on Anglesey with Lligwy being very close. There are also plenty of footpaths for walking, including the remains of the Iron Age village of Din Lligwy. Other attractions on Anglesey, which is an easy place to get around, include Beaumaris Castle, Pili Palas and, on the other end of the island, Newborough Model Village and the Sea Zoo at Brynsiencyn.

✘ children restricted to certain areas
✓ family room
✓ garden
✓ garden toys
✓ lunchtime meals
✓ evening meals
✓ food lunchtime and evening
✓ children's menu
✓ bottle warming
✓ no smoking area
✘ accommodation
✓ nearby camping and caravan sites
✓ nappy changing – women's toilets
✘ entertainment
✘ children's certificate
✓ high chairs
✘ time limit

### RED WHARF BAY

## Ship Inn

Red Wharf Bay, Pentraeth, Anglesey LL75 8RJ
**T** 01248 852568
*Licensees*: Andrew and Eve Kenneally
*Opening times*: 11–3, 6.30–11 (11 Sat, summer); 12–10.30 Sun
*Real ales*: **Adnams Bitter**; **Greene King IPA**; **Tetley Burton Ale**, **Tetley Imperial**
*Directions*: one mile off A5025, follow road to beach

Traditional old inn which overlooks the massive sweep of Red Wharf Bay – including a good sandy beach. Hard to believe that this was a busy port in the Middle Ages, given the peaceful nature of the place today. The Ship Inn reflects the history of the bay with plenty of shipping artifacts, while the old-fashioned atmosphere is complemented by wooden beams, old church pews and real coal fires in the winter.

Children are allowed everywhere apart from around the lounge bar area, while the no-smoking 'cellar bar' (actually at the back of the pub) and 'old kitchen' are designated as family rooms. There is also a dining room which opens weekend evenings.

As for food, the **kids' menu** is an impressive mix of 'real food' such as salmon and fettuccine, roasted vegetable pasta alongside the more traditional sausage and chips and baguettes. Some of the main menu's dishes can be served in smaller portions, such as curries and bolognese, as well as small roasts at Sunday lunchtime. Food is served midday–2.30pm, 6pm–9pm (6.30pm winter) Monday–Saturday, and all day Sundays throughout the year. The pub can get busy at weekends so do arrive in good time to get a table if eating.

This is a great area for long sandy beaches including Red Wharf Bay and Llanddwyn, or further up the coast at Benllech – the beach there has rock pools where toddlers can spend many a happy hour with their nets.

- ✓ children restricted to certain areas
- ✓ family room
- ✗ garden
- ✗ garden toys
- ✓ lunchtime meals
- ✓ evening meals
- ✓ food lunchtime and evenings
- ✓ children's menu
- ✓ bottle warming
- ✓ no smoking area
- ✗ accommodation
- ✓ nearby camping and caravan sites
- ✗ nappy changing
- ✗ entertainment
- ✗ children's certificate
- ✓ high chairs
- ✗ time limit

# CONWY

## Mulberry

Conwy Marina, Conwy LL32 8EP
**T** 01492 583350   **F** 01492 572440
*Licensee*: Gincarlo Girometti
*Opening times*: 12–11; 12–10.30 Sun

*Real ales*: **Robinson's Best, Hartley's XB**; seasonals
*Directions*: Conwy Marina is signed off the A55

Large purpose-built pub owned by Robinson's which was opened with the marina in the 1990s. It gets its name from the artificial harbours (mulberries) built for the D-Day landings in World War Two, sections of which were constructed on this part of the coast; check out the old pictures on the wall of the mulberries during construction and in use in France. There's also a copy of a letter from Monty to the troops promising them 'good hunting' when they engage the Nazis. Inside, there's a big open bar with a raised no-smoking area; upstairs there's a dining space with a separate entrance.

Children are allowed in a designated area in the bar near the no-smoking area, where there is a Lego table with bricks. Families also enjoy the outside verandah which overlooks the marina with views over the River Conwy towards Deganwy and beyond that the Great Orme's Head at the seaside resort of Llandudno.

Food is served lunchtimes and evenings, with a **kids' menu** offering familiar choices with chips; on Sunday lunchtimes there is also the option of a suitably-sized roast.

Despite its relative newness, this is a comfortable and friendly pub with a soothing view of water. There's lots to do in the area, including the magnificent Conwy castle which still has its town walls. There are two beaches at Llandudno, where there is also a farm park on the outskirts of the town. The Great Orme headland has a tram ride at the top, bronze age copper mines (fascinating for older children) and stunning views of the Irish Sea and Anglesey (keen-eyed children might also catch sight of the elusive goats).

- ✓ children restricted to certain areas
- ✗ family room
- ✗ garden
- ✗ garden toys
- ✓ lunchtime meals
- ✓ evening meals
- ✓ food lunchtime and evenings

- ✓ children's menu
- ✓ bottle warming
- ✓ no smoking area
- ✗ accommodation
- ✓ nearby camping and caravan sites
- ✓ nappy changing – disabled toilet
- ✗ entertainment
- ✗ children's certificate
- ✓ high chairs
- ✓ time limit – 9pm

- ✗ children restricted to certain areas
- ✗ family room
- ✓ garden
- ✗ garden toys
- ✓ lunchtime meals
- ✓ evening meals
- ✓ food lunchtime and evenings
- ✗ children's menu
- ✓ bottle warming
- ✗ no smoking area
- ✗ accommodation
- ✓ nearby camping and caravan sites
- ✗ nappy changing
- ✗ entertainment
- ✗ children's certificate
- ✗ high chairs
- ✗ time limit

## LLANFIHANGEL GLYN MYFYR

## Crown Inn

Llanfihangel Glyn Myfyr LL21 9UL
T 01490 420209
*Licensee*: Michael Morley
*Opening times*: 7 (12 Sat)–11; closed Mon;
12–10.30 Sun
*Real ales*: beer range varies
*Directions*: on B5105

Former hotel built at the beginning of the 19th century, the Crown Inn can be found in a lovely spot beside the River Alwen, where it has trout fishing rights. Inside it's traditional rustic decor with low beams and dark furniture. There's a bar, games room and snug and children are welcome everywhere; there are a few jigsaw puzzles to entertain them. Outside there's a beer garden at the back with terraced gardens which lead down to the river, so keep an eye on toddlers.

Food is served Saturday and Sunday lunchtimes and evenings and every evening in the week. There is no kids' menu, but small portions of the traditional bar food can be served; these include chips with egg and sausage or beans on toast. There are no Sunday roasts. This is very much a local pub in a small farming community and very welcoming to children, though it might be more suited to older ones.

No accommodation but the pub has its own space for camping. Good walking country, especially in the Clocaenog Forest, while the pub owns five acres of woods and river banks so you don't have to go far for a stroll. Also nearby is Llyn Brenin where there are picnic tables, archaeological trails and a visitor centre.

# GWYNEDD

## LLANRUG

## Glyntwrog Inn

Llanrug, Caernarfon LL55 4AN
T 01286 671191
*Licensees*: Dave and Gill Rochell
*Opening times*: 11–11; 12–10.30 Sun
*Real ales*: **Greene King IPA; Young's Special**
*Directions*: on A4086, just outside the village

Spacious pub with excellent views of Snowdonia. Inside there's a large and comfortable informal lounge, a no-smoking eating area and a public bar; there's also a games room. Children are allowed throughout, though most families would probably find it more comfortable in the lounge. Outside, there's a garden with tables and play equipment, including a slide, tyre swings and a climbing frame.

The **kids' menu** ranges from tomato soup to sausages, chips and beans and spaghetti bolognese; smaller portions off the specials board can be provided where possible. Roast dinners are available on Sundays, with smaller portions for children. Food is served 12pm–3pm and 5pm–9pm daily.

There are plenty of attractions within a few minutes drive including Caernarfon Castle, the excellent Greenwood Centre (where children can build their own dens in the woods and enjoy monster outdoor slides), Electric Mountain (the pumped-water hydro-electric storage power station in the middle of a mountain) and canoeing on Lake Padarn.

- ✘ children restricted to certain areas
- ✘ family room
- ✔ garden
- ✔ garden toys
- ✔ lunchtime meals
- ✔ evening meals
- ✔ food lunchtime and evening
- ✔ children's menu
- ✔ bottle warming
- ✔ no smoking area
- ✘ accommodation
- ✔ nearby camping and caravan sites
- ✘ nappy changing
- ✘ entertainment
- ✔ children's certificate
- ✔ high chairs
- ✘ time limit

## WAUNFAWR

# Snowdonia Parc Hotel and Brewpub

Waunfawr, Caernarfon LL55 4AQ
**T** 01286 650218    **F** 01286 650409
**E** karen@snowdonia-park.co.uk
www.snowdonia-park.co.uk
*Licensee*: Karen Humphreys
*Opening times*: 6 (opens at 12 in the summer and on Sat throughout the year)–11; 12–10.30 Sun
*Real ales*: **Mansfield Dark; Marston's Bitter**, Pedigree; **Snowdonia Welsh Highland Bitter**; seasonal beers
*Directions*: The pub is on the A4085, four miles south of Caernarfon on the road to Beddgelert

Situated on the Waunfawr stop on the Welsh Highland Railway line, this spacious and very child-friendly brew-pub is the former home of the Victorian station master. It occupies an idyllic setting, right on the edge of Snowdonia National Park, with views of the mountains.

There are three rooms in the pub and children are allowed in two of them: half the dining lounge and the large family room (both no smoking), the latter of which has a fantastic selection of large toys, such as small pedal cars and rockers and other toys for small children. These are replaced at regular intervals, and in summer lots of the toys go to the outside Wendy House. The main bar is child-free at all times and children are required to leave both gardens and licensed premises at 10.30pm. Outside, there is a playground with a proper soft surface and big swings, a slide and a roundabout for older ones. It is next to the railway line so that parents can sit and supervise their children and watch the steam engines manoeuvre in order to take the carriages back to Caernarfon. There is a bouncy castle in the adjacent garden and a Wendy House for younger children. The pub also has its own touring and camping site attached.

There is a full **kids' menu** with familiar choices, while some child-sized adult meals are available all the time, namely roast beef or lamb or scampi, chips and salad. During the summer there are roast lunches available all week, including local beef, lamb and a chicken fillet mozzarella dish; the large full menu is also available all day Sunday and every evening. The kitchen is open from 11am-8.30pm every day during the summer. Please phone to check opening times in the winter, as in the autumn and winter the pub is not normally open during weekday lunchtimes, but if you ring a couple of days before, Karen will open. There's a small brewery here which produces its own excellent beers.

This is a beautiful part of North Wales and places for the family to visit include Caernarfon Castle, Portmeirion Village (where *The Prisoner* TV series was filmed), the Greenwood Centre and of course the Welsh Highland Railway.

- ✔ children restricted to certain areas
- ✔ family room
- ✔ garden
- ✔ garden toys
- ✔ lunchtime meals
- ✔ evening meals

✓ food lunchtime and evenings
✓ children's menu
✓ bottle warming
✓ no smoking area
✗ accommodation
✓ nearby camping and caravan sites
✗ nappy changing
✗ entertainment
✗ children's certificate
✓ high chairs
✓ time limit – 10.30pm

## WEST WALES

LLANGOEDMOR

# Penllwyndu

Llangoedmor SA43 2LY
**T** 01239 682533
*Licensee*: Lynne Davies
*Opening times*: 12–11 (2–11 winter); 12–11 Sat
all year round; 12–10.30 Sun
*Real ales*: **Brains Buckley's Best Bitter**; **Tetley
Burton Ale**; guest beer
*Directions*: four miles east of Cardigan on the B4570

Even though this quiet country pub is over
200 years old, it was closed between 1926
and the 1980s. Now happily open and
thriving, it retains a traditional slate floor
in the bar, wooden beams, log fires in the
winter and a few rustic novelties on the wall
including a trombone and an ancient gun.
By the way, the pub's name translated into
English is 'head of the blackthorn'.

There's a public bar, games room and
dining area with children allowed everywhere,
though they'll probably want to make for
the secure garden at the back of the pub
with its views towards the Preseli Hills.

Honest bar food is served between
12pm–3pm and 6pm–9pm throughout the
summer and on Saturdays and Sundays all
year round, while in the winter it is only
available in the evening. The **kids' menu** has

the usual nuggets, burgers and sausage with
chips and beans, while small portions off
the main menu are available. These include
ham and chips, curries, sandwiches, and
lasagne. Sunday lunchtimes sees the main
menu, a few specials and the kids' menu.

The small village of Llangoedmor is just
outside Cardigan and within easy reach of
the coast where there are ample
opportunities for bird and dolphin
watching. Other attractions close by
include the Welsh Wildlife Centre at
Cilgerran and the Felinwynt Rain Forest and
Butterfly Centre near Aberporth.

✗ children restricted to certain areas
✗ family room
✓ garden
✗ garden toys
✓ lunchtime meals
✓ evening meals
✓ food lunchtime and evenings – not in winter
✓ children's menu
✓ bottle warming
✗ no smoking area
✗ accommodation
✓ nearby camping and caravan sites
✗ nappy changing
✗ entertainment
✗ children's certificate
✓ high chairs
✓ time limit – 9pm

LLANSAINT

# Kings Arms

13 Maes Yr Eglwys, Llansaint,
near Kidwelly SA17 5JE
**T** 01267 267487
**E** morris_kingsarms@hotmail.com
*Licensees*: John and Debbie Morris
*Opening times*: 12–2.30, 6.30–11 (closed Tuesday
in winter); 12–2.30, 6.30–10.30 Sun
*Real ales*: **Worthington Bitter**; guest beers

Charming and traditional pub dating back
to the 18th century, which can be found
next to the mediaeval village church.
Inside, the decor is 'olde worlde' with jugs
hanging from the low beams and local
photos on the walls. During the winter
there is a welcoming log fire.

There is no family room as such, but children are allowed in the restaurant, part of which is no smoking, while there's a secure beer garden for them in the summer. The **kids' menu** offers familiar choices with chips and beans, while older children can choose from a general menu which includes gammon, garlic chicken, breaded plaice and scampi. Food is served lunchtime and evening all week, apart from Tuesdays in the winter when the pub is closed all day. There's plenty to do in the area, with Pembrey Country Park, Oakwood Theme Park, Kidwelly Castle and the National Botanical Gardens all close to hand.

✓ children restricted to certain areas
✗ family room
✓ garden
✗ garden toys
✓ lunchtime meals
✓ evening meals
✓ food lunchtime and evenings
✓ children's menu
✓ bottle warming
✓ no smoking area
✓ accommodation
✓ nearby camping and caravan sites
✗ nappy changing
✗ entertainment
✗ children's certificate
✓ high chairs
✗ time limit

## PENNANT

# Ship Inn

Pennant SY23 5JW
**T** 01545 570355
*Licensee*: Stephen Wakley
*Opening times*: 6 (12 Sat)–11; closed Mon; 12–3, 7–11 Sun
*Real ales*: beer range varies
*Directions*: 300 yards south of B4577

Licensee Stephen Wakley has three kids under eight and works on the philosophy that if the kids are enjoying themselves then parents will enjoy themselves as well. The family's own children are also part of the pub: 'we don't want to shut them out upstairs,' he says. This generosity extends to the fenced-off garden which leads down to the River Arth. As well as an old tractor (stripped of all harmful metal bits), Stephen's children's own toys are usually out there for customers' young ones to play with (full marks for sharing!).

The pub is an 18th-century alehouse which is a bit hidden away, but it is full of character and atmosphere with oak beams and lots of local photos. Inside, there's a single big bar and a games room which doubles up as a family room. Children are allowed everywhere and there are board games available including backgammon, dominoes and shut-the-box which is a particular favourite with young customers.

Only one real ale is served and tends to be a session beer from regionals and micros throughout the country.

As for food, there are no chips but sandwiches can be made to order in the summer on most evenings and at weekend lunchtimes. A friendly and unpretentious hostelry which attracts both locals and visitors, many of whom come from the nearby caravan park in the summer.

The beaches of Cardiganshire are close by, while Aberaeron Wildlife and Leisure Park and the Fantasy Farm Park at Llanrhystud are both short drives away (if in different directions).

✗ children restricted to certain areas
✓ family room
✓ garden
✓ garden toys
✗ lunchtime meals
✗ evening meals
✗ food lunchtime and evenings
✗ children's menu
✓ bottle warming
✗ no smoking area
✗ accommodation
✓ nearby camping and caravan sites
✗ nappy changing
✗ entertainment
✗ children's certificate
✓ high chairs
✓ time limit – 9pm

### RHOS

# Lamb Inn

Rhos SA44 5EE
**T** 01559 370055
**E** chris_lamb@fsmail.net
*Licensee*: Meriel Lewis
*Opening times*: 12–2.30, 5.30–11; 12–11 Fri &
Sat, Mon–Thurs summer; 12–10.30 Sun
*Real ales*: **Banks' Original; Greene King Old
Speckled Hen; Taylor Landlord; Worthington
Bitter**; guest beer (occasional)

Even though the original building was
constructed 300 years ago, the Lamb Inn
made a name for itself after its 1960s
refurbishment when it was nicknamed 'the
little Ritz in Wales'. Then, I'm told, it was all
tuxedos and ballgowns. Nowadays, it's been
remodelled again with lots of inside and
outside brickwork, flagstones and a
cobblestone effect floor.

The walls are busy with shelves of
bottled beers, old shop signs and other
curios, while children are well-catered for
with a play area (the former kitchen), which
is done up to resemble a jail. Unlike the real
thing, it's full of toys and a great magnet for
youngsters. Once you've prised them out of
there, they are allowed anywhere in the
pub, except for the immediate bar area,
including a no-smoking area off the bar and
a games room. There is also a dining area.

The garden is at the front and even though
it is gated it is recommended you keep an
eye on wandering toddlers.

Food is served midday–2.30pm,
6pm–9.30pm, and the **kids' menu** includes
bangers and mash, chicken nuggets and
other familiar favourites with chips, while
the main menu offers small portions of the
likes of pasta, soup, salad, scampi and chips,
sandwiches and jacket potatoes. Sunday
lunch is restricted to a choice of three roasts,
with a child-sized portion always possible.

A useful stop on the road south to
Carmarthen, but it's also on the edge of
good walking country and half-an-hour
from the beaches of Cardiganshire.

✗ children restricted to certain areas
✓ family room
✓ garden
✗ garden toys
✓ lunchtime meals
✓ evening meals
✓ food lunchtime and evening
✓ children's menu
✓ bottle warming
✓ no smoking area
✓ accommodation
✗ nearby camping and caravan sites
✗ nappy changing
✗ entertainment
✗ children's certificate
✓ high chairs
✗ time limit

# Index

## AMENITIES

**East Anglia**
Accommodation 22, 28, 30
Bouncy castle 19, 21, 25
Brewpubs and brewery taps 26
Camping and caravans 18
Clowns 25
Colouring books, toys or games 16, 21, 23, 29
Entertainment 25
Firework displays 25
Karaoke 21
Mooring facilities 18
Outdoor play area 17–25, 27, 28
Pets corner 17, 20, 21

**London**
Colouring books, toys or games 34, 36, 37
Firework displays 37
Outdoor play area 34, 35

**Midlands**
Accommodation 42, 47, 51, 58, 66, 67, 74
Bouncy castle 42, 43, 68, 71, 72, 75
Brewpubs and brewery taps 49, 54, 72, 74
Camping and caravans 47, 63, 67, 70
Colouring books, toys or games 42, 44, 45, 46, 48, 50, 51, 53, 58, 60, 61, 64, 65, 69, 71
Easter egg hunts 72
Entertainment 42, 57, 69,
Farm animals 54, 64
Firework displays 56, 57
Football pitch 44, 63
Indoor play area 61
Magicians 42
Miniature railway 43,
Outdoor play area 42–50, 52, 54–70, 72, 73, 75
Pets corner 43, 69
Traditional pub games 48, 50, 55, 63, 64, 68

**North East**
Accommodation 82
Colouring books, toys or games 80, 83
Outdoor play area 82

**North West**
Accommodation 88, 90, 91, 92, 93, 97, 98
Bouncy castle 89, 90, 96, 97, 99

Brewpubs and brewery taps 98
Colouring books, toys or games 90, 93, 94, 96, 99
Entertainment 89, 90, 99
Indoor play area 88, 96
Magicians 90, 97
Outdoor play area 89, 90, 93, 95, 96, 97, 99
Pets corner 95, 99
Traditional pub games 94

**South**
Accommodation 105, 107, 108, 115, 116
Bouncy castle 113, 116
Brewpubs and brewery taps 113, 121
Camping and caravans 109
Colouring books, toys or games 105, 107, 110, 111, 113, 114, 117, 119, 121
Conker competition 120
Outdoor play area 104–121
Pets corner 105
Traditional pub games 117

**South West and West Country**
Accommodation 128, 130, 134, 139, 141, 142, 143, 145, 147, 149, 153, 156
Bouncy castle 130, 153
Brewpubs and brewery taps 140
Colouring books, toys or games 127, 128, 132, 134, 135, 136, 139, 140, 142, 144, 146, 148, 150, 153
Entertainment 146
Indoor play area 130, 134
Museum 128, 144
Outdoor play area 128, 129, 131, 132, 134, 135, 137, 140–143, 145–151, 153–156
Pets corner 129, 140, 143
Traditional pub games 139, 144
Trampoline 130

**Yorkshire**
Accommodation 161, 163, 164, 166, 168, 169
Bouncy castle 167, 169
Brewpubs and brewery taps 162, 167
Camping and caravans 164, 167
Colouring books, toys or games 160, 164, 165
Indoor play area 167
Karaoke 165
Outdoor play area 162, 163, 164, 166, 167, 169

**Scotland**
Accommodation 174–182, 184–189, 192–196

Bouncy castle 187
Brewpubs and brewery taps 196
Colouring books, toys or games 174, 180, 181, 183, 184, 186, 188, 189, 193, 194
Indoor play area 186
Magicians 180
Miniature railway 182, 192
Mooring facilities 187
Outdoor play area 176, 186, 192–194
Traditional pub games 189

**Wales**
Accommodation 209, 210, 217, 218
Bouncy castle 203, 204, 215
Brewpubs and brewery taps 215
Camping and caravan facilities 210, 214, 215
Clowns 202
Colouring books, toys or games 203, 211, 213, 215
Entertainment 203
Indoor play area 205, 207, 218
Magicians 202
Outdoor play area 202–208, 210–212, 214, 215, 217
Traditional pub games 217

## NEARBY ATTRACTIONS

**East Anglia**
Adventure play areas 19
Animal attractions/sanctuaries 18, 21, 22, 25, 28, 29
Aquariums 19, 23
Birdwatching 21, 22, 30
Country walks 17, 18, 20, 21, 22, 24–29
Environmental centres 24
Gardens 16
Historical recreations 24, 25
Historic buildings 23, 27
Historic towns, cities and villages 16, 18, 19, 26, 29
Leisure parks 26, 28
Museums and collections 16–18, 21, 24, 28
Narrow-boating 24, 26
Nature reserves 19, 21, 29
Seaside resorts/beaches 19, 21, 22, 23, 24, 29
Shopping 26
Small railways and steam engines 22, 24
Waterside locations 18

**London**
Canalside walks 34
Country walks 36
Historic buildings 34, 36
Museums and collections 34–36
Narrow-boating 34

**Midlands**
Adventure play areas 49, 58
Animal attractions/sanctuaries 42, 43, 44, 62, 73
Battlefields 59
Bird parks 50, 53
Canalside walks 45, 58, 59, 68, 71
Castles 66
Country walks 46, 47, 50, 51, 53–56, 58–65, 67, 68, 69, 71, 72, 73
Environmental centres 67
Farm attractions 50, 52, 74
Historic buildings 43, 44, 46, 55, 64, 69, 70
Historic towns, cities and villages 46, 48–51, 56, 58–60, 63–66, 69, 71, 75
Leisure parks 68
Local landmarks 48
Local traditions 47, 57
Museums and collections 42, 46, 49, 51, 54, 59, 69, 70, 71, 75
Narrow-boating 58
Nature reserves 73
Outdoor activities 51
Plane-spotting 54, 65
Small railways and steam engines 53–55, 64, 66, 73
Sports events/grounds 55
Swimming pools 42, 43
Theme parks 61, 68, 69

**North East**
Country walks 81, 82
Historic towns, cities and villages 80, 82
Leisure parks 83
Museums and collections 82
Nature reserves 84
Seaside resorts/beaches 83
Small railways and steam engines 82
Sports events/grounds 83
Theme parks 81

**North West**
Animal attractions/sanctuaries 92
Bird parks 91
Canalside walks 89, 91
Country walks 88, 90–94, 96
Cycling 93, 94
Historic buildings 96, 99
Historic towns, cities and villages 95, 99
Lake cruises 93
Leisure centres 94
Local landmarks 91
Museums and collections 88, 90, 92, 93, 95
Narrow-boating 89
Plane-spotting 97
Seaside resorts/beaches 97, 100
Shopping 89, 95
Small railways and steam engines 91, 92
Sports events/grounds 99
Theme parks 89, 94, 96, 98

**South**
Animal attractions/sanctuaries 109, 113
Bird parks 118
Castles 120
Caves 107
Country walks 104–109, 111, 112, 114–122
Farm attractions 109
Gardens 110
Historical recreations 110
Historic towns, cities and villages 115, 119, 120, 122
Leisure centres 106
Local landmarks 116, 120
Model villages 112
Museums and collections 108, 109
Seaside resorts/beaches 110, 112, 113, 118
Small railways and steam engines 105
Sports events/grounds 116
Theme parks 104, 105, 110, 116

**South West and West Country**
Adventure play areas 131, 132, 156
Animal attractions/sanctuaries 129, 133, 136, 139–142, 145, 148, 150, 152, 154
Aquariums 131, 142, 143
Bird parks 130, 131, 133, 155
Birdwatching 136, 153
Castles 129, 137, 148
Caves 146, 151
Country walks 127, 134, 136, 138–141, 143, 145–149, 151, 153, 155
Environmental centres 131, 132
Farm attractions 132, 139
Gardens 129, 130, 131
Go-karting 132
Historic buildings 130, 138, 141, 152, 154, 155, 156
Historic ruins 156
Historic ships 148
Historic towns, cities and villages 137, 140, 142, 144, 148, 155
Lakeside attractions 128, 153
Leisure parks 134, 142, 147, 155
Local landmarks 128, 130, 145
Model villages 132, 141
Museums and collections 124, 129, 137, 138, 140, 142, 144, 145, 148, 150–152, 154, 155
Seaside resorts/beaches 130, 132, 134, 135, 141, 142, 144, 145, 149, 150
Shopping 142, 151
Small railways and steam engines 127, 133, 146, 150, 153
Sports events/grounds 145
Theme parks 128, 129, 133, 135–137, 140, 143

**Yorkshire**
Aquariums 160, 161, 165
Birdwatching 169
Canalside walks 167
Castles 165, 167
Country walks 162–169
Gardens 163
Historic towns, cities and villages 164
Museums and collections 160, 162, 164, 168

Narrow-boating 167
Science adventure centre 166
Seaside resorts/beaches 165
Shopping 167
Small railways and steam engines 165, 167
Sports events/grounds 165
Swimming pools 168
Theme parks 162
Waterside locations 167

**Scotland**
Aquariums 183
Battlefields 174, 196
Birdwatching 183, 191, 193
Boat trips 181, 187
Canalside walks 193
Castles 179, 182, 184
Children's golf 191
Country walks 174–183, 185–187, 189, 190, 192–196
Cycling 178, 180, 183
Historic buildings 177, 178, 185
Historic towns, cities and villages 174, 176, 178, 188–190, 192, 193
Leisure centres 181
Local traditions 184, 187
Museums and collections 175, 180, 183, 189, 191, 192, 194, 195
Narrow-boating 193
Nature reserves 175, 182
Outdoor activities 175, 176
Plane-spotting 183
Puppet theatre 195
Seaside resorts/beaches 181, 183, 187, 193–195
Small railways and steam engines 185
Swimming pools 184

**Wales**
Animal attractions/sanctuaries 206, 216
Aquariums 212
Birdwatching 210, 216
Castles 205, 208, 212, 213, 215, 217
Country walks 202–215, 217, 218
Craft centre 211
Environmental centres 215
Farm attractions 202, 207, 211, 213, 217
Gardens 217
Historic buildings 206
Historical sites 205, 208, 211–213
Historic towns, cities and villages 202, 211, 215
Lakeside activities 209, 214, 215
Leisure centres 207
Leisure parks 217
Local traditions 204, 210
Model villages 212
Museums and collections 202, 209
Outdoor activities 208, 209, 215
Seaside resorts/beaches 203, 211, 212, 213, 217, 218
Shopping 211
Small railways and steam engines 215
Theme parks 204, 208, 217

# Join CAMRA

If you like good beer and good pubs you could be helping to fight to preserve, protect and promote them. CAMRA was set up in the early Seventies to fight against the mass destruction of a part of Britain's heritage. The giant brewers are still pushing through takeovers, mergers and closures of their smaller regional rivals. They are still trying to impose national brands of beer and lager on their customers whether they like it or not, and they are still closing down town and village pubs or converting them into grotesque 'theme' pubs.

CAMRA wants to see genuine free competition in the brewing industry, fair prices, and, above all, a top quality product brewed by local breweries in accordance with local tastes, and served in pubs that maintain the best features of a tradition that goes back centuries.

As a CAMRA member you will be able to enjoy generous discounts on CAMRA products and receive the highly rated monthly newspaper *What's Brewing*. You will be given the CAMRA members' handbook and be able to join in local social events and brewery trips. To join, complete the form below and, if you wish, arrange for direct debit payments by filling in the form overleaf and returning it to CAMRA. To pay by credit card, contact the membership secretary on (01727) 867201.

Full single UK/EU £16; Joint (two members living at the same address) UK/EU £19; Single under 26, Student, Disabled, Unemployed, Retired over 60 £9; Joint retired over 60, Joint under 26 £12; UK/EU Life £192, UK/EU Joint life £228. Single life retired over 60 £90, Joint life retired over 60 £120. Full overseas membership £20, Joint overseas membership £23. Single overseas life £240, Joint overseas life £276.

Please delete as appropriate:

I/We wish to become members of CAMRA.

I/We agree to abide by the memorandum and articles of association of the company.

I/We enclose a cheque/p.o. for £       (payable to CAMRA Ltd.)

Name(s)

Address

 

 

Postcode

Signature(s)

CAMRA Ltd., 230 Hatfield Road, St Albans, Herts AL1 4LW

## Instruction to your Bank or Building Society to pay by Direct Debit

Please fill in the whole form using a ball point pen and send it to:

Campaign for Real Ale Ltd
230 Hatfield Road
St. Albans
Herts
AL1 4LW

Originator's Identification Number

| 9 | 2 | 6 | 1 | 2 | 9 |
|---|---|---|---|---|---|

Reference Number

| | | | | | | | | | | | | | | | | | |
|---|---|---|---|---|---|---|---|---|---|---|---|---|---|---|---|---|---|

Name of Account Holder(s)

Bank/Building Society account number

| | | | | | | | |
|---|---|---|---|---|---|---|---|

Branch Sort Code

| | | | | | |
|---|---|---|---|---|---|

Name and full postal address of your Bank or Building Society

To The Manager                    Bank/Building Society

Address

Postcode

**FOR CAMRA OFFICIAL USE ONLY**
This is not part of the instruction to your Bank or Building Society

Membership Number

Name

Postcode

**Instructions to your Bank or Building Society**
Please pay CAMRA Direct Debits from the account detailed on this instruction subject to the safeguards assured by the Direct Debit Guarantee. I understand that this instruction may remain with CAMRA and, if so, will be passed electronically to my Bank/Building Society

Signature(s)

Date

Banks and Building Societies may not accept Direct Debit instructions for some types of account

✂ - - - - - - - - - - - - - - - - - - - - - - - - - - - - - - - - - - - - - - - - - - - - - - - - - - -

**This guarantee should be detached and retained by the Payer.**

## The Direct Debit Guarantee

- This Guarantee is offered by all Banks and Building Societies that take part in the Direct Debit Scheme. The efficiency and security of the Scheme is monitored and protected by your own Bank or Building Society.

- If the amounts to be paid or the payment dates change CAMRA will notify you 10 working days in advance of your account being debited or as otherwise agreed.

- If an error is made by CAMRA or your Bank or Building Society, you are guaranteed a full and immediate refund from your branch of the amount paid.

- You can cancel a Direct Debit at any time by writing to your Bank or Building Society. Please also send a copy of your letter to us.

# Other books from CAMRA

*The CAMRA Books range of guides helps you search out the best in beer (and cider) and brew it at home too!*

## Buying in the UK

Our books are available from bookshops in the UK. If you can't find a book, simply order it from your bookshop using the ISBN number, title and author using details given below. CAMRA members should refer to the CAMRA newspaper *What's Brewing* for details of special offers. CAMRA books are also available by mail-order (postage free in UK) from: CAMRA Books, 230 Hatfield Road, St Albans, Herts AL1 4LW. Cheques made payable to CAMRA Ltd. Telephone credit card orders to **01727 867201**.

## Buying outside the UK

CAMRA books are also sold in many book and beer outlets in the USA and other English-speaking countries. If you have trouble locating a particular book, use the details below to order with your credit card (or US$ cheque) by mail, email (info@camra.org.uk), fax (+44 1727 867670) or website (www.camra.org.uk). The website will securely process credit card purchases. Carriage of £2.00 per book (Europe) and £4.00 per book (US, Australia, New Zealand and other overseas) is charged.

## UK Booksellers

Call CAMRA Books for distribution details and book list. CAMRA Books are listed on all major CD-ROM book lists and on our Internet site: www.camra.org.uk

## Overseas Booksellers

Call or fax CAMRA Books for details of local distributors. Distributors are required for some English language territories and rights are available for electronic and non-English language editions. Enquiries should be addressed to the managing editor.

---

## Good Beer Guide

ROGER PROTZ

CAMRA's annual guide to the best 4,000 pubs in the UK. A third of the entries change every year and all the descriptions are brought up to date by CAMRA branches who visit all the pubs in the guide. Real ale quality has to be of the highest order to get into the guide and branches are looking for top quality in all respects if a pub is to be listed.

*800 pages approx*
Published annually in September.

## Good Bottled Beer Guide

JEFF EVANS

The definitive guide to real ale in a bottle:

- *Every UK bottle-conditioned beer*
- *tasting notes to help you choose*
- *the background to each beer*
- *where to buy the beers*
- *key dates in beer history*
- *how to buy, store and serve bottled ales*
- *the best foreign beers*

Highly commended by the British Guild of Beer Writers, the *Good Bottled Beer Guide* is for those who like to try the most creatively brewed beers in the world. More than 300 to choose from, all from the comfort of your armchair!

**£8.99** *(224 pages)*
ISBN 1 85249 185 X

## India Pale Ale

(Homebrew Classics series)

CLIVE LA PENSÉE and ROGER PROTZ

Roger Protz goes on an historical hunt for the origins of the most famous British beer of all time – IPA. He uncovers the original brewery where IPA was devised as an export for the colonies, an invention that made its brewers extremely wealthy men.

Brewer La Pensée conjures up the smells and sounds of breweries and brewers spanning three centuries, making their version of IPA.

**£8.99** *(196 pages)*
ISBN 1 85249 129 9

## 50 Great Pub Crawls

BARRIE PEPPER

Visit the beer trails of the UK, from town centre walks, to hiking and biking and even a crawl by train to trackside pubs! Barrie Pepper, with recommendations from CAMRA branches, has compiled a 'must do' list of pub crawls, with easy to use colour maps to guide you, notes on architecture, history and brewing tradition to entertain you.

**£9.99** *(256 pages)*
ISBN 1 85249 142 6

## Brew Your Own British Real Ale at Home

GRAHAM WHEELER *and* ROGER PROTZ

This book contains recipes to replicate some famous cask-conditioned beers at home or to customise brews to your own particular taste. Conversion details are given so that the measurements can be used world-wide.

**£8.99** *(194 pages)*
ISBN 1 85249 138 8

## CAMRA's Good Cider Guide

DAVID MATTHEWS

CAMRA's guide to real cider researched anew for cider's fifth Millennium. Features on cider around the world, and cider-making, plus a comprehensive and detailed guide to UK producers of cider. The brand new listing of outlets includes pubs, restaurants, bars and small cider makers – with full address and contact numbers. Also provided are details of ciders available and, where appropriate, items of interest in the pub or area.

**£9.99** *(400 pages)*
ISBN 1 85249 143 4

ASK IF IT'S
CASK ✓

## CAMRA's London Pubs Guide

LYNNE PEARCE

The guide to CAMRA's favourite London pubs, chosen because they sell traditional real ale, often brewed in the capital itself. The guide points you to the features you will want to discover on your trip around London: the architecture, personalities, history, local ambience and nearby attractions.

Practical aids include transportation details and street level maps, information about opening times, food, parking, disabled and children's facilities, plus the range of beers.

Feature articles include a history of brewing in London, a guide to London's best pub food, and London pubs with stories to tell. What could be better?

**£9.99** *(224 pages)*
ISBN 1 85249 164 7

## Heritage Pubs of Great Britain

MARK BOLTON *and* JAMES BELSEY

It is still possible to enjoy real ale in sight of great craftsmanship and skill. Feast your eyes and toast the architects and builders from times past. This full-colour 'coffee-table' production is a photographic record of some of the finest pub interiors in Britain. As a collector's item, it is presented on heavy, gloss-art paper in a sleeved hardback format. Photographed by architectural specialist Mark Bolton and described in words by pub expert James Belsey. Available only from CAMRA – call 01727 867201
(overseas +44 1727 867201)

**£16.99** *(144 pages, hardback)*

## Home Brewing

GRAHAM WHEELER

Recently redesigned to make it even easier to use. The classic first book for all home-brewers. While being truly comprehensive, Home Brewing is also a practical guide which can be followed step by step as you try your first brews. Plenty of recipes for beginners and hints and tips from the world's most revered home brewer.

**£8.99** *(240 pages)*
ISBN 1 85249 137 X

## Brew Classic European Beers at Home

GRAHAM WHEELER *and* ROGER PROTZ

Keen home brewers can now recreate some of the world's classic beers at home. Brew superb ales, stouts, Pilsners, Alt, Kölsch, Trappist, wheat beers, sour beers, even fruit lambics. Measurements are given in UK, US and European units.

**£8.99** *(196 pages)*
ISBN 1 85249 117 5

## Dictionary of Beer

CAMRA

A unique reference work. Where else would you find the definitions of: parachute, Paradise, paraflow and paralytic? Or skull-dragged, slummage and snob screen? More than 2000 definitions covering brewing techniques and ingredients; international beers and breweries; tasting terms; historical references and organisations; slang phrases and abbreviations; culinary terms and beer cocktails; and much more.

**£7.99** *(208 pages)*
ISBN 1 85249 158 2